e-mail Forensics:
Eliminating Spam, Scams
and Phishing

Les Hatton

**Professor of Forensic Software Engineering,
Kingston University, London**

Bluespear Publishing,
United Kingdom

Published by Bluespear Publishing, United Kingdom

— BluespearPublishing.com

ISBN 978-1-908422-00-2

Typography

This book was prepared using the open source system LaTeX.

Revision information

```
Revision: $Revision: 1.24 $
Date:     $Date: 2011/08/25 15:12:18 $
```

Dedication

As with all of my writing, this book is dedicated to my family, Gillian, Leo, Felix and Isabelle. Computer scientists can easily lose track of how important it is for systems to do what they are supposed to do in plain language, without undue incident and without de-humanising the end user. My family never let me forget this very important lesson even though they make me work in the garden shed where they can't hear my swearing.

Executive summary

If you're reading this in a shop and fail to buy a copy[1], at least read this page. It might save you at some stage.

> An e-mail is generally about as private as shouting your message across a crowded room to a friend. **Never** forget this.

> Nearly everything in an e-mail can be spoofed i.e. forged, and this is exactly what spammers, scammers and other abusers do in order to get their stuff into your mailbox.

> The essence of spamming and phishing by e-mail is to entice you to give away details of yourself either by responding directly, or by clicking on a toxic link buried in the e-mail. No responsible organisation should ever ask you to do this. If you suspect that one has, ring them up and give them an earful for being stupid. It's not uncommon.

> **Never** supply any details requested by an e-mail. That's **never**. There is no legitimate reason for this. So if ever you get led into revealing anything (and some scamming e-mails are astonishingly credible), just pause before you hit "Send".

> "Please pass on to 25 of your friends" ... Don't !

If you take heed of the rest of the advice in this book, your junk mail will fall to around 3 per 1,000,000 received with negligible loss of genuine mail.

---

[1] Shame on you :-)

Executive summary

The essence of Forensics

"Those who cannot remember the past are condemned to repeat it".

George Santayana, (1863-1952)

"Examine things of the past, and obtain the new knowledge and the opinion from there."

Ancient Japanese proverb[2]

"The real essence of software forensics is painstaking work to identify patterns coupled with the ability to build tools quickly and reliably to exploit those patterns, hopefully teasing out others."

"Having your own server is the world's best executive toy."

Me, (2011)

---

[2]http://japanesekanji.nobody.jp/idiom/onkochishin.htm for other examples.

The essence of Forensics

About the author

Although mail filtering was an unintended research area for me, it was an essential distraction to secure my e-mail and it happened to use techniques I had learned in other areas.

I originally trained as a mathematician at King's College Cambridge and later at Manchester University where I was introduced to the complexities of atmospheric fluid flows. Following a brief spell at the Met Office, I relocated to Houston, Texas as a research geophysicist with a major American geophysical contractor. During this 15 year period, I bathed in computational analytic methods and signal processing. Finding almost continual problems with computer systems software, I eventually switched careers and have studied the forensic aspects of software systems failure ever since. After spending most of my life in industry, I now hold a part-time chair in this area at Kingston University, London, although I still keep my hand in with computational physics.

Like nearly everybody nowadays, I rely in my work on the sanctity of my e-mail so when this sanctity was threatened a couple of years back by the volume of junk, I decided to apply the forensic techniques I have deployed for many years to unravel the peculiarities of software systems failure, in order to secure my e-mail. This book is the result. I confess that it's partly for me. Writing things down after a long period of hard work is extraordinarily satisfying but I hope it's useful for you too. It is as down to earth as I can make it.

About the author

Acknowledgements

First, I would like to thank all the many spammers over the years who by their relentless crap eventually conspired to render my e-mail unusable, forcing me to do something about it. Do keep sending it. For the few of you who don't already appear to have my address, it's lesh@oakcomp.co.uk.

For reasons I won't go into here, I am very excited about the progress we have made with open source, particularly in it's reliability and ease of interfacing. After switching from Word ten years ago, (there are still some papers I wrote which I can sadly not recover), I started to use LaTeX[3] and it's splendid graphical interface Kile[4] and this is the first book I have written using it. All of the tricky stuff in writing, bibliography, indices and so on is very easy in LaTeX and stunningly reliable. Line diagrams were prepared using xfig and image editing was carried out by the Gimp. The scripts are either bash (.sh) scripts or Perl scripts (.pl) and the C programs were compiled and tested using the GNU C compiler gcc. The book itself and it's embedded programs were revision controlled using rcs. What a pleasure it is to acknowledge all the many people who have contributed to this wonderful collective achievement.

The work of Perl-meisters everywhere (particularly Gisle Aas and Sean Burke) for effectively removing the complexities of dealing with HTML and MIME formatting in e-mails allowing me to focus on the forensics. Terrific job.

John Graham-Cumming for his many writings on the measurement, categorisation and treatment of the spam epidemic.

This project allowed me to come into serious contact with the open source mailing system Postfix[5]. My experiences with this have been uniformly excellent. It is rock solid, easy to understand and easy to work with and

---

[3]http://www.LaTeX-project.org/
[4]http://kile.sourceforge.net/
[5]http://www.postfix.org/

Acknowledgements

enhance which is why I chose it as my implementation here. It is a great testament to the skills of it's designer Wietse Venema.

I read voraciously during the three years I have been trying to recover my e-mail address and lots of people contributed in one way or another including Tom Anderson, Mike Andrews, Eddie Bishop, Michiel van Genuchten, Leo Hatton (who read the entire book and made endless suggestions to improve it), Rob Mellor, Tim Mortimer as well as any number of contributors to various forums on the web, too numerous to mention.

Lastly I must acknowledge Mats Nilsson and the other stalwart members of the erudite Akkurat Dining Philosophers' club, Stockholm, Sweden without whom I would have drunk far less splendid Belgian beer and might have finished this book somewhat earlier.

Preface

The word *forensics* has a legal connotation and as such there are various forms of forensic analysis which can be carried out with e-mail. There appear to be no official definitions so I will use the following. The first and most important as far as this book is concerned is *preventative forensics*. In preventative forensics, we analyse the dynamic nature of incoming toxic e-mails with the intention of discovering patterns to reduce the probability of such an e-mail even reaching a prospective victim to a negligible level, (the target in this book is less than 4 junk mails delivered per million sent). Toxic e-mails are intimately associated with the law; spam is illegal to non-business addresses in numerous countries and scams and phishing, (see later for detailed definitions), are simply fraudulent. They seek to steal from innocent parties.

In *investigative forensics*, we may be trying to determine the provenance of a particular e-mail to determine if it is genuine as part of a legal investigation.

Whilst techniques for both of these kinds of forensic analysis tend to be similar, the nature of the material is rather different. In the former, we are analysing many received e-mail messages for patterns whereas in the latter we tend to spend our time poring over enormous logs trying to piece together the trajectory of a particular e-mail to determine it's provenance. I will talk a little about this later but the vast majority of this book concerns *preventative forensics* as this is by far, the bigger problem.

The seeds of this book were sown after being progressively besieged by spam passed on by my previous ISP. I have had my primary e-mail address for about twenty years and it's visibility has gradually grown - it is very difficult to hide forever whilst still ensuring that it is exposed to people who you would actually like to hear from.

Eventually it got to the stage where they refused to handle it anymore even with well-known anti-spam procedures, and a short discussion with them led to their suggesting that I change my punch-drunk e-mail address to avoid this uninvited plague, (or take it elsewhere). It seems unacceptable to me to be driven away from my own address because of the perpetrators of the tsunami of junk which washes backwards and forwards around the internet so I resolved to find out more with the goal of receiving exactly what I wanted to receive; no more and no less. There are surprisingly few books on this subject so as is often the case in modern internet computing, the best way of finding out more is to set yourself up with a dedicated server and learn the hard way. The main problem of course is that computing science is not strong on the scientific method so I had no idea what works and how well - we are not in general a critical discipline. After crashing and burning several times, I finally began to learn.

This book is an account of these experiences. If you follow it's advice, all of which is based on empirical measurements over a period of 3 years, you can reduce the number of spams, scams, phishing mails or malware attempts which reach your inbox to an occasional one every now and then, with a very small chance of losing wanted mail[6]. I am not claiming that this is the best but it's certainly good enough for me at the present threat level and it's very considerably better than most of the commercial systems I have tried so I hope it's useful. It has to be. Through much of this period, my mail server got hit daily by between 20,000 messages (a quiet day) and 100,000 messages (a bit noisy), nearly all of which were directed at me and were junk. Consequently, my systems have to be very nearly perfect in identifying and dealing with junk automatically, otherwise my mailbox would be unusable. Of a total volume of 7.5 million junk messages directed at me in the last 10 months, only 37 made it to my inbox. It's nice to feel wanted but there are limits.

I am fully aware that the book may be read by the very people who have been bombarding my various mail addresses for years. However I share the same view as Ross Anderson who in his well-known book "Security Engineering", [1] summarises a discussion of this particular conundrum by saying

> "In short, while some of the bad guys will benefit from a book such as this, they mostly know the tricks already, and the good guys will benefit much more."

---

[6]The chance is never zero however so I take no responsibility if you do lose some. You must ultimately decide your own acceptable limits of what is and what is not junk and the parts of the system which need to be trained will reflect this judgement.

If you want to be ahead of the game and hang on to your valuable e-mail address, read on ...

Les Hatton,
New Malden, August 2011, http://www.leshatton.org/.

Preface

Contents

Contents

Contents

1 The rise of e-mail

e-mail is one of those simple technologies which arise and so quickly become part of your life that you wonder how you ever did without it in the first place. At the same time as enabling communication, it has changed the entire environment in which people communicate.

Perhaps it's most obvious characteristics are it's speed of delivery and the fact that it is buffered. This simply means that if you can't pick a message up temporarily, it is stored for you until you can. Unlike telephone calls, it is also self-logging in that you can easily keep a copy of everything you receive or send. (My mailboxes have accumulated gigabytes of data over the years).

Unlike Facebook and Twitter for example, the technology is also independent of any commercial interest. It is perfectly possible to send and receive e-mails using only open source software. Indeed a very significant percentage of all e-mails travelling round the net (regrettably including much of the junk also) are transmitted in this way. My own mail systems use a server running Centos Linux and KMail clients on machines running openSuSe Linux and Ubuntu. These software systems are rock-solid, cost nothing and are easy to use.

Even more glaringly obvious however is that the transmission of e-mails is also essentially free by which I mean when you have paid the basic internet connection costs, it generally doesn't matter how many e-mails you send - and you can send an awful lot down a typical outgoing broadband connection of say 1Mbits per second,(incoming speeds are usually much higher). A character takes up around 10 bits on a communication line so that your broadband connection is capable of delivering perhaps 100,000 characters or around 15,000 of your words of wisdom per second. I could comfortably e-mail my life's work in a few minutes.

1.1 The threat

Unfortunately, such speeds and economy mean that it is the perfect medium for sending vast amounts of unsolicited mail in it's various forms. Even worse, it is the primary attack vector of choice amongst the criminal fraternity as they produce ever more ingenious toxic payloads to add to e-mail in order to claim their victims. At the time of writing this section, the Wall Street Journal[1] ran a report of a very recent international crime ring which led to arrests in the US, the UK, Ukraine and the Netherlands. Their attack method was an interesting combination. First of all they targeted victims apparently using a piece of toxic code called the "Zeus Trojan" embedded in email messages and attachments. Once installed on the victim's machine, this software eavesdropped user names and passwords from banking and brokerage accounts.

A second phase of the attack then performed a denial of service on victims' telephones using automated dialling systems so that no communication was possible between the bank or broker and the victim. Whilst this was in operation, they then raided the accounts using the stolen user names and passwords and passed these on to other parts of the crime ring to drain. Some of the attacks went on for as long as a week and a total of around $70 million stolen. This is sophisticated and highly coordinated crime and according to some experts, the tip of the iceberg. Although the usual warnings were issued about keeping your virus software up to date and so on, the only real protection for this is to keep the e-mails away from your computer in the first place.

As we will see, it is much easier to keep them off your computer than trying to repair the damage after they are already installed. These and many other threats associated with e-mail are the prime reason for writing this book and I will expand on this in great detail later.

Before that, it is worth commenting briefly on a couple of other matters which although annoyances, pale into insignificance against the threat backdrop.

---

[1]9th October 2010

1.2 Think before you send

Many people reading this book will have experienced that moment when they have reacted perhaps too quickly, included the wrong people on a circulation list or even sent it to the wrong person, immediately regretting it. It's hard to do that with a letter, a far more measured means of communication.

I will use the word viscosity (borrowed from the world of atmospheric fluid dynamics where I started my career), to describe the resistance of a communication medium in the following sense.

- High viscosity communication. Written letter sent by slow mail. For example in the 19th century, this may have taken months to reach the desired destination. Such communications automatically require a serious engagement of the brain before putting pen to paper to remove as many mistakes as possible. The cost of any mistake is simply too high.

- Medium viscosity communication. Written letter sent to arrive say overnight. Writing a letter usually requires engaging the brain but the increased rapidity of the communication means that such a letter could be informal and perhaps hurried. Mistakes are not typically as expensive as with high viscosity communication.

- Low viscosity communication. Text messages or e-mails are typically turned around so quickly that they invite little if any thought beforehand. It is indeed very common to find that the person you send it to hardly reads it all, missing things which you may need responses to. These are at least in part responsible for the informal nature of much of modern communication[2] and contain many indiscretions and mistakes. Whereas a couple of written letters a day would have been considered a lot, it is not uncommon for individuals to compose and send tens or even hundreds of e-mails or text messages a day. Many of these might be copied needlessly to third parties or even sent needlessly to the primary party. In big companies, it is interesting to speculate just how much of it has any value at all.

We live in an era of low viscosity communication so a few more comments might be appropriate.

---

[2]Such as being called "Chief" by your students occasionally.

1.2.1 e-mail pollution

Whilst it has no doubt transformed our lives, e-mail has not been without it's problems, not the least of which is e-mail overload. The central theme of this book is of course junk mail which Anne-Françoise Rutkowski and Michiel van Genuchten term *external pollution* in [48]. Using data collected within a sub-unit of a multinational corporation they point out that internal or *e-mail pollution* is also a significant problem, in other words people send each other far too many pointless e-mails, for example by adding unnecessary recipients via the CC list.

Even without the growing spam problem, such internal e-mail pollution was leading to massive overloads on managers with some reporting several thousand unread genuine messages. In this book, I will offer no advice for this other than to pass on the three rules they recommend:-

Rule 1 No more reply to all because this leads to e-mail avalanches.

Rule 2 No more copies than originals. Don't just add anybody who might be interested.

Rule 3 No more e-mail fights. Talk it through instead.

I will also give some idea of how these can be enforced within the infrastructure I will describe later.

1.2.2 e-mail blindness

As many e-mail users will know, it is very easy to miss something in the middle of an e-mail. They are scanned quickly by the reader because there are so many and the likelihood of all points in a relatively long e-mail being answered or even read is not high. This is part of a wider problem of ECO (Emotional and Cognitive Overload) discussed in an interesting and very recent article, [47].

Perhaps the best thing is to keep e-mails simple and short with perhaps only one main point if you want them to be answered in full.

1.2.3 e-mail subject obfuscation

I put this in as a personal irritation. The scenario is this. Somebody e-mails you with a particular subject in the Subject: line. As the discussion develops and diversifies, more people enter, the subject changes but *not* the Subject: line. This just has an endless succession of "Re:" before the original and long irrelevant subject. I do it myself. Wouldn't it be so much nicer to make the Subject: line reflect the content of the e-mail[3].

1.3 A little history

e-mails are no longer a new technology, although unusually in computing, they remain a dominant means of communication both personally and corporately, in spite of the appearance of SMS (text) messages on mobile phones and more recently social interaction through Facebook, Twitter and so on.

The first e-mails were sent in the early 1970s and looked very much the same as they do today. They are based around standard protocols. A protocol is simply an agreed way whereby two or more systems can communicate. I am being deliberately very general about systems here. A very good example of an early system communication protocol is the key originally passed between trains on single track railways. The idea here is that a single key belonged to that piece of track. A train was not allowed to enter the single track unless the driver had the key. On exiting, the driver handed the key over to a driver wishing to travel in the opposite direction. Since there was only one key, only one train could be on the single track at any one time. Nowadays this is replaced by electronic signalling software but the principles are the same.

As I will describe shortly, e-mails are exchanged in between computers using somewhat more complicated protocols which each computer has to follow in order for the e-mail to be passed correctly. The sending protocol is known as SMTP (Simple Mail Transfer Protocol) and the receiving protocols are POP3 (Post Office Protocol) and IMAP (Internet Message Access Protocol). You shouldn't normally have to know this stuff but if you ever have to set up a mobile phone with a mail provider not in the phone defaults, then it won't do any harm to understand what the words mean[4].

---

[3]We are talking revolutionary concepts here.

[4]Whenever the instructions say "contact your system administrator", a mythical being almost impossible to find when you need one, this is the bit you need to know

1.4 A gentle reminder on privacy

In general, an (unencrypted) e-mail is about as private as writing your innermost thoughts on a holiday postcard and handing it to a complete stranger to post for you or alternatively, shouting them across a crowded room to another. If you haven't yet come across a postcard, another way of thinking of it is as a letter with the message written on the outside of the envelope. It is in other words, completely open. Although it is possible to encrypt them to make them private, this is rarely the case and the vast majority are in what is known as *plain text*, i.e. readable by anybody. In spite of this, people are frequently very indiscreet about what they write, assuming a level of privacy which is in practice, non-existent. I have personal experience of former acquaintances and colleagues writing astonishingly indiscreet messages to others unaware that they can not only be read easily by third-parties but that they are also often backed up for legal or governance reasons. The result is that they can be at best highly embarrassing and at worst very damaging indeed[5].

The assumption of privacy (which in practice is often illusory) seems a feature of low viscosity communication methods with Facebook and Twitter both being notorious for such indiscretions[6]. You see precisely the same thing with mobile phone users who bellow their deepest secrets in crowded areas under the touching assumption that nobody is listening[7].

1.5 Obscurity is no help

Your e-mail address is your brand and is an exceptional asset. We live in a privileged generation where quite often you can still get your name or something closely recognisable in your own country's domain. This won't continue for very long as more and more people take up the technology. You will want to keep your e-mail address as a life-long asset and you can give it to somebody in the full knowledge that they can find you easily and quickly

---

[5] It's not just individuals who behave like this. Most law practices for example, freely transmit confidential information by e-mail with a disclaimer at the end. This may be OK for FAX transmissions which are difficult to eavesdrop but is completely unacceptable for e-mail messages almost all of which pass in clear across the net readable by anybody !

[6] To the extent now of encouraging web-sites on the subject as at http://willmoffat.github.com/FacebookSearch/.

[7] If you find this irritating and you can't move, start reading aloud from a book next to them. Within a couple of sentences, they will be too distracted to talk.

in the world by a number of communication channels which have bridging protocols to the e-mail system just using that address, (mobile phones and so on). It is not only your unique identifier but as technology progresses it will identify your location and perhaps other details about you, (which hopefully you have chosen to share).

Ultimately, your e-mail address will gradually creep out. For example, it is relatively common for people to get their hotmail accounts and mailing lists hijacked[8]. As a result, the junk mailers will get their hands on your e-mail address at some stage, either directly by stealing it or indirectly because you are on the mailing list of somebody who has had their's stolen. If you are careful with your passwords, you shouldn't get it stolen unless there is a major break-in but it's very likely it's existence will be advertised to the junk mailers. At this point, you could move on and get a new address which means you have to tell your valid contacts, a chore you can do without in a busy life. Alternatively, you can follow the advice in this book and armour-plate it so that junk mail does not get through and does not interfere with your valid mail.

To delay the leaking out of your valuable e-mail address, it is common for people, (even academic computer scientists), to obfuscate the way their address appears on their web pages, for example, lesh@oakcomp.co.uk might be lesh (at) oakcomp (dot) co (dot) uk. In my view this is ultimately a complete waste of time as junk mailers have even been known to employ labour in underdeveloped countries to transcribe them by hand. Not only that, but not everybody knows the correct format for an e-mail[9]. It is better to face up to it and use your full e-mail address. Sooner or later, they will get it anyway so you might as well be ready and waiting.

1.5.1 Slowing e-mail diffusion

If you do want to put off the evil day as long as possible because your ISP isn't much use at defending your address, it is worth noting that some

---

[8]About every three weeks, this happens to an acquaintance. You know this as soon as you receive an apparently normal message from them, usually CC'd to other friends who you may know, but the content is toxic - either spam or one of the many kinds of scam.

[9]Some years ago, a distinguished but elderly scientist unfamiliar with the ways of the web, wrote to me by post after failing to contact me by e-mail when he typed lesh (at) oakcomp (dot) co (dot) uk into his newly acquired copy of Outlook ! So the only person who was fooled by it, was the very one I wanted to hear from.

practices cause your e-mail address to leak out to the junk mailers much more quickly than other practices. For example, as noted by my colleague Rob Mellor [33], quoting an e-mail address on a web-site in the form of both Hyper Text and Markup Language as

```
<a href="mailto:lesh@oakcomp.co.uk">lesh@oakcomp.co.uk</a>
```

or, as Hyper Text only

```
<p>lesh@oakcomp.co.uk</p>
```

very quickly invited large amounts of spam due to the practice of *ripping*, whereby automated robots cruise around the web looking for easy pickings such as an obvious e-mail address.

Note that it is awfully easy to write a robot to do this. All it needs to do is incorporate a little bit of Perl looking for this pattern

```
#
#       Read web page text into $webtext.
#
...
while($webtext =~ m/(w+)@(\w+)/ig)
{
#
#       Hoover away.
#
        my      $uridom    = lc $2;
#
#       Sometimes people screw up the format.
#
        $uridom            =~ s/^www\.//;

        ++$hoover_email{$uridom};
}
```

As mentioned above, obfuscating the e-mail as

```
<p>lesh _AT_ oakcomp DOT co dot uk</p>
```

helps for a little while until somebody paid to look for this stuff manually finds it and translates it and then sells it. Then it's public property.

You can also slow the process of diffusion down by using Javascript which opens up a web page to which there are no links from the main site, (known as an *orphan page.*), and therefore defeating the rippers as follows:-

```
<script language="JavaScript">
function popup(URL) {window.open(URL,'popup')}
</script>
...
<a href="javascript:popup('orphan.html')">succulent e-mail address</a>
...
```

where orphan.html contains

```
<a href="mailto:lesh@oakcomp.co.uk">lesh@oakcomp.co.uk</a>
```

I won't say any more about slowing things down here as, as I have stated above, ultimately it's futile if you want to hang on to your e-mail address indefinitely.

1.6 The legal view of junk mailing

In short, if you are tempted, spamming and it's many derivatives are illegal in most jurisdictions. For example, in Europe, it became illegal on 31 October 2003[10]. The act left it up to individual European members to implement. In the UK, laws came into being on the 11 December 2003[11] providing for a fine of 5,000 pounds in a Magistrate's court (although unlimited if tried by a jury) but continued to allow spamming of commercial addresses for which they were roundly criticized, by amongst others, Spamhaus. In other countries in the EU, for example, Italy, much heavier penalties were prescribed including fines up to 90,000 Euros and jail sentences of up to three years.

In the USA, the CAN-SPAM[12] deals with the same issue and is both broad in scope and punitive in nature.

---

[10]Directive 2002/58/EC of the European Parliament and of the Council of 12 July 2002 concerning the processing of personal data and the protection of privacy in the electronic communications sector, http://eur-lex.europa.eu/LexUriServ/LexUriServ.do?uri=CELEX:32002L0058:EN:HTML, and have a look particularly at Article 13.

[11]http://news.bbc.co.uk/1/hi/technology/3120628.stm

[12]http://en.wikipedia.org/wiki/CAN-SPAM_Act_of_2003

For a general description of laws around the world, this site[13] contains considerable further detail.

1.6.1 What is legal and what isn't

In essence, most jurisdictions have decided

- Unsolicited e-mails sent to a business address are legal provided:-
  - They are not anonymous or deliberately obfuscated.
  - They give ample and obvious opportunity to unsubscribe and that such unsubscription takes place promptly and permanently.

- Unsolicited e-mails sent to a private address are illegal.

There may be variations in detail but this seems to capture the initial legal thrust against spamming practices. Unfortunately, other aspects of the law sometimes conspire against each other to public detriment as will now be seen.

1.6.2 Freedom of Information and address harvesting

This short case history details one such example whereby existing legislation is uncomfortable with regard to spamming activities. In the United Kingdom, two particular Acts of Parliament interact to give undesirable side-effects in some cases.

First of all, note the following acronyms:-

- DPA, (Data Protection Act, 1998)

- ICO, (Information Commissioner's Office of England and Wales)

- FOIA (Freedom of Information Act, 2000)

- PECR (Privacy and Electronic Communications EC Directive 2003)

The problem is that FOIA 2000 allows a Freedom of Information request to be placed on any public organisation, which must then handle it an appropriate manner, disclosing the requested information unless it can present a considered argument to the contrary.

---

[13] http://spamlinks.net/legal-laws.htm

10

Early in 2010, such a request was made to every Higher Education Institution (HEI) in the UK for the e-mail addresses of every employee, numbering perhaps a million e-mail addresses altogether. This of course is a very valuable asset in the bulk mailing world. A number tried to deny the request using DPA 1998 but such requests are not deemed sufficiently strong by the ICO.

To cut a long story short, many HEIs have apparently complied and only two, (Sheffield-Hallam[14] and Kingston University[15]) have been successful, using arguments detailed in the Appendix, (p. 310) and based on an earlier request[16].

So what is wrong with this ? After all, the requester had claimed that the addresses would only be used for bulk mailing purposes associated with academic freedom of information, an apparently laudable goal. The real sting in this follows from:-

- The massive rise in scamming attacks detailed elsewhere in this book.

- *Successful FOIA requests are considered to place the corresponding information with the **public at large**.*

In other words, the release of such information is very likely to increase the number of successful scamming attacks, which given the central role of e-mail in public organisations and potential disruption of their activities on behalf of the public, would not be in the public interest.

This topic needs to be taken seriously given the threat levels. As I write this, it is 11am and my main server has already received (and rejected) over 11,000 junk mail messages today. Another 15-20,000 will arrive during the rest of the day at current levels of activity. More worryingly, about half of these will be scamming attacks.

1.7 The fall or rise of spam ?

On numerous occasions, both death *by* spam and death *of* spam have been forecast. Neither have come to pass - extremes rarely occur in the real

---

[14]http://www.ico.gov.uk/ /media/documents/decisionnotices/2011/fs_50344341.ashx
[15]http://www.ico.gov.uk/ /media/documents/decisionnotices/2011/fs_50315973.ashx
[16]http://www.informationtribunal.gov.uk/DBFiles/Decision/i101/MoD.pdf

world, which just muddles along in the middle somewhere most of the time
- "The report of my death is an exaggeration" as Mark Twain put it the
first time he was incorrectly feared dead.

As will be discussed individually and in much more detail later in this
book, various techniques have evolved to deal with junk mail. We can split
them up into several principle categories.

1.7.1 Content filtering

The earliest attempts at this involved simple keyword or phrase matching,
for example looking for "cheap loans" or whatever. Gradually this evolved
into weighted checks for numerous phrases associated with junk and the
appearance of the very widely used SpamAssassin. This kept pace for a
while and still forms part of the front-line defences of many mail servers
but a new content filtering technique appeared in 2002 following an influential proposal by Paul Graham utilising Bayesian statistical methods, (more
later). It was argued (with some considerable evidence), that the adaptive
nature of these methods meant that junk mailers will be forever involved
in catch-up. Indeed the success of these methods embedded in a mixture
of other analytic techniques forms the backbone of this book. Carefully
implemented, they are truly successful at present with no signs of failing as
yet.

1.7.2 Collaborative filtering

In collaborative filtering, a mail server collaborates with other mail servers
which store junk mail characteristics. In effect a collaborating server says,
"I've just received this. Is it anything like any of the other junk you have
received ?".

1.7.3 Reputation analysis

There are a number of organisations on the web which maintain active lists
of mail servers which are implicated in junk mail at any one time. Many of
these are free to use for non-commercial use and some for commercial use
also although subscription for commercial use is usually very reasonable.

Probably the best known of these is Spamhaus[17].

---

[17] http://www.spamhaus.org/

1.7.4 Sender Authentication

This comprises a grab-bag of techniques based on the principles of *Sender Authentication*. The comprehensive white paper published by Meng Weng Wong[18] paints the backdrop for this. Again I will discuss this in more detail later, when I discuss the Domain Name System in enough detail to see it's relevance in junk mailing (on p. 30). For now, I will just give some general principles.

The main principle is very simple and is exemplified in Figure 1.1 on p. 14. When a sending mail server (indicated in the figure by "sending MTA"[19] sends a mail on behalf of say, somebody@sender.com to a receiving MTA, the receiving MTA gets (amongst other things) two pieces of information. It gets the domain name of the e-mail which is being sent (sender.com) and it also gets the IP address of the sending MTA (X.X.X.X). Sender authentication is then simply a process whereby the receiving MTA can extract information from the internet infrastructure[20] to say whether the IP address X.X.X.X is allowed to send mail from sender.com or not. The idea is that if it is not, the mail should be simply rejected on the grounds that the MAIL FROM: address has been spoofed by person or persons unknown.

This along with related techniques to be described shortly, was expected by the author of the white paper to end spam effectively, (by the end of 2005 according to the white paper although this appears somewhat tongue in cheek. I hope it was.).

1.7.5 Network properties

In a recent paper, Beverly and Sollins [3] investigate the possibility of identifying a piece of junk mail from it's transmission characteristics (TCP/IP) as it travels across the web. The principle behind this is that junk mailers must send a large volume of mail very quickly usually from various hi-jacked machines (botnets) before they get shut down by collaborative filtering systems as described above. As they discover, this tends to lead to characteristic signatures in various transmission time properties allowing them to identify junk mail quite effectively without even looking at it.

---

[18]http://www.pobox.com/whitepaper.pdf.

[19]MTA = Mail Transfer Agent as will be defined in the next chapter.

[20]I will expand on what I mean by internet infrastructure shortly but this teasing reference will do for now.

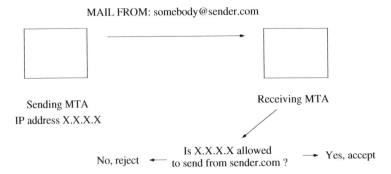

Figure 1.1: Illustrating the essential principle of sender authentication. MAIL FROM: is part of the SMTP protocol which is used by sending and receiving MTA (Mail Transfer Agents) to talk to each other.

This independent view is very likely to be complementary to the techniques discussed later in this book.

1.7.6 Challenge-Response

There are some organisations which offer a challenge-response service. It works like this

- I send a message to somebody at say challenge-response.org.

- I get an automatic e-mail back telling me that my message has been quarantined and that I have to do something like click on a link on a web-site to release it or something.

At this point, I give up. In the parlance of junk mail measurement, the system has clocked up a FP (False Positive) (p. 82 if you can't wait) because it has driven off a genuine e-mail. In effect the other party is expecting me to sort out their spam filtering for them. I thought at first I was being a tad sensitive about this but it was pleasing to see that others felt the same way[21] [22] [23].

---

[21] http://www.jgc.org/antispam/02282005-60dfea1d4f36a4071c21d1ba86f5e988.pdf
[22] http://kmself.home.netcom.com/Rants/challengeresponse.html
[23] http://email.about.com/cs/spamgeneral/a/challenge_resp.htm

Perhaps the worst thing about it is that it is capable of substantial abuse by junk mailers as follows.

- Such systems rely on the From: or the Envelope Sender address, both of which can be abused, p. 29.

- As John Graham-Cumming points out, most people will use and therefore have white-listed[24] Yahoo or Amazon to allow them through and so a junk mailer could forge these as a From: address and go straight through.

- Junk mailers can fake challenges and send you through to a toxic link for your response.

- Junk mailers can *backscatter* off them, p. 182.

They are in other words ineffectual against junk mailers and they irritate genuine users although you still find people depending on them. I really don't like them and never confirm them. If somebody wants to make it a little bit harder to contact them, that's fine, I won't bother, life's complicated enough. I believe it is everybody's responsibility to sort out their own junk without unloading the problem on somebody else.

1.7.7 The current reality

For all sorts of reasons, as we will see, none of these methodologies has killed off spam however. *By definition, any killer technique worth it's salt must undermine the economics of junk mailing to the point where it no longer has any value to the junk mailer.* It is certainly true that by using a combination of techniques (which in this case feature Bayesian content filtering at their heart), I see almost no junk in my valid mailboxes[25]. However my mail servers were bombarded at around the rate of 300,000 junk mails per domain per week each throughout much of 2010. In the summer of 2010, (I am writing this bit in October), it peaked at over 1,000,000 junk mails per domain per week each for two dizzy months[26]. It is clear then that we have failed in general. The only sane conclusion of this is that most people simply do not use or have access to these techniques. If they did, no doubt the junk mailers would evolve other techniques[27].

---

[24] A list of users who you are happy to hear from and discussed in more detail later.

[25] Around 3 falsely categorised messages per million to be precise.

[26] It must be the heat.

[27] There is some current evidence of this in that junk mailers are undermining sender authentication methods by their success at infiltrating valid machines and networks.

So, the most likely scenario is that it won't go away and it won't overwhelm us. Instead, all the evidence currently suggests that the perpetrators and the defenders will continue locked in an ever-evolving arms race. On the one hand, scamming has a long history of success and the digital world simply opens up a wider and cheaper marketplace in spite of the efforts of forensic analysts to deny them the opportunity. On the other hand, if you use the best techniques, you won't see any. On average however, there remains enough business to keep on sending junk so you may as well get used to the idea.

As a personal footnote to this chapter, if it disappeared tomorrow, I think I would be left with an intense feeling of loss after three years of watching it's ever-changing character and marvelling at the ingenuity of thieves. However that's a selfish thought and if I can contribute in some small way to it's ultimate demise, that would suit me fine. There are lots of other interesting problems to work on.

And now to work ...

2 How it all works

In order to protect yourself, it's best to know how e-mail works. If you are not inherently technical, don't worry, it is written to be as simple as possible without leaving anything important out. Although we have by both necessity and also choice, added several layers of complexity, it remains at it's heart very simple.

2.1 Sending a message from A to B

Figure 2.1 (p. 19) illustrates a typical route which e-mails might take. It works like this.

- The sender sitting at computer A composes an e-mail message. The computer is merely a representation here. It could be a PDA, mobile phone or whatever. A fancier name for the mail software you use to create the e-mail is a MUA (Mail User Agent). Examples of MUAs include Outlook (Windows), Mail (Mac OSX), Mozilla Thunderbird (all) and kmail (Linux). There are lots of others but these are the ones I use most often. The sender then presses send. We will suppose the sender's own e-mail address is me@sender.com. Mails are sent using a protocol called SMTP.

- The senders's computer A wraps an envelope around the message, adds an address to the envelope in a standard form (more of this later but have a quick look at Figure 2.2 (p. 26) if you want to jump ahead a bit) and sends the message to a sending mail server, (known as an MTA (Mail Transfer Agent)). The sending MTA could be one of the free ones, hotmail, yahoo or whatever, the mail server provided by your Internet Service Provider (ISP) or your own as we will discuss later. If you are using webmail, the MUA is usually running on the sending MTA itself.

  The sending MTA checks that the sender address (you) is valid and then checks the destination address for validity which it does using something called a DNS (Domain Name System) lookup. This simply takes the destination address say myfriend@destination.com, splits off the myfriend@ bit to leave destination.com and then looks up the IP address corresponding to this on the relevant DNS databases which are themselves servers located in various parts of the world and look like big telephone directories with entries like:-

destination.com 123.213.132.001

(It's a little more complicated than this but this will do for now. Note that a forward DNS lookup provides destination.com and gets back 123.213.132.001 and a reverse DNS lookup provides 123.213.132.001 and gets back destination.com)

- The sending MTA then sends the message to the machine holding the IP address 123.213.132.001 which then is known as the receiving MTA.

- The receiving MTA checks the myfriend@destination.com address and delivers it to the mailbox of the user myfriend using an MDA (Mail Delivery Agent) (which we will assume exists for now). Although I have shown it separately, the Mail Store is just a bit of disc space usually on the MTA somewhere.

- The user myfriend checks his mail using the mail software (MUA) on his computer B to talk to the MDA and read or download his message using protocols called POP3 or IMAP. Again don't worry about these for now. Note also that the MDA and the receiving MTA are different bits of software although often resident on the same physical machine.

And that's it. Of course it can get a bit more complicated than this for example if mails are rejected somewhere in the route or if some servers simply pass messages on to other servers (relaying), but this will do for now and I will repeatedly refer back to Figure 2.1 to jog your memory.

2.2 Nerd corner: talking to a mail server

As a fully paid up Babylonian[1], it came as a great (and pleasant) surprise to me that you can pretend to be a mail server and talk to another mail

---

[1]Babylonians learn by sticking their fingers in electric sockets in comparison to Aristotleans who learn by thinking great thoughts and abstractions. Aristotleans can light

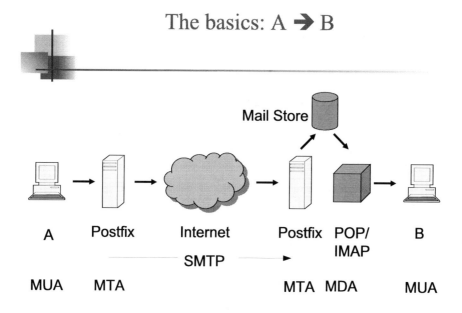

Figure 2.1: A typical route through the web for e-mails sent by A and received by B.

server. Many of you may be thinking I should get out more (I should) but this simple transaction tells you much about the mail system.

In general I am a big fan of software protocols which are in human-readable form because for one thing, they are much easier to test and for another, you can learn how they work much more quickly. There was once a time when computer scientists persuaded themselves that machine-only readable protocols full of digital gibberish were more efficient and therefore preferable but I am glad those days have mostly passed. Much of the web runs on human-readable protocols such as http: (HyperText Transfer Protocol), ftp: (File Transfer Protocol) and smtp: (Simple Mail Transfer Protocol) just under the surface and it is only when you delve down deep into the dark world of TCP/IP that it becomes streams of digits flying around in squadrons called packets, (this is a big subject so I will say little more than go and read as much as you need of [24]). You have to talk hexadecimal[2] to exist in this world and we do not need to. Let's meet the mail protocols and appreciate them in a little more depth.

2.2.1 The protocols

This is probably why the original protocols arose in this form although their exact form is described in documents known as RFCs. An RFC (Request For Comment) document is a publicly available document which describes the protocols which mail software must speak in order to communicate with one another. They are not required nor are they normative but they are exceptionally influential. There are several ones relevant to this book, which collectively form part of the IP (Internet Protocol) suite:-

SMTP RFC 821 describes the SMTP protocol[3]. This is the protocol used for transferring e-mail between MTAs and also sending outgoing mail from your MUA to the MTA responsible for sending it on.

Headers RFC 822 describes the allowable format of the headers like From:, To: and so on[4].

---

up light bulbs with the sheer force of their personality whereas Babylonians tend to walk around in a confused state much of the time. The great 20th century physicist Richard Feynman had much to say on this but unfortunately I can't remember the reference and I couldn't find it but I think it's in his wonderful book on Quantum Electrodynamics[14]. If you can only afford either this book or that one, buy that one.

[2]You need to take your socks off to count in base 16.

[3]http://www.faqs.org/rfcs/rfc821.html

[4]http://www.faqs.org/rfcs/rfc822.html

POP3 RFC 1939 describes the POP3 protocol[5]. This is one of the protocols used for incoming e-mail from the receiving MTA to your MUA.

IMAP RFC 3501 describes the IMAP protocol[6]. This is the more modern protocol used for incoming e-mail from the receiving MTA to you MUA, (although in the case of IMAP it remains on the MTA).

MIME RFC 2045, 2046, 2047, 2049, 4288 and 4289 describe the MIME protocols[7]. MIME stands for Multi-purpose Internet Mail Extensions and this series of linked RFCs explains how rich content, (for example, video, photographic, audio and other content as well as the many kinds of document such as Word, pdf and so on) is transported by e-mail.

Together these protocols have bent a bit under the strain since the definitions in some cases twenty years ago, but have managed to adapt sufficiently to keep the innovation moving. OK, we have a spam problem but if you removed the e-mail system over-night, much of modern society would be crippled[8].

2.2.2 An actual SMTP conversation

I am now going to send a message from a normal e-mail address alice@send.com to bob@receive.com. (This is simulated so the domain names and IP addresses are bogus). To do this you just type in the bold face lines in what follows in a terminal window on Linux or in the Command Line window in Windows.

---

[5]http://www.faqs.org/rfcs/rfc1939.html
[6]http://www.faqs.org/rfcs/rfc3501.html
[7]http://www.faqs.org/rfcs/rfc2045.html etc
[8]I was in Egypt on holiday in January 2011 during the demonstrations and the internet was taken down throughout the country. It was like losing a limb.

```
$ telnet receive.com 25
Trying 127.0.0.1...
Connected to receive.com.
Escape character is ']'.
220 receiver.com ESMTP Postfix
HELO send.com
250 send.com
MAIL FROM:<alice@send.com>
250 Ok
RCPT TO:<bob@receive.com>
250 Ok
DATA
254 End data with <CR><LF>.<CR><LF>(In English, an
empty line)
Your mail message goes here followed by a .
.
250 Ok queued as ...
quit
221 bye
Connection closed by foreign host
$
```

Figure 2.2.2 shows a transaction with a MTA using the SMTP protocol. You type the bold face commands. Note that there can be multiple RCPT TO: commands issued for several recipients although there is only one in this case.

That's it. You have now talked to a mail server in exactly the same way as your mail software does using the SMTP protocol. Wasn't that nice. Transactions can be rather more complicated than this but the minimum you have to do is to say HELO[9], revealing who you are; say MAIL FROM: telling it who the mail is coming from; say RCPT TO: telling it who you want the mail to go to and then say DATA to give it the message body (i.e. the bit you write including any attachments). The other mail server was responding with a numeric code such as "250" which is one of the responses it gives when it's happy with what you sent, (see the Appendix p. 302 for more on these codes).

---

[9]or it's more modern equivalent EHLO - it's bset nto ot ask.

There are few other bits of the SMTP protocol which it is useful to know about.

The VRFY command

The original intention of this was to be able to verify that a user existed before attempting to send them an e-mail message. Nowadays unfortunately, it is primarily used by junk mailers to identify valid addresses to squirt junk at. The modern view therefore is that it should be disabled in the receiving MTA[10]. For example on my Postfix server, it is disabled and you get the response

```
VRFY ericthehedgehog
502 5.5.1 VRFY command is disabled
```

The EXPN command

This expands mailing lists and is nowadays not used for similar reasons to VRFY.

Extended SMTP

The original SMTP (defined by the late Jon Postel in the 70s), has proved very robust but one important thing which was missing was some kind of password authentication. This was added later in what became known as Extended SMTP and it's associated HELO command, EHLO. You indicate to the receiving SMTP that you would like to use this by issuing the EHLO command:

```
EHLO send.com
```

This invites the receiving MTA to describe what facilities it supports, each one returned on a line of it's own as the following example shows

```
250-receive.com
250-PIPELINING
250-SIZE 104857600
```

---

[10]In Postfix you can either disable it with disable_vrfy_command = yes in main.cf or you can rate-limit it using the smtpd_junk_command_limit = 10 or something. If you are not quite sure what these mean, you can look ahead to p. 134

```
250-ETRN
250-AUTH LOGIN PLAIN
250-ENHANCEDSTATUSCODES
250-8BITMIME
250 DSN
```

The sending MTA then knows what it can use, although details of this are not important here.

That's all you really need to know about SMTP.

2.3 Headers and Content

When I first started with mails, one thing confused me initially and that's the distinction between headers, content and the envelope. The confusing thing is that the envelope is a bunch of extra headers and the thing the envelope is wrapped round is other headers plus your content. Confused ? Let me explain.

A mail message is defined in RFC 822 as:

A message consists of header fields and, optionally, a body. The body is simply a sequence of lines containing ASCII[11] characters. It is separated from the headers by a null line (i.e., a line with nothing preceding the CRLF (i.e. carriage return and line feed characters)).

2.3.1 Headers

So we have established that headers are everything that appears before the first empty[12] line. The (slightly) confusing thing is that the headers you see in a raw e-mail come partly from the mail software you used to compose your e-mail (MUA) and partly from the envelope that the sending MTA

---

[11] American Standard Code for Information Interchange.

[12] Lest I become sloppy, it is tempting to use the phrase 'blank line'. However, this could mean a line full of space characters, (what you get when you hit the space bar). This is not an empty line. In e-mails, an empty line separates the header from the body. An empty line is simply two newline characters next to each other with the first one terminating the previous line and the second one terminating the empty line. Confusingly, newlines are traditionally indicated by <Carriage return> <Line feed> on some machines (Windows) and just <Line feed> on others (Linux). Fortunately this shenanigans is hidden from you.

adds in Figure 2.1 (p. 19). In other words in the raw e-mail, the headers you can see partly came from your entries in the To:, From:, Subject: and other fields which you specified in your mail client, added to the envelope headers which come from the details of the SMTP transaction, (HELO, MAIL FROM:, RCPT TO:) shown in Figure 2.2.2 on p. 22. We will see which is which later.

2.3.2 Content

The content is the body of the message, which is basically everything after the first blank line. This can be in several pieces, (what is called a MIME message) and the pieces might be a bit of text, a Word document, a bit of rich text dressed up in HTML or any of a large number of other things. Each bit is separated by the MIME separator, a bit of random text placed there by the original composing software to split up your message appropriately. (The program on p. 285 of the appendix can read these.)

2.3.3 The mail envelope

The sending MTA wraps up your message with the envelope which is a few bits of information necessary to pass it through the system. The process is shown in Figure 2.2 (p. 26). These pieces are derived from the telnet conversation shown on p. 22.

2.3.4 A real e-mail message in the raw

Now let's have a look at one in the raw. Normally all you see is the mail body which is the bit right at the end and this will normally be rendered by your mail software to look nice as shown in Figure 2.3 (p. 26).

To understand the subterfuge which underlies spam and the multitude of scams, we have to look a little deeper. It's a bit daunting but is actually simpler than it looks at first sight. I have blanked out a few identifying characteristics but it is in every other regard a genuine e-mail. Note that the references to "sending MTA" and so on refer directly to Figure 2.1 (p. 19). As you can see, there is a fair amount going on behind the scenes for the bit that you actually look at in Figure 2.3 (p. 26). Here it is broken down into simple sections.

First of all, the following are the envelope headers added by the receiving MTA. Note that Return-Path: is the MAIL FROM address.

The basics: Headers and Content

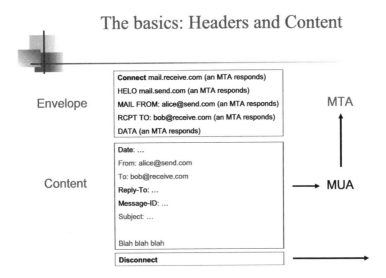

Figure 2.2: Indicating the separation of envelope and content. The content is a mixture of headers and your mail message assembled by your mail software (MUA - Outlook and the rest), and then wrapped up in an envelope containing details of the HELO discussion between the MUA and the sending MTA. Normally you can only see your message (including any attachments) and a few headers such as From:, To:, cc:, Date: and Subject:. The rest is normally hidden. In the case of the Outlook webmail program, it is hidden so effectively that it can't be found, thus depriving the user of possibly important information.

Figure 2.3: The nice version of the e-mail whose raw content is shown below.

```
Return-Path: xxxx@blueyonder.co.uk
Delivered-To: lesh@oakcomp.co.uk
Received: by localhost.oakcomp.com (Postfix, from userid 1016)
    id 40A386597F; Thu, 15 Jul 2010 13:20:15 +0100 (BST)
```

Next, the X-Spam-xxxx headers are added by the well-known SpamAssassin software (more later) running on the receiving MTA. The capitalised codes like HTML_MESSAGE are codes which SpamAssassin inserts after inspecting your e-mail. The score of -0.7 is pretty good. The bigger the score, the more suspicious it is and anything over about 5 is definitely flakey.

```
X-Spam-Checker-Version: SpamAssassin 3.3.1 (2010-03-16) on
    localhost.oakcomp.com
X-Spam-Level:
X-Spam-Status: No, score=-0.7 required=5.0 tests=HTML_MESSAGE,
    RCVD_IN_DNSWL_NONE,SPF_PASS,
    T_RP_MATCHES_RCVD ...
```

Next, grey-listing information is added. This is another sophisticated spam reducing process and is also running on the receiving MTA, (more later on p. 139).

```
X-Greylist: delayed 2903 seconds by postgrey-1.33 at
    localhost.oakcomp.com; Thu, 15 Jul 2010 13:20:12 BST
Received: from smtp-out5.blueyonder.co.uk
    (smtp-out5.blueyonder.co.uk [195.188.213.8])
    by localhost.oakcomp.com (Postfix) with
      ESMTP id E40A365970
    for \textless lesh@oakcomp.co.uk\textgreater;
    Thu, 15 Jul 2010 13:20:11 +0100 (BST)
```

That concludes the first part of the complete e-mail message with annotation and is the part added by the receiving MTA at the end of the process. Now we will deal with the headers added by the sending MTA. (Note that the most recently added headers appear at the top).

```
Received: from [172.23.170.136] (helo=anti-virus01-07)
    by smtp-out5.blueyonder.co.uk with smtp (Exim 4.52)
    id 1OZMfM-0001vk-La; Thu, 15 Jul 2010 12:31:48 +0100
Received: from [92.234.192.14] (helo=brokenheart)
    by asmtp-out1.blueyonder.co.uk with smtp (Exim 4.52)
```

```
    id 1OZMfH-0001cM-DV; Thu, 15 Jul 2010 12:31:43 +0100
Message-ID: <000f01cb2411$4c7b8b00$0ec0ea5c@brokenheart>
```

The following are the headers added by your mail composing software based on what you type. Note that the From: may be different from the Return-Path:

```
From: "xxxx" <yxzzy@blueyonder.co.uk>
To: "yyyy" <yyyy@juniperhillblues.co.uk>,
    "zzzz" <zzzz@oakcomp.co.uk>
Subject: Hallo
Date: Thu, 15 Jul 2010 12:31:40 +0100
```

Your message has multiple bits so here the separator (boundary) is defined.

```
MIME-Version: 1.0
Content-Type: multipart/alternative;
    boundary="----=_NextPart_000_000C_01CB2419.AD1D1DE0"
```

The following just identifies the mail composing software the sender used.

```
X-Priority: 3
X-MSMail-Priority: Normal
X-Mailer: Microsoft Outlook Express 6.00.2900.3664
X-MimeOLE: Produced By Microsoft MimeOLE V6.00.2900.3664
Status: R
X-Status: N
X-KMail-EncryptionState:
X-KMail-SignatureState:
X-KMail-MDN-Sent:
```

Finally, here's the empty line put in by your composing software and then your message.

```
                        <----- empty
Greetings folks ...
```

This concludes the second part showing the items added by the sending MTA along with your original message and therefore concludes the e-mail.

Now here is the really bad news.

> Nearly everything you see above can be spoofed i.e. forged, and
> this is exactly what spammers, scammers and other abusers do in
> order to get their stuff into your mailbox.

To be more specific,

Bits that can be spoofed

- Subject:

- Date:

- Message-ID:

- From:

- To:

- CC:

- BCC:

- Received: (except the most recent)

- Any arbitrary headers, X-Mailer: and so on.

- Content

Bits that can NOT be spoofed

- The most recent Received: (i.e. the topmost)

- Originating mail server, specifically it's IP address

- Subsequent timestamps

It is therefore the nature of e-mails that the only things that can't be
spoofed are things you can't normally see, (none of the above list is visible
in Figure Figure 2.3 (p. 26)). Before having a look at the kind of things
which junk mailers get up to, I will just give a bit more detail about how
it all works. Feel free to skip this if you wish and jump to the start of the
next chapter on p. 35.

2.4 A little more detail you can skip

2.4.1 The role of the Domain Name System

I wasn't going to include this section at first but I struggled with this for some time, so I thought it would be useful as a kind of struggling person's guide to how you find your way around the Internet. In short, the Domain Name System (DNS) is absolutely fundamental to the functioning of the Internet.

Let me approach it by describing the process of acquiring a domain name, (**uisgebeatha.info**), which is one of mine. If you didn't know, *uisge beatha* is the Scots Gaelic word for whisky, (literally water of life).

1. You need to register it. The first challenge is to understand the difference between Registry, Registrar and Registration, (I did tell you that you could skip this bit.)

   - *Registry*: An organisation responsible for looking after a top level domain, (such as .info in my case), also known as a *TLD*. In Internet speak, the top-most part of a domain name is the rightmost part, (see below).

   - *Registrar*: These basically act as agents for one or more of the registries. There are lots of them and these are the people you get your brand spanking new domain name from. In exchange only for a little money, they check your domain name is available, collect your contact details and register the domain. At the same time, if you have them available and have any idea of what I am talking about yet, they will take the details of the *name servers* for these domains. If you don't have them, they will assign two of their own name servers to handle your domain which can be changed when you do understand what you are doing, (More later). All this information is used to register your domain name and other details with the registry which handles the top-level domain you have chosen, (.com, org, .info or one of the country ones such as (.co).uk).

   - *Registration*: This is simply the act of registering your domain name where you tell the Registrar to register it on your behalf with the Registry.

2. So it's registered. Assuming you want a web-site, you then need somewhere for your domain to live. For most people, this means finding a

hosting company, of which there are thousands, to give you a bit of space on their server and make sure that everybody knows that your domain name points to that bit of space. They will charge you for this in general, but it's usually peanuts.

At this point you find that you now have something called an IP address, which as an example, I will take to be 111.112.113.114. So all of a sudden you have your domain name uisgebeatha.info *and* an IP address. The IP address will be one of a fairly large number, (called a subnet) which your ISP has previously been allocated, (also by a process of registration which essentially registers the domain name 114.113.112.111.in-addr.arpa). Your ISP will have some kind of infrastructure (zones - more shortly) which takes responsibility for associating this IP address with your domain name and therefore allowing it to be found. If you change ISPs and move your site elsewhere, the domain name stays the same but the IP address will change. Unless you are going to go native and manage your own name servers, this is all you need to do, (or know).

Name servers

Surprisingly, people do not find it easy to memorise 12-number sequences. Instead, when we browse the web or send an e-mail, we would like to use meaningful names instead. The Domain Name System (DNS) is at the heart of this using a wonderful delegated system originally created by Paul Mockapetris, a researcher at the Information Sciences Institute (ISI) in 1983. First, you need to know a couple of other very widely used words.

- *Resolver*: One of the essential functions of the DNS is to take your easily remembered uisgebeatha.info, (I might have picked a better example here), and convert into it's currently assigned IP address which can then be used to find your machine[13]. The Resolver, (or name server as they are also known), is sublimely ignorant of all the underlying excitement. It's job is simply to turn a domain name into an IP address for those domains which it is responsible for or, if it doesn't know, to suggest another name server which might know.

- *Delegation*: This embodies the essential beauty of the system. If a small number of servers had to handle all the domain name to IP

---

[13]By traversing the infrastructure underlying the IP address, (it's called TCP/IP and it's a *big* subject filled with exotic animals like routers, gateways, packets, MAC addresses, protocol layers and so on, [24])

address conversions on the Internet, the whole thing would grind to a rapid halt. Instead, a small number of servers, (known as the root servers), handle TLDs and a few others and delegate the rest to servers further down in the system. In other words, a particular server is responsible for some part of the domain name system, (often a small number of related names). This process is called *delegation*. If you want to handle your own name servers, you just have to make sure they announce the domains they are handling and the IP addresses they correspond to, (in what are called it's zone files). The rest is handled by this delegation system.

The bottom line in all this excitement is that when we browse the web, meaningful names such as google.com are resolved at any one instant using the DNS into a particular computer IP address. With e-mail, we e-mail friend@somedomain.com and the sending MTA will use the DNS to find the IP address of the receiving MTA so that it can communicate with it.

In the IP address 111.112.113.114, 111 is known as class A, 112 as class B and 113 as class C[14], although allocating by these is wasteful so a format known as CIDR (Classless Inter-Domain Routing) is now used. Each number can go from 0 up to 255 giving up to 4 billion (2^{32} possibilities). In practice there are reserved internal networks, (for example 192.168.0.0 - 192.168.255.255) which help to increase the address space by associating one external IP address with one of these internal networks but as the world moves towards making everything have an IP address, we will run out quite soon. A technology called IPv6 is waiting in the wings for when we do. This has 128 bits in 8 16-bit chunks. It is therefore capable of addressing 2^{128} or 340,282,366,920,938,463,463,374,607,431,768,211,456 entities. I am reliably informed that this is enough to give every atom on over 100 earths it's own IP address. It is widely believed that the human race will have died out due to ATMS (Automated Telephone Menu Syndrome) long before this address space runs out.

That's probably as much as you need to know although it should be noted that it is a little more complicated than this because the net has to balance it's loads. It also has to be redundant and the information is therefore distributed amongst many nodes so that if some are lost, the referral system still works OK. On top of this, the whole infrastructure of name registry and maintenance was built.

---

[14]Defined by RFC 791 in 1981 with the 114 part left undefined for later.

Given that we rely completely and utterly on the sanctity of the DNS system, it is timely to remember that it occasionally has problems[15]. These lead to successful man in the middle attacks whereby A thinks they are talking to C, but they are actually talking to B who passes the conversation on to C so that neither A nor C realise.

---

[15]http://www.wired.com/politics/security/commentary/securitymatters/2008/07/securitymatters_0723

.

3 Scams, spam and other abuses

3.1 Overview

The principle reason for writing this book was because of the massive rise in scams, spam, phishing, identity theft and similar[1]. By far the most efficient way of delivering these toxic packages is by e-mail. I will use *junk mail* as an umbrella term for any kind of unwanted e-mail and give lots of real examples of these. This is also a health warning. The methods junk mailers use change very rapidly to combat improvements in protection systems. In other words, what we have is an arms race. At the moment, if you know what you are doing, it's very hard for junk mailers to get anything through. If you don't you will be overwhelmed by it.

Of course, most of the scamming techniques described below have been used since time immemorial in one form or another, the differences being that e-mail is a wonderful gift to a scammer because it is so efficient at reaching it's intended victims and as we have now seen, nearly everything can be spoofed.

A huge industry of anti-virus, anti-spam, anti-phishing products and the like has grown out of this. Unfortunately, most of these run on the recipient's machine shown as B in Figure 2.1 (p. 19). Some are good and some not so good but the fundamental problem is that they are always playing catch-up to the latest threat. *The ones delivered by e-mail should never get this far and that is the principle philosophy of this book.* That does not mean to say that these products have no value. Real protection requires defence in depth. Toxic e-mails should never get to you but if they do, and nothing is perfect, then they should not be able to poison your machine or lure you off anywhere nasty.

---

[1] Although this will be expanded on shortly, for the present just note that a scam is trying to hoodwink you into handing over money; spam is trying to get you to buy stuff you very likely do not want; phishing is attempting to get you to reveal financial details about yourself which can be sold on, such as credit card details and identity theft is the theft of personal details for all sorts of nefarious purposes. Naturally, these categories overlap but this rough distinction will do for now.

3.2 Know your enemy: examples of junk mail

There follows copious examples of this kind of thing sent to my own mail server[2]. Each is presented and analysed forensically. What we are looking for is sufficiently general patterns occurring which we can use to design defence systems of long-term value. Here I will merely identify the form of such mails and offer some forensic comments. Rules to remove these will be discussed under advanced content filtering later.

First however:-

The founding principle of junk mailing is to get through your mail defences without being trashed and then get you to click on a toxic link, visit a web-site, supply some information or persuade you to install something nasty on your machine without realising it.

As we will see, this will always be their Achilles heel.

3.3 UCE or UBE

UCE is the standard acronym for Unsolicited Commercial Email. It was once distinguished from something known as UBE, (Unsolicited Bulk Email), based on the volumes it is normally shipped in[3]. I am not so sure that distinguishing between them in this way is useful to the thread of discussion in this book so I will not and will refer to it hereafter as UCE.

The main defining characteristic of UCE is that it is *not anonymous*. The sender is genuinely trying to sell you something and makes no attempt to hide their name, contact details or other forms of identity. No attempt is made to spoof the e-mails even though they may have been delivered by a mailing organisation on behalf of the sender. In general, such a supplier will also be covered by prevailing laws on the supply of goods and services.

---

[2]For an even more copious set of examples see the excellent web source http://www.virusbtn.com/resources/spammerscompendium/index, accessed 22-Aug-2010. I do not break down this section with such fine-grained granularity because it has not been necessary to do this yet. The techniques described in this book take them *all* out. At the moment.

[3]The Usenet abuse FAQ as quoted on p. 19 [56] distinguishes by defining UCE as commercial in nature but not implying massive numbers based on the fact that several ISPs then specified thresholds for UCE.

Such organisations usually comply with Web standards and include an unsubscribe link in their mails. How you treat them depends entirely on the kind of product or service which is being pushed and whether or not you are an administrator or an end-user. An administrator should tag them as generic bulk mail on the receiving MTA so the end user can decide what to do when it finally reaches their mailbox. One person's favoured UCE can easily be another person's anathema. Tagging them as bulk mail simply informs the user that they are clean even if they unwanted.

A UCE mailer will cherish it's mailing list as an important business asset. e-mail addresses are gathered from trade shows, business cards, personal contacts and bought in from hopefully reputable sources. In other words they are qualified and should only contain addresses of people who are generally interested in the product. If a UCE mailer does not do this, they are in great danger of being blacklisted and this can really damage their ability to distribute[4].

A typical bulk mailer might send out 20,000 e-mails twice a week to it's qualified distribution list.

For UCE I wish to receive, you can use the presence of "unsubscribe" somewhere in the body of the mail to identify them, (after you have made sure there is nothing worse in there). This may also be re-worded as "do not wish to receive further ..." or something similar. It's a pretty reliable indicator and if junk mailers steal it, they will fall foul of later checks and get elevated to spam or worse. This is relevant to either the administrator of a mail server or the individual mail user.

Looking in the body of those I do not wish to receive, they are often sent by bulk-mailing companies who get hold of your e-mail address somehow, perhaps because you have shown interest in a particular product, and then bombard you with all kinds of other products you couldn't conceivably want. In this case, you can extract the domain name of the bulk-mailing company from the mail body (a small number of these are responsible for a lot of UCE), and reject anything from them. The administrator of a mail server should not do this though, it is an individual user's choice. Remember one user's UCE is another user's junk.

---

[4]I will discuss blacklisting in much more detail later but here I will simply note that it only takes one rogue address to make it onto a blacklist for the sending MTA to become blacklisted and this can take some time to correct.

3.4 Spam

UCE can be annoying but it doesn't do you any harm and companies sending bulk mail will normally act reasonably responsibly if you unsubscribe from their lists although you may not want to admit you exist, in which case don't unsubscribe, just discard.

Spam is an entirely different beast for the following reasons.

The sender is deliberately obscured I suppose there is almost a sense of fairplay about UCE. People make their living selling reasonable quality things which you might actually want. When the sender is deliberately obscured however by using a wide and evolving variety of techniques we will see shortly, that unbroken line is crossed.

You must not respond However much you are tempted to respond with language not normally used in polite company, you must not. You are simply telling the spammer that the address you are using is a good one. This means they can sell it on to others who want to spam you or worse, attempt to scam you. The way to defeat junk mailing is to deprive them of any feedback whatsoever, by not responding and/or by de-fanging (i.e. disabling the nasty bits) of their HTML pages - this is the real art of spoofing[5].

Volumes The volumes shipped by spammers are incredible. It is not uncommon for mailings of several million to be sent in one session. On my server, it fluctuates from day to day and week to week as can be seen on Figure 3.1 (p. 39), nearly all of which are received and silently discarded as described later. A recent estimate of 183 billion a day for the total amount of spam as of January 2010 can be found here[6]. This appears to be currently doubling around every two years.

---

[5]There is a wonderful example of this in a far more serious context, the second World War. In "Most Secret War" by R.V. Jones, [25], he describes one particular occasion where radar jamming was so successful by German engineers that a key Allied radar station in the Mediterranean was rendered completely useless. The operators of the radar station asked for advice as to what could be done. Professor Jones told them to simply keep the radar switched on operating as normal even though it was completely useless. After three days, the German engineers switched their jamming systems off because they thought they were not working, ruefully discovering the truth when they met up with Professor Jones after the war and asked him. So the lesson is NEVER give a junk mailer an even break.

[6]http://en.wikipedia.org/wiki/E-mail_spam

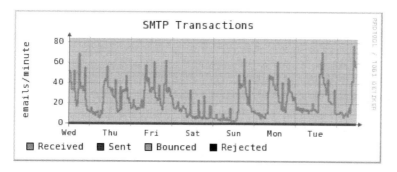

Figure 3.1: A week's worth of joy in August 2010. The relentless futility of all this energy can be seen by noting that the genuine mail activity of processed mails all collects invisibly down the bottom of the graph whilst the upper curve represents the junk that is received and nearly all of which is immediately binned. The spamming activity here is running at around 99.9% of all e-mail.

The cyclic nature of this blizzard changes. At the moment it tends to peak in the mornings here, and then die away during the day. The pattern was rather different when I started as can be seen on Figure 5.1 (p. 121) where you often got weekend peaks. This just reflects the nature of the primary junk mailers responsible and the time zones in which they operate. After a relatively quiet summer, things are now hotting up again. The day before I wrote this particular section on 24-Aug-2010, a sudden peak of 150,000 e-mails hit my server during a day with more than 11,000 an hour for several hours. Nearly all of these were aimed at a single domain. What an astonishing waste of time and energy. It's like listening to heavy rain on windows.

You may wonder about the economics of this. The success rate of such a mailing for Viagra or one of the other meds which flood the net is believed to be tiny. We can actually estimate it as follows.

Supposing you want to make a living at this and the thing you are pushing on somebody else's behalf costs say 20 dollars for which you might get 2 dollars commission on each. It might take you a couple of days to set up and deliver such a mailing so let's assume that you would like to earn 400 dollars a day to cover your living and

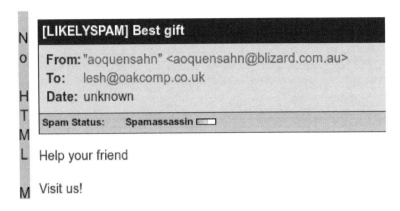

Figure 3.2: A typical piece of spam. Your "friend" here is a male body part south of the nose. By using this very indirect reference, the junk mailer hopes to defeat filtering mechanisms. This is a forlorn hope as we will see when we discuss statistical filtering methods.

your cost of equipment[7]. You therefore need to contact 400 people willing to buy this product in your mailing. However spammers might send out 4 million mails to achieve this, so the hit rate will only be around 0.001%. The other 3,999,600 have no interest whatsoever. If these numbers sound staggering, on average my mail server alone received 50,000 - 150,000 such mails *every* day whilst this book was in preparation, most of which is directed at me[8]. From these some 100 legitimate mails emerge but much more on this later.

3.4.1 Run of the mill rubbish - body parts etc.

Figure 3.2 (p. 40) is a fairly typical piece of spam advertising sites often in China and selling medicines which allegedly transfer most of the blood in your body to one unusual location.

It's not at all obvious where it comes from and the From: address shown is entirely bogus. In fact, this is a multi-part mail message (MIME format)

---

[7]If it was a lot more lucrative than this, there would be legions of people doing it and competition would force the price back down.

[8]Perhaps I shouldn't complain. According to http://en.wikipedia.org/wiki/E-mail_spam, the most spammed person on the planet is Jef Poskanzer, owner of the domain name acme.com, who was receiving over one million spam e-mails per day in 2004.

and the second part shown in Figure 3.4 (p. 43), contains the payload, a piece of HTML which will drag you off kicking and screaming to a site in China, http://gikpa.cn/. This mail is a couple of years old and the site no longer exists. In fact, such sites are often open for hours only until complaints close them down, (assuming the ISP hosting them takes any notice of your complaint, which is pretty rare in my experience, especially in some parts of the world).

As can be seen in Figure 3.4 (p. 43), kmail, the mail client (i.e. MUA) I am using here, identifies the presence of the HTML and alerts me to the fact that such messages can be toxic. Nowadays, most mail clients will offer you the option to display or even discard such HTML messages, (known in the trade as *de-fanging* as mentioned earlier). In Outlook 2007, options to disable links and other functionality in potential phishing messages are available as are warning levels for the presence of suspicious links.

Backscatter

Notice that there is no point in trying to respond to this because the only e-mail address is either completely bogus (in this case the domain does not exist), or it is an innocent party as the From: field can be anything the spammer chooses. This is called mail address hi-jacking and is so common as to defy comment. I will discuss how junk mails should be processed later but one possibility is to return them to their sender. Of course if this is the innocent party, the first thing they know is they get hundreds of bounced messages[9] from people they have never heard of. This is called backscatter and happens to most people who have had the same e-mail address for a long time. An example of somebody using my address is shown in Figure 3.3 (p. 42).

As we will see later, backscatter is also a potent way of delivering junk indirectly.

It's pretty simple to identify this sort of stuff. All you have to do is extract the embedded link and sniff at it in various ways including finding out which country it is from[10], whether it is listed on existing blacklists,

---

[9]These are also known as a NDR, (Non-Delivery Report or Receipt), a DSN, (Delivery Status Notification) or a NDN, (Non-Delivery Notification).

[10]There are countries, for example Nigeria and Bulgaria, from either of which I have yet to receive a legitimate e-mail. This is by no means a prejudicial statement, it is based simply on analysing the mail records on my mail server. Country of origin filtering is

Figure 3.3: An example of a bounce of a Viagra advert apparently sent by me, so the bounced message comes back to me. These can be blocked and will need to be if somebody does this with your address big-time, (i.e. thousands of messages). Note that the From: address here is lesh@ci.rosenberg.tx.us which is spoofed. The address lesh@oakcomp.co.uk appears as the Reply-To: field in the original spam, (when you send an e-mail, you can give different From: and Reply-To: addresses).

Note: This is an HTML message. For security reasons, only the raw HTML code is shown.
message then you can activate formatted HTML display for this message by clicking here.

```
<!DOCTYPE HTML PUBLIC "-//W3C//DTD HTML 4.0 Transitional//EN">
<HTML><HEAD>
<META http-equiv=Content-Type content="text/html; charset=koi8-r">
<META content="MSHTML 6.00.2900.3198" name=GENERATOR>
<STYLE></STYLE>
</HEAD>
<BODY>
Help your friend<br>
<a href="http://gikpa.cn/v/">Visit us!</a>
</BODY></HTML>
```

Figure 3.4: The second part of the spam message shown in Figure 3.2 (p. 40). This is the payload. You can see the squiffy link near the bottom as href="http://gikpa.cn/". Note that the warning box put in at the top of this e-mail is added by my MUA, kmail. If I press on the button to activate the HTML formatting, I will tell the perpetrator that their message has been received because it will fetch any embedded images and this information will be recorded on their servers.

whether it has any relationship with the From: address and how old it is. A combination of these gives a pretty accurate assessment as will be seen later.

3.4.2 HTML and works of art

Allowing HTML (Hyper Text Markup Language) in messages makes them look pretty but unfortunately opens up numerous opportunities for innovative spam at the same time. Figure 3.5 (p. 44) is an excellent example. It is a pleasure to receive such spam and I wish my students were this good at HTML.

The second part of the e-mail is in HTML format and looks like Figure 3.6 (p. 44)

The true artistic value of this e-mail jumps out when you allow your mail client (MUA) to render this upon which you get Figure 3.7 (p. 45).

---

very useful as one of the gene markers of junk.

43

Figure 3.5: I received a considerable number of these in mid 2008, all with the little smiley face. This is the text part.

```
<!DOCTYPE HTML PUBLIC "-//W3C//DTD HTML 4.01 Transitional//EN">
<html><head> <title> </title>

<META http-equiv=Content-Type content="text/html; charset="iso-8859-1">
</head>
<body>

<p>
Salut,<br></p><b>
</b>
<br><br><table width="115" cellspacing="2" cellpadding="6">
<tr>
<td nowrap="nowrap" bgcolor="#B7F0BC"><strong>V</strong> </td>
<td align="center" bordercolor="#441D8E" nowrap="nowrap" bgcolor="#B9BCF0">I<font
color="#B9BCF0">r</font></td>

<td valign="baseline" bordercolor="#E71C1C" bgcolor="#F0E8BC"><i>A</i></td>
<td align="center" bgcolor="#F0C6BC" valign="top"><em>G</em><font color="#F0C6BA">x</font> </td>
<td bgcolor="#F0D7BC" bordercolor="#F67B73" align="left" nowrap="nowrap" valign="middle">
<em>R</em><font color="#F0D7BC">w</font> </td>
<td bordercolor="#66D5B9" bgcolor="#EEBCF0" valign="top" align="left" nowrap="nowrap">
A</td>
</tr>
</table>
<br>
<a name="#rpwr"> </a><table><tr><td>WWW</td><span name="#prrr"> </span><td>.</td><strong>
</strong><td>NEVOB</td><span name="#wqrr"></span><td>.</td><span name="#tqqw">
</span><td>COM</td></tr></table><span> </span><br><strong> </strong><p><strong>
</strong></p><strong> </strong>
<p><strong> </strong></p>
</body></html>
```

Figure 3.6: This is the HTML part of Figure 3.5 (p. 44) in it's raw form.

Figure 3.7: The rendered version of Figure 3.6 (p. 44)

Much as it grieves me to trash messages like this[11], business is business. To block things like this, you have to parse the HTML properly and then you finish up with characteristic single and multiple letter combinations which are easy to get rid of as will be seen later. Since you can't get the HTML to behave properly unless you do this[12], I guess that's the end of those. Pity - compared with what follows they were real works of art.

3.5 Scams

Although I am generally a very easy-going person, scams really bring out the worst in me. To put it in a nutshell, people who prey on others like this forfeit any rights to be treated decently as far as I am concerned.

There are hundreds of variants of these as described at useful internet sites[13],[14]. Each variant has to convince you of some deal and appeals to the most basic of human instincts, e.g. greed, desperation or whatever.

They are easy to deal with if you remember one thing and one thing only:-

> Anything that sounds like a fast buck is a fast buck. It just isn't you that's going to make it.

I have *never* heard of a genuine one of these but in spite of this simple advice, people still apparently get caught by this kind of stuff. There is an excellent site[15] which poses a few examples in the form of a short test. If you don't get 10/10, you should worry[16]. If you do get 10/10, you should worry because tomorrow there will be new ones to worry about.

---

[11] We had a little battle over about 3 weeks as progressively more exotic HTML variations were sent before I found out how to block them generically. It was like losing an old friend.

[12] At least I don't think you can, but I await your next instalment with bated breath whoever you are.

[13] http://www.consumerfraudreporting.org/

[14] http://www.scamwatch.gov.au/

[15] http://www.sonicwall.com/phishing/

[16] I did but I'm a cynical, suspicious old man. :-)

3.5.1 Banking scams

It would be very simple if banks simply stopped contacting customers by e-mail. However, there are legitimate reasons for sending mails but NOT for account details in any shape or form, EVER. It is perfectly possible to do such transactions in an entirely secure way but the effort of recognising the toxic ones is simply too much for the layperson.

Such scams vary from the useless to the fairly sophisticated. Figure 3.8 (p. 48) is a fairly useless one.

Incredibly, spammers hang on to such templates over a considerable time. Figure 3.9 (p. 49) shows almost the same thing from 18 months earlier, although this was a little more imaginative in it's From: address.

Even something as bad as this is still dangerous if you allow your MUA to render the HTML message to make it look pretty as can be seen in Figure 3.10 (p. 50)

Note that HSBC is not being singled out here - these are actual e-mails. All banks are scammed like this in a bid to get as many valid sets of account details as possible. Just one is enough to pay for the inherent costs of mailing so it can be a lucrative business although it is very easy to stop as we will see later.

Figure 3.11 (p. 51) illustrates a slightly different twist on the basic bank scam.

As a final warning against allowing pretty e-mails to fool you, sometimes the links are made explicit and are sufficiently similar to be fairly convincing. Figure 3.12 (p. 52) is an example of one these. I have annotated it to show you where the link points but it contains the word "Barclays" to attempt to give you confidence. In actual fact it points to a non-standard port (port 4903) on the site www.personal.barclays.co.uk.userset.net, which astonishingly still exists, (the mail is a couple of years old). This corresponds to the IP address 174.137.125.36 and is based in Seattle, USA no doubt waiting to be used again. No doubt there are many others - this IP address was hosting 3,899 domain names at the time of writing in August 2010.

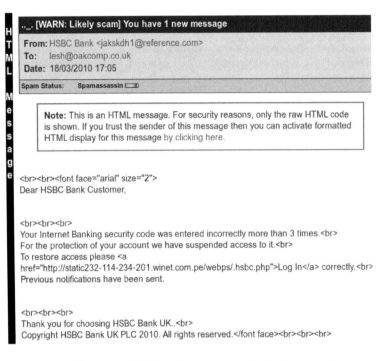

Figure 3.8: This is a HTML-only message which is cause for concern on it's own. As most good mail clients (MUAs) should make squiffy links visible as here in kmail, you can see that the link is based in Peru (it ends in .pe, the TLD (Top-level Domain) for Peru) and has nothing to do with the bank. Neither has the e-mail address. The perpetrator is a complete idiot. If only they were all this bad.

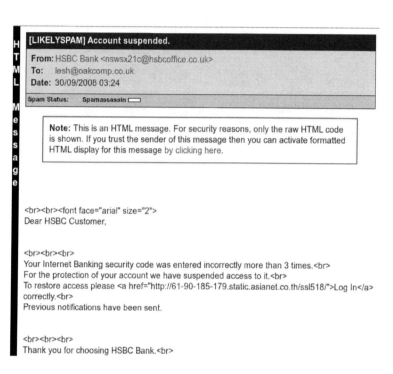

Figure 3.9: Almost the same template as in Figure 3.8 (p. 48) from 18 months earlier.

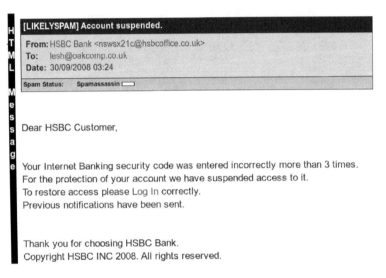

Figure 3.10: The mail shown in Figure 3.9 (p. 49) after rendering by the MUA to make it look pretty. As can be seen from the unrendered form, the seductive "Log In" points to http://61-90-185-179.static.asianet.co.th/ssl518/, a web server in Thailand this time so our spammer is using servers all over the place to carry out his or her noble work.

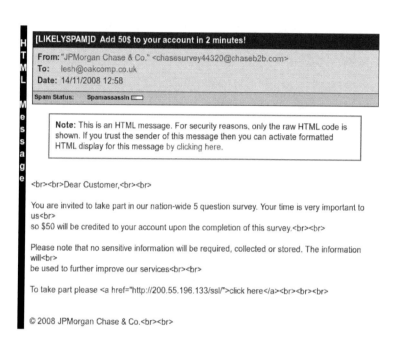

Figure 3.11: In this case, the tease is a $50 reward for filling out a survey. Unfortunately, after going to the effort of thinking of a From: address with "chase" in it somewhere, it goes on to say it will be credited to your account but no details collected, whatever that means. Nice try chaps but no cigar.

Figure 3.12: A credible scam with toxic link containing the word "Barclays". The link actually points to www.personal.barclays.co.uk.userset.net which is nothing to do with Barclays.

3.5.2 Upfront fees, prizes and so on

There are a wide variety of these. They vary from the bombastic simplicity of the infamous 419s to much more sophisticated approaches. Here are some examples.

419s

I love these. The only problem with good mail filtering is that it deprives you of the joy of reading the deranged ramblings of these low-grade scammers. These are called 419s after section 4.1.9 of the Nigerian penal code as most of these attempts used to come from Nigeria although the rest of the world has joined in now with Hong Kong a recent entrant in the idiocy stakes.

It is a real culture shock to read these. They are so transparently stupid as to defy the imagination. They usually take the form of assisting the perpetrator to transfer some vast amount of money from somewhere you wouldn't rush to visit and for which you will get a substantial take. What beats me is the reasoning offered which is something like "I hab no left leg as it hab been nawed off by a lion but I hab 20 million dollars stashed away in da empty trouser leg and I wish to inves in your beutiful counry." They're priceless.

However, latterly whoever sends this nonsense has been buying time from botmasters with lots of relatively clean machines[17], so they have to be filtered on content. It isn't usually that hard but the volumes are pretty breathtaking.

Figure 3.13 (p. 54) is an early classic example of the genre. Capital letters tend to figure prominently in these missives as do appalling spelling, a generally simple outlook on life and a dogged determination which would not disgrace the handbag salesmen who pursued me relentlessly through the Souk in Tangier ruining a recent visit[18].

I would not personally recommend this but there are now sites for people who indulge in baiting such scammers[19]. My preference is to consign all such messages to the trash where they belong. Meanwhile, they grind away

---

[17]More on this later

[18]May your handbags turn to dust and your ripped-off Guns and Roses CDs turn out to be Cliff Richard.

[19]For example, http://www.419eater.com/

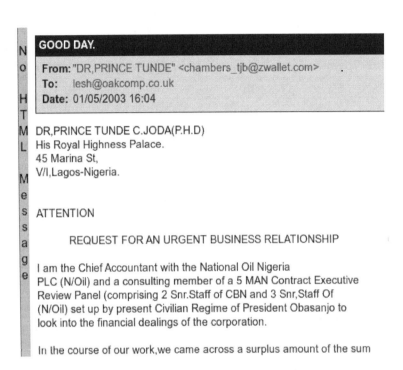

GOOD DAY.

From: "DR,PRINCE TUNDE" <chambers_tjb@zwallet.com>

To: lesh@oakcomp.co.uk

Date: 01/05/2003 16:04

DR,PRINCE TUNDE C.JODA(P.H.D)
His Royal Highness Palace.
45 Marina St,
V/I,Lagos-Nigeria.

ATTENTION

REQUEST FOR AN URGENT BUSINESS RELATIONSHIP

I am the Chief Accountant with the National Oil Nigeria
PLC (N/Oil) and a consulting member of a 5 MAN Contract Executive
Review Panel (comprising 2 Snr.Staff of CBN and 3 Snr,Staff Of
(N/Oil) set up by present Civilian Regime of President Obasanjo to
look into the financial dealings of the corporation.

In the course of our work,we came across a surplus amount of the sum

Figure 3.13: Note that you have to get in as many titles as possible. The perpetrator of this seems to think it will help. I love the P.H.D. bit. It is unclear if he is a Jedi spammer or not although he has the right name. Another slant is to play the religious card as in Figure 3.14 (p. 55).

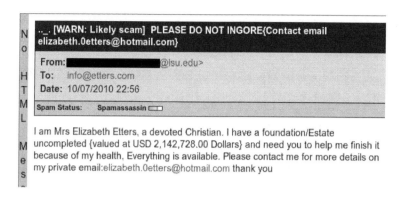

Figure 3.14: Another theme is the religious devotee in the belief that this will add credibility. What are these people on ?

on their curiously mixed theme of personal hardship whilst managing to salt away a few million bucks on the side which they are desperate to share. Sad really but not as sad as the people who get caught out by this. It beggars the imagination.

Loans

These are all characterised by some or all of the following:-

- They aren't interested in your credit history. The Subject line will say something like "Bad Loans ?". It's hard enough getting money out of legitimate lenders these days when you are a good credit risk. Expecting to have it thrown at you by person or persons unknown stretches the credulity just a tad.

- The fees are never disclosed.

- Copy-cat names in the From: address trying to add credibility.

A recent example is shown in Figure 3.15 (p. 56). The content is naive with mismatched From: (wilkes.edu) and embedded domain names (discuz.org). Worryingly, I have had to anonymise the From: address as it is real and the sending MTA matches this domain name and is clean so must have been compromised in some way. This automatically leads to a higher load on the receiving MTA which must reject stuff like this mostly by content filtering which as will be seen is done relatively late in the chain of filters. It's not hard forensically, just more expensive but reflects what will

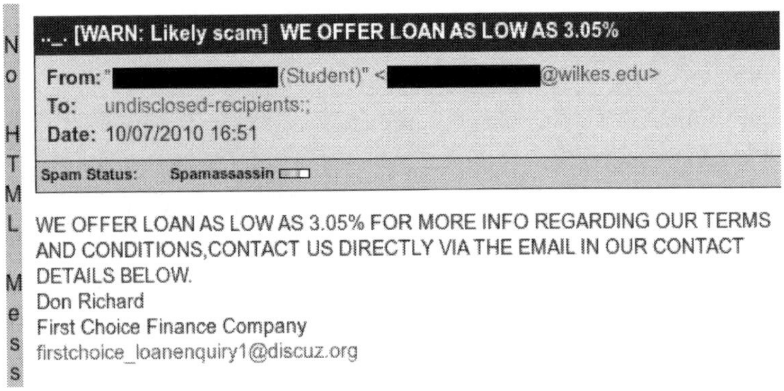

Figure 3.15: The content here is pretty naive but worryingly, it arrived via a clean machine as discussed in the text.

almost certainly be a growing trend of more computer power spent to turn back the tide of this junk.

Cheque overpayment scams

In essence these involve somebody sending you a cheque for your services (you might give guitar lessons for example) which is deliberately too much. They then ask you to refund the difference and then mysteriously their original cheque bounces. Surprise, surprise.

An example is shown as Figure 3.16 (p. 57), (I used to teach guitar and a number of tutors in my tutor registry received this).

Lottery and Sweepstakes

A fairly common theme is the idea that you have been selected out of the millions on the Internet by somebody you have never heard of with several different e-mail addresses for a huge prize in a competition that you paid nothing to enter and of which you have never heard. Yes, very likely.

Figure 3.17 (p. 57) is a typical example gleaned from my mail server from a little while ago. It wouldn't fool a hamster. These things work by getting you to send some kind of fee upfront to transfer the non-existent funds into your account. Alternatively, if you are daft enough to supply your personal information, they may try to steal it in which case it comes under identity theft, (see below).

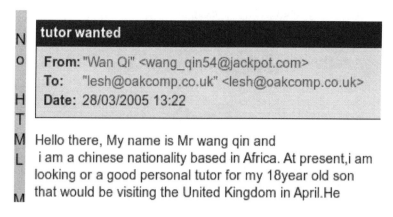

Figure 3.16: This is a standard template for this kind of thing. Another giveaway is that it says in a later part of the e-mail that replies should be addressed to a yahoo.com account.

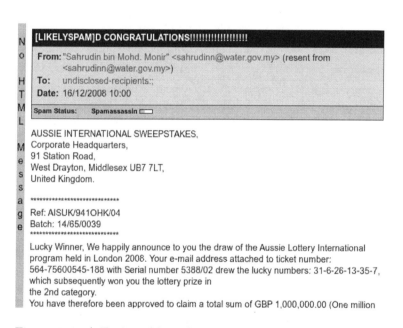

Figure 3.17: A From: address from Malaysia, a reply to somebody on hotmail and an Aussie lottery in West Drayton; oh please ... another intellectual giant hits the ether.

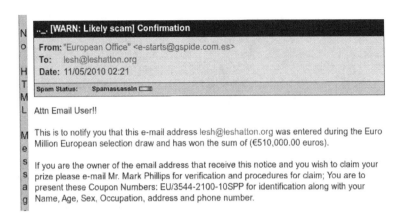

[WARN: Likely scam] Confirmation

From: "European Office" <e-starts@gspide.com.es>
To: lesh@leshatton.org
Date: 11/05/2010 02:21

Spam Status: Spamassassin ▭▭▯

Attn Email User!!

This is to notify you that this e-mail address lesh@leshatton.org was entered during the Euro Million European selection draw and has won the sum of (€510,000.00 euros).

If you are the owner of the email address that receive this notice and you wish to claim your prize please e-mail Mr. Mark Phillips for verification and procedures for claim; You are to present these Coupon Numbers: EU/3544-2100-10SPP for identification along with your Name, Age, Sex, Occupation, address and phone number.

Figure 3.18: Nearly as bad as Figure 3.17 (p. 57).

Figure 3.18 (p. 58) is a recent example; same theme, same nonsense.

As we will see later, these can be filtered using a mixture of the conflict between the various domain names supplied, the vocabulary, and sometimes the headers.

Unexpected gifts

These often feature packages allegedly from reputable companies such as DHL to add a little credibility but they again feature the strange (and forensically very revealing) combination of mismatched contact details and standard wording.

An example is shown as Figure 3.19 (p. 59). The bizarre combination of contact details along with the relatively common phrasing used easily allow it's detection.

Laundering

In a laundering scheme, you may be offered the opportunity to work from home. This opens up several ways of scamming you. You may be requested to make an upfront payment. You may be overpaid and asked to refund the difference. Sometimes, these are actually used to launder real money and such money would then pass through your account. Another twist on this nasty activity is to claim you have been sent money which you haven't

.._. **[WARN: Likely scam] Telephone: +234-803 957 0118 Mtcn:602 539 0872**

Date: 25/07/2010 08:41
From: Western Union Office <alessandra.jatta@fastwebnet.it>
To: undisclosed-recipients:;
Reply to: wum.transfer.unit@w.cn

This email contains the senders name and also the MTCN. Please get this
information and locate any western union office closest to you for
immediate pick up, so as to enable us expedite action in sending another
5000.00 USD as you are aware that we will be sending you 5,000.00 USD until
the entire amount is completed. Do call me once you pick up the funds.

Manager: Mr. Daniel George

Email: alice_ford@live.com

Figure 3.19: A typical recent example of an unexpected gift. Note here the From: address which appears to come from Italy although it features a spurious reference to Western Union and the Reply-to address which is in China and finally the embedded contact link to live.com. The To: field is also anonymous.

and then to ask for a refund. Ultimately, any of this may finish up with an unpleasant visit from the Fraud squad.

An example is shown in Figure 3.20 (p. 60). The rest of the e-mail is a form requesting personal details which you have to send. These WILL be used for nefarious purposes.

I have a particular dislike of these. If greed causes you to fall for one of the other kinds of scam discussed here then that's your problem - if you play with fire, you expect to get your fingers burnt. However, hard-working people under financial stress will often seek home-working as a way to improve their lot rather than gambling or the lure of the fast buck. The people who send these are preying on that work ethic.

A variant of this is the so-called Mystery shopping scam. In this you will be contacted out of the blue to do some mystery shopping. You will receive an apparently legitimate cheque for say 350 pounds to check out retailer services. Your first assignment will be to test out a money transfer agency, (with your own money). That's the last you ever see of that and the original 350 pound cheque bounces. An example of this is shown as Figure 3.21 (p.

··_. [WARN: Likely scam] Work From Your Desk And Earn 10% Commission Nov-Dec/Apply Within

Date: 06/11/2009 01:20

From: "Better Digital Technology" <btkltd@live.com>, "<kmtil@biznetvigator.com>"@obav05.netvigator.com

To: info@biznetvigator.com

Better Digital Technology Co., Ltd
HEAD OFFICE
Better Digital Technology Co., Ltd
Address: Build 1, Hua Feng Industrial Zone,
71st District, Bao An, Shenzhen, China
website: www.better-int.com

Hello Sir/Madam,

Season's Greetings. I' m Mr. Nathan Lee by name. I represent the above named Company based in China. My company manufacture Car DVD Player, Car LCD Monitor,Car DVD And LCD Combo, Car Amplifier (digital) Car HID Xenon Kit,Car alarm Parking Sensor,Car rear view camera (system),GPS player and Steering wheel remote. and many more in China.

I want you to work for the company either from your office desk on lunch break hour or from home at your comfort and make 10% (pay as you go) salary on every transaction payment you re-direct for the company. You do not have to spend a dime and if handle 4 payments, you get paid 4 times and you do not run any personal expense. We pay you for everything. Your salary on each payment after other expenses we would pay you for is estimated at 300 - 400 Dollars. Just Imagine if you work 3 or 4 times a week.

Figure 3.20: Again note the bizarre collection of contact e-mail addresses which define the forensic signature of many scams.

> **.._. [WARN: Likely scam] Become Our "MYSTERY SHOPPER"**
> Date: 05/09/2009 01:39
> From: "Mystery Shopper Inc." <mystery.shopper@mall.org>
> To: undisclosed-recipients::
> Reply to: mystery.shopper@luxmail.com
>
> Need an extra INCOME?
> EARN NO LESS THAN 200.00 British Pounds
>
> Become our "MYSTERY SHOPPER" :
> Earn [NO LESS THAN 200.00 British Pounds] Per Venture:
> It is Very Easy and Very Simple:
> No Application fees:
>
> Here's your chance to get paid for shopping and dining out.
>
> Your job will be to evaluate and comment on customer service in a wide Variety of shops, Stores,
> restaurant and services in your area.
>
> Mystery shoppers are needed throughout the UK. You'll be paid to shop and dine out-plus, you
> can also get free meals, free merchandise, free services, free entertainment, free travel and
> more. Great Pay. Fun Work. Flexible Schedules.
>
> No experience required.
>
> If you can shop-you are qualified!
> Let me explain to you what it entails
> What is a mystery shopper?

Figure 3.21: The Mystery shopping scam. It's the usual collection of mismatched e-mail addresses and the offer of work.

61).

3.5.3 Tax and other refunds

The bogus tax refund is an example of identity theft but is so common that it is worth a section to itself. My mail server received one of these every month until I blocked them because they no longer presented any forensic interest[20].

An example of one of them is shown as Figure 3.22 (p. 62) although they are all very similar. This is a particularly nasty and well-crafted one. The e-mail exhorts you to fill out a form which is attached as a HTML document. The form displays like a web-page and encourages you to fill in your credit card details to get your refund. Further burrowing into the form reveals that all the graphics are extracted from the legitimate HMRC web-site for

---

[20]I've since unblocked them as I missed them.

Figure 3.22: One of many HMRC (Her Majesty's Revenue and Customs service in the U.K.) scams promising a refund. The link is a form urging you to fill in your credit card details for the refund.

credibility but the form is sent off to the IP address 208.101.9.140 which is in the USA[21].

3.6 Phishing and identity theft

Phishing is one of the fastest growing criminal activities of all. The name covers identity theft in it's many forms as well as the large-scale technologies used to automate it, (for example botnets and so on). There is nothing new about this other than the fact that technologies such as e-mail help to make it extraordinarily efficient.

---

[21]The full embedded link is http://208.101.9.140/ securepl/images/index3.php". Yes, I have reported this abuse but very few ISPs ever answer, presumably because they are swamped.

The figures involved in this crime are beginning to beggar the imagination. A quick search on the web revealed these statistics quoted at[22].

- 886 The average dollar loss per Phishing Victim (Gartner, Dec 17, 2007)

- 3.6 Billion The total dollar loss of all phishing victims over a 1 year period (Gartner, Dec 17, 2007)

- 3.2 Million The number of people who fell victim to phishing scams over that same 1 year period (Gartner, Dec 17, 2007)

- 8.5 Billion The estimated number of phishing e-mails sent world-wide each month (SonicWALL, 2008)

- 32,414 The number of phishing web sites that were operational in May 2008 (Anti-Phishing Working Group)

Well, it's not going to reduce any time soon. Note in particular the estimated number of phishing e-mails sent each month. These numbers are equalled only by the amounts which ordinary people have had to spend on bailing banks out since 2008.

3.6.1 Identify theft

The number of different ways this can be done means that you can never drop your guard but there is a very simple rule.

Never supply any details requested by an e-mail. That's **never**. There is no legitimate reason for this. So if ever you get led into revealing anything (and some scamming e-mails are astonishingly credible), just pause before you hit "Send" and ask yourself who is doing this.

Identity theft can take a large number of variants and the type of information solicited includes contact details, passport details (yes indeed, some will actually ask you to send a copy of your passport), bank details (including your test questions!) and login details.

---

[22]http://www.sonicwall.com/phishing, accessed 03-Aug-2010.

The threat landscape – recent example

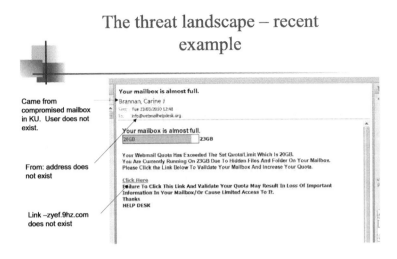

Came from compromised mailbox in KU. User does not exist.

From: address does not exist

Link –zyef.9hz.com does not exist

Figure 3.23: A recent attempt to persuade myself and colleagues to hand over their login details. This evaded the commercial e-mail filtering services which my university uses (MessageLabs).

Figure 3.23 (p. 64) shows an example where login details for e-mail are being scammed. This passed straight through a commercial e-mail filtering service even though there are a number of forensic clues on which to reject it. For example, the recipient is unknown, the sender does not exist and the body of the e-mail contains a short-lived scrambled target under the "Click here" link, (http://zyef.9hz.com/).

However, as it got through the MessageLabs commercial filtering system, there is an expectation amongst users of this system that the mail is in some sense OK and several colleagues asked if this was genuine or not at the time. Unfortunately, the sense of security is enhanced because it is not very obvious in Outlook how to view the raw mail. All of these factors add up to an increased likelihood of somebody clicking on the link and compromising their login details, and so it goes on.

Another example is shown in Figure 3.24 (p. 65). Forensically, this class of e-mail is pretty easy. For example, it contains the word "BENIN" in

N
o

H
T
M
L

M
e
s
s
a
g
e

.._. [DANGER: Toxic links] YOUR ATM MASTER CARD PAYMENT//
Date: 10/06/2009 15:49
From: 92van164 <92van164@ac-bongo.nl>
To: undisclosed-recipients:;

Attention: Dear

I have been waiting for you since to come down here and pick your Bank Draft of
$2,500,000.0usd but did not heard from you since that time then I went and deposited the Draft
with OCEANIC BANK PLC OF BENIN here in Cotonou, Benin Republic, because I travelled to
Japan to see my boss and will not come back till next month end.

I have arranged with them to make your payment to you with their new ATM MASTER CARD
which you can use to withdraw your money in any ATM MACHINE around the globe/world. You
have to contact the Oceanic Bank Plc Of Benin with your full contact informations such as
follows:

1. FULL NAME:
2. ADDRESS WERE YOU WANT THEM TO SEND THE ATM CARD
3. PHONE AND FAX NUMBER
4. YOUR AGE AND CURRENT OCCUPATION
5. COPY OF YOUR INTERNATIONAL PASSPORT.

However, Kindly contact the below person who is in position to release your ATM Master CARD.

E:mail(oceatmd@sify.com)
REV. DR. KEN CHUKWU
DIRECTOR, ATM PAYMENT DEPARTMENT OCEANIC BANK PLC OF BENIN PHONE
NUMBER:(+229-93-0002-85)

Figure 3.24: Note that this one is asking for passport details. Although also
a 419, it's a classic scam to steal your identity, (and if you are
daft enough to send it, skim a bit of money off you at the same
time).

capitals, (I have never had anything legitimate from BENIN); anything
with a sify.com embedded link should be canned, (it's an ISP in Chennai,
India and features in many scams and spams); it claims to have come from
the Netherlands as do many of the Lottery Prize scams; it asks for personal
details .... need I go on.

A much more subtle and very recent one received by my son in Singapore
is shown in Figure 3.25 (p. 66). This one is subtle indeed. In it's rendered form (as most mailers show), it looks like a perfectly reasonable order
confirmation from amazon.com. Of course in this case, he hadn't ordered
it. However, the links on this page are a crafty mixture of legitimate ones
(pointing to parts of amazon.com), and a toxic one (http://kupsucv.com/)
which lies under the order reference numbers and also the suppliers. Click
on one of those and it's probably going to act out a refund via your credit

Figure 3.25: This looks a perfectly innocuous order confirmation from amazon.com. Unfortunately, some of the links are not what they seem.

card details.

Forensically, it's not difficult but only if the mail systems have the right protection in place, (with my son's ISP, they obviously didn't). In this case, kupsucv.com was already recorded on various RBLs[23] on the web as a persistent offender. Failing that, the clash of names between the legitimate amazon links and this obviously bogus one could be picked out. However in other respects, it's carefully crafted and is likely to have claimed a few victims. As such, it is a warning of the way things are going and forensic analysts can't rest on their laurels.

Figure 3.26 (p. 67) shows the mixture of links on a small part of the HTML form of this message including a cheeky little invitation to turn off HTML messaging by once again visiting the toxic link.

As a loose graphical summary of the previous sections, Figure 3.27 (p. 68) shows the various threat vectors of an incoming e-mail according to it's toxic content, (links, attachments, e-mails and sometimes combinations)).

---

[23]Real-time Black Lists but see later.

```
</p><p>
<font face="verdana,arial,helvetica" size="-1">
If you ever need to return an order, visit our Online Returns Center: <a
href="http://www.amazon.com/returns">www.amazon.com/returns</a>
</font>
</p><p>
<font face="verdana,arial,helvetica" size="-1">
Thanks again for shopping with us.
</font>
</p><p>
<font face="verdana,arial,helvetica" size="-1">
<b>
<a href="http://kupsucv.com/">Amazon.com</a></b>

<br><b>
Earth&apss Biggest Selection
</b>
</font>
</p><p>
<font face="verdana,arial,helvetica" size="-1">
<img
src="https://images-na.ssl-images-amazon.com/images/G/01/x-locale/common
width="17" height="15" border="0">
Prefer not to receive HTML mail?


<a href="http://kupsucv.com/">Click here</a></font>
```

Figure 3.26: Note the annotated mixture of links. This is a small part of this carefully crafted page.

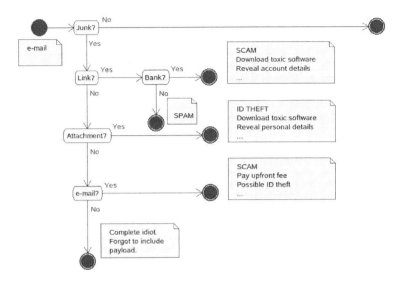

Figure 3.27: Simplified threat vectors for an incoming e-mail.

3.6.2 Botnets, trojans and other nasties

First a word or two about botnets. A botnet is a collection of computers attached to the internet which, unknown to their owners, are actually controlled by a third party called a *botmaster*. They gain control of such machines by persuading the owners to compromise their machines in some way by unwittingly installing a piece of software called a *trojan horse* or *backdoor* without realising it. The botmaster can then use this trojan to control the computer[24] and make it send e-mail messages, steal data from it, steal keystroke information or even direct the whole botnet to launch a denial of service attack[25] on a legitimate site which they see as a threat. Botmasters also sell time on their botnet(s) to other spammers and scammers.

Botnets can contain tens or even hundreds of thousands of machines around the planet. They can be installed in a number of ways but always require you to execute a piece of software on your own machine without realising it. This can be done by getting you to click on a toxic link in an

---

[24]Often by using IRC - Internet Relay Chat servers

[25]By trying to overwhelm the target with connections from thousands of compromised machines.

Figure 3.28: An attempt to force me to install a trojan.

e-mail or on a web-page or in some cases by sending you a file with a teasing name which when you click on it, installs the trojan.

An example of this latter case is shown in Figure 3.28 (p. 69). In this case the attachment is a compressed file in .zip format as widely used on the web but if I expand this on a machine which allows me to install software as administrator, it will install a trojan. Linux machines do not allow this but it is only relatively recently with Vista and Windows 7 that Microsoft machines have become a little more robust against this.

The forensic response in this case is to quarantine and then analyse the zip file. Such toxic payloads will be sent very widely and there are distributed web databases which contain signatures of known toxic payloads. It is also quite simple to store the first line of these payloads and compare payloads across messages on a server, (you usually get multiple hits). That and the fact that it claims to have come from a photo/video site (blender.com) entirely unrelated to it's alleged source UPS, a reputable world-wide parcel service, is enough.

Some statistics on botnets

These were gleaned relatively recently from the Internet for 2010 alone.

- Mariposa botnet (Spain, Mar 2010) had details of 800,000 people gleaned from a staggering 12.7 million machines[26].

- Lethic (Jan, 2010)[27], Mega-D (Nov 2009)[28], Torpig (May, 2009)[29], McColo (Nov, 2008)[30] all taken down (if but temporarily) after efforts by security researchers.

- Waledac (US, Feb 2010)[31] (hundreds of thousands of PCs) used for sending hundreds of millions of spam messages each day.

At the time of writing, (December 2010), there has been a sudden and dramatic fall in botnet activity. This is clearly visible in the data[32] on p. 252 and was widely reported[33]. This appears to be due to the dramatic drop in spam volumes emanating from the Rustock botnet, (responsible for about half of all junk mail at around 45 billion junk mails a day throughout 2010, down to about 1% of this number suddenly in December 2010), and also the Lethic and Xarvester botnets. The reason for this is unknown but Rustock has in the past on an irregular basis throttled back before a major new offensive. There is also speculation that they may introduce technology changes to make attacks more successful or possibly address parallel markets such as the social networking sites,[34].

Fingerprinting mail servers

If you ever wondered how researchers identify botnets, the method is known as SMTP fingerprinting. Computers in a botnet are simply controlled by the botmaster. They each run the botmaster's particular junk mail software, which is often hand-crafted and so by fingerprinting the nature of the junk mail software, a particular computer can be identified as belonging to that botnet.

---

[26] http://www.guardian.co.uk/technology/2010/mar/03/mariposa-botnet-spain, accessed 26-Jul-2010

[27] http://www.m86security.com/labs/i/Lethic-botnet–The-Takedown,trace.1216 .asp, accessed 26-Jul-2010

[28] http://en.wikipedia.org/wiki/Mega-D_botnet, accessed 26-Jul-2010

[29] http://en.wikipedia.org/wiki/Torpig, accessed 26-Jul-2010

[30] http://en.wikipedia.org/wiki/McColo, accessed 26-Jul-2010

[31] http://news.bbc.co.uk/1/hi/technology/8537771.stm, accessed 26-Jul-2010

[32] For a little while, I thought it was just me but it turns out to be global.

[33] http://www.bbc.co.uk/news/technology-12126880, accessed 06-Jan-2011

[34] http://www.networkworld.com/news/2009/011609-researcher-two-big-botnets-gone.html?page=1, accessed 06-Jan-2011

To determine what to fingerprint, cast your mind back to the discussion of an SMTP conversation as described on p. 21. When you connect to port 25 (it's inbound port) on a mail server[35], the first thing it does is to identify itself. This response is not standardised and varies wildly. A simple response might be:-

```
220 xxxx.com ESMTP Postfix
```

which tells you that xxxx.com is using Postfix[36]. It could equally well be

```
220 xxxx.com ESMTP Postfix; Eureka, it's Thu 06 Jan 2010 14:00:00
```

It turns out that this on it's own isn't really good enough but, as Ken Simpson and Stas Bekman report[37] using the EHLO command and also issuing invalid commands reveals enough about the mail server set up to distinguish around 85% of all mail servers, (in their case).

3.6.3 How do you protect yourself ?

In a sense this is an easy question to answer. I know I am repeating myself but I don't think you can repeat these messages often enough given the scale of abuse so I will summarise it in a single set of points and this is true whether you are a seasoned junk mail detector or just another user trying to make reasonable use of the amazing resources of the Internet.

- *Never* give your details away to anybody requesting them by email.

- *Assume* that all e-mail offers of cash prizes, other prizes and so are bogus. Just ignore them.

---

[35]Make sure it's a mail server. If it isn't, you won't get a response. To find the mail server for a domain, simply type in % dig MX xxxx.com, and then telnet to that. More details on p. 271

[36]This is set by the smtpd_banner parameter in Postfix and is by default = myhostname ESMTP mailname

[37]http://oreilly.com/pub/a/sysadmin/2007/01/05/fingerprinting-mail-servers.html?page=1, accessed 06-Jan-2011

- If you want to buy anything, stick with suppliers you trust with websites which are professional and which are in a country which is bound by a legal protection system for product and services which you trust. I don't personally go this far but you can be even more paranoic and deal only within the country in which you live so that the transaction falls entirely under your own legal regime. Under the 1979 Sale of Goods Act and the 1994 Supply of Goods and Services Act, the UK has a very strict regime thankfully. The USA and most European countries have similarly strict legislation. Some other parts of the world will too but I am less familiar with them.

- *Don't* use HTML rendering in your e-mail unless you are confident that your MTA and MUA are set up so that you are safe. Remember at least some of the following could happen:-
  - You could be directed to a bogus site
  - You could pick up a virus through a rogue image or some other embedded nastiness.
  - At the least, by activating an invisible *web bug*, (p. 310), you tell the junk mailer that you exist and their junk made it through your defences.

- *Never* respond to junk however tempting. Silence is golden from your point of view and is a slow death to a junk mailer.

- If you want to find a good deal, use a comparison site you trust.

I know some of the above won't be popular with marketeers but until the public at large is better protected against all this dross, it is far better to be safe than sorry.

DON'T pass this on to 25 of your friends ...

Finally, we have all seen these. They are always carefully crafted around something which will excite a sympathetic, humorous, threatening or similar response. For example, they may tell of somebody's plight and play on people's good nature to pass it on and "save" somebody. It might be an environmental cause; a joke; something about speed cameras and sometimes even good advice. You also see subject lines "HACKER WARNING - PLEASE READ ALL" with an instruction to pass a warning on to your friends. However, the vast majority of them are designed by the baddie simply to harvest mail lists because you will usually CC: all those friends on the one mail. In other words your good nature is being exploited, the essence of junk mailing.

This is one of the ways they work. Supposing, you can get an average of 5 people to pass them on at each level and it lasts for maybe 10 passes. You have then covered up to $5x5x...x5 = 5^{10}$ which is an astonishing 10 million, (assuming that people's friends don't overlap and so on). Some proportion of these machines will already have been compromised so a baddie somewhere will be able to harvest the mail lists from those machines. You can quickly see that they are likely to get a fairly large number of nice shiny new e-mail addresses to add to their collection and start attacking directly or sell on to other spammers. Think of it as milking cows.

Figure 3.29 on p. 74 illustrates one form of this process. Evil botmaster X contacts some set of already compromised machines in it's botnet with a forged message inviting response from friends. Each user of a compromised machine passes on this message in good faith without realising they have been compromised or that the message is phoney. Anybody the compromised machines contact whether on the CC or BCC line will have their e-mail addresses sent back to X simply because they have been compromised with spyware. As the mail sweeps out, some uncompromised machines will unwittingly forward the message to a compromised machine which then reports back their e-mail addresses to X. For example, compromised machine A contacts friend B who themselves contacts friends C and D. Unfortunately, D then contacts other friends one of whom is compromised machine E. E then sends back to X the e-mail addresses of D and B, and possibly C also if a CC line was sent by B. Similarly, F sends back G and H. J and possibly I (if H used a CC line) are returned by K, and so the process fans out.

It is a common misconception amongst ordinary users that e-mail addresses on BCC (Blind Copy) lines cannot be seen in this process. Unfortunately, these are visible in the initial transaction from the sender's PC to the sending MTA as shown on the left hand side of Figure 2.1 (p. 19). If the user's PC is compromised, off they go to the botmaster just like any others, *including any in the body of the e-mail itself*. The new e-mail addresses are then either sold on or subjected to phishing attacks attempting to induct them into the botmaster's botnet.

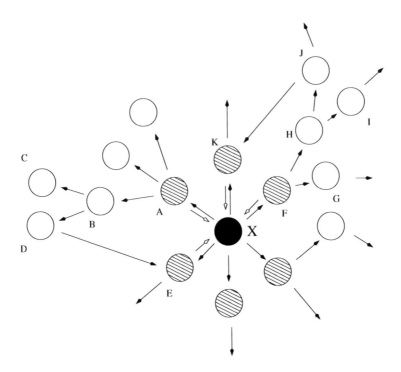

Figure 3.29: How evil botmasters milk their botnets. The botmaster is shown at the centre as X and the compromised machines are shaded.

This is an ongoing process. In spite of advising everybody I know not to do this, about one every two weeks comes sweeping by. Please don't pass them on and try to warn the sender that they are just being used in a rather unpleasant way.

3.7 Responsible bulk mailing

Can there be such a thing as responsible bulk mailing or is it an oxymoron ? Well, if you run a business or you work for one, (which covers most people), you rely on selling products and services to other people. In an ideal world, people sell things they really believe bring a benefit and people buy things that then confer that benefit.

When sales and marketing stick reasonably close to these ideals, things work quite well. People earn a living selling useful things and their customers come back for more because they trust their suppliers. I know there are some hard-liners who might disagree but I believe bulk marketing through e-mail has a very important role to play in building business.

On the other hand, when these principles are broken (and they are emphatically broken by junk mail which is close to the snake-oil salesmen of old or worse), then we finish up with something really ugly and junk mail is really, really ugly. It costs all of us a fortune both in paying for extra infrastructure to give enough bandwidth for legitimate activity and also in the enormous amount of time people spend trying to find the e-mails they want amidst the ocean of stuff they do not want. All this for a relatively small number of greedy unscrupulous individuals.

Responsible bulk e-mail will use all of the following.

3.7.1 Carefully scrutinized e-mail lists

When you place your business card in a supplier's box at a conference *or* you subscribe to a particular mailing list for a guitar shop[38] *or* you request information and supply your e-mail address *or* even when you book a flight online and give your e-mail address whilst ticking the box requesting further information be sent in future, then you are inviting contact. That is not junk, that is an expression of interest in a business relationship which a supplier is entitled to exploit.

---

[38]and don't we all ...

Maintaining e-mail lists

A word or two here is in order. A carefully vetted e-mail list is a major company asset. They cost a lot of money to assemble and an equally large amount of money to maintain. Vigilance is essential because one single rogue e-mail address included in a restricted mailing from a company's mail server can cause that server to be listed on an RBL. While it remains on that RBL, UCE to customers who really would like to hear from you is de-railed. I have seen it happen. This raises some simple precautions which can be taken as follows.

- Keep your e-mail addresses in a database with fields to indicate where they came from, when they were acquired, when they were last sent to, the degree of trust and any other information relevant to your business. That way if you have rogue ones, you can quickly identify the source. As an example, an e-mail address acquired from a business card at a trade show is of an entirely different quality to an e-mail entered on a form on a web-site unless it subject to challenge-response[39].

- Do not assume that third-party lists have the same degree of care lavished on them as you are prepared to do with your own however much you paid for them. There is a fair chance they will contain toxic e-mail addresses.

- Discard anonymous addresses - Google, Yahoo and so on. They are more trouble than they are worth and are hacked worryingly frequently[40].

3.7.2 Ample opportunity to unsubscribe

In every e-mail, it should be made abundantly clear how to unsubscribe if and when you lose interest in a particular relationship. Removal should be prompt, efficient and polite. Only really stupid companies will continue to mail you. Even if this is through incompetence, it is still junk mailing.

---

[39] In other words, any e-mail submitted to your site is not accepted until it has been confirmed by e-mailing it and receiving a positive confirmation that the request did indeed come from them and that they would like to receive future mailings. Not all is rosy with challenge-response however as noted earlier and it is not unknown for malicious entries or even spamtraps to be entered into web-forms requesting more details of a product or service.

[40] At the time of writing, three acquaintances have had their's hacked and junk is being funnelled through them in spite of complaints to the host. In one case, this has been going on for weeks, (see page 278 for the sordid details).

There are even RBLs which trace failures to carry out unsubscribe requests and blacklist the offenders[41].

3.7.3 No transitive relationships

As was mentioned briefly elsewhere, third-party marketing companies may handle lots of businesses. Supposing I purchase a product from company A so that there exists a business relationship between me and them $Me \longleftrightarrow A$. If a third-party marketing company M acts for A, then a further relationship $A \longleftrightarrow M$ exists. If company M then assumes that this means a business relationship $Me \longleftrightarrow M$ then exists just because I dealt with A, then they are plain wrong. What they do of course is start sending you junk from company B who they also deal with but you have no interest in whatsoever. Some even have the cheek to suggest that you have signed up to this relationship. This is a breach of trust. Complain both to M and the company they represent, A.

3.7.4 Obvious legal presence

Their contact e-mails give full detail of where they are based and how they can be contacted and they do not use anonymous sources such as Google or Yahoo mail.

As far as I am concerned, companies which adhere to these responsible principles are free to contact me whenever. Companies which buy my e-mail address from a junk mailer may get through once. Anonymous parties who buy my e-mail address from a junk mailer won't get through at all[42].

3.8 Investigative forensics

Although this book is primarily about preventative forensics, I will say something here about a related concept which is carried out in criminal investigations when trying to determine the provenance of a particular e-mail.

---

[41] http://www.lashback.com/support/UnsubscribeBlacklistSupport.aspx for example.
[42] But I *will* use you for defensive research.

3.8.1 Identifying marks

In essence, we are trying to track e-mails through the logs of the servers through which the e-mail under study is alleged to have passed. *The standard assumption here is that the logs are sacrosanct.* The logs are maintained automatically in time-sequential order by the servers and if they are interfered with, successful forensic investigation might be severely if not fatally compromised.

A couple of identifying marks can be used in forensic work. These are

Message-ID header

This header has the format

```
Message-ID: <alphanumeric-characters@more-alphanumeric-characters>
```

In other words, it looks something like an e-mail address. Here are a few examples

```
Message-ID: <TNT118-DS196906AC26631F473CC61CDAD0@phx.gbl>
Message-ID: <001d01fbfc6a$fd25b3e0$fa711ba0$@com>
Message-ID: <49872.68.147.30.20.1302904548@oakcomp.co.uk>
```

RFC 2822 has this to say.

> *Though optional, every message SHOULD have a "Message-ID:" field.*

and, if present,

> *The "Message-ID:" field provides a unique message identifier that refers to a particular version of a particular message. The uniqueness of the message identifier is guaranteed by the host that generates it (see below). This message identifier is intended to be machine readable and not necessarily meaningful to humans ...*

Furthermore, if it is present and the e-mail is replied to, the reply SHOULD contain (again it's optional), "In-Reply-To: " and "References: " headers which specifically reference the original "Message-ID:". Obviously this is less than perfect but if the servers are compliant, it gives us an identifying mark.

ESMTP ID

This is usually a hexadecimal string, changed regularly and inserted in each of the Received: lines by the corresponding server. Here is an example of one from my own server with the identification E7B946597E

```
Received: by localhost.oakcomp.com (Postfix, from userid 1016)
  id E7B946597E; Thu, 14 Apr 2011 18:28:08 +0100 (BST)
```

So how do we use these identifying marks ?

3.8.2 Matching entries with logs

I will talk more about rummaging in logs later but these identifying marks can be used to match corresponding entries in the time-sequential mail logs of a server. Here is an example of a Received: trail from one valid e-mail showing the identifiers, followed by the corresponding entries taken from the mail logs of my server, (it's from a friend so I have hidden the e-mail address).

From the mail header ...

```
Received: by localhost.oakcomp.com (Postfix, from userid 1016)
  id E7B946597E; Thu, 14 Apr 2011 18:28:08 +0100 (BST)
Received: from snt0-omc4-s5.snt0.hotmail.com
          (snt0-omc4-s5.snt0.hotmail.com [65.55.90.208])
  by localhost.oakcomp.com (Postfix) with ESMTP id 68F0E6597A
  for <lesh@oakcomp.co.uk>; Thu, 14 Apr 2011 18:28:04 +0100 (BST)
```

and from the logs ...

```
...
Apr 14 18:28:05 localhost postfix/qmgr[20404]: 68F0E6597A:
  from=<xxxx@yyyy>, size=8832, nrcpt=1 (queue active)
Apr 14 18:28:08 localhost postfix/pickup[4712]: E7B946597E:
  uid=1016 from=<xxxx@yyyy>
Apr 14 18:28:08 localhost postfix/qmgr[20404]: E7B946597E:
  from=<xxxx@yyyy>, size=9372, nrcpt=1 (queue active)
...
```

Note that the Received: lines are in reverse order, (latest first), whereas log entries are in normal order, (latest last).

3.8.3 Traversing the received trail

As was mentioned earlier, (p. 29), only the latest Received: header can be trusted. In investigative forensics we walk down the Received: trail looking for inconsistency. It may well be that the Received: trail itself is consistent as in the genuine message above or it may contain lines like

```
...
Received: from jollybogus.com
         (snt0-omc4-s5.snt0.hotmail.com [65.55.90.208])
 by localhost.oakcomp.com (Postfix) with ESMTP id 68F0E6597A
 for <lesh@oakcomp.co.uk>; Thu, 14 Apr 2011 18:28:04 +0100 (BST)
...
```

where the "from" does not match the reverse DNS lookup of 65.55.90.208, a hotmail server. Sometimes, we need the co-operation of the system administrators of the servers in these "Received" trails to check their own log entries for consistency trying to find the point at which a bogus e-mail was injected. This may be particularly difficult where proxies (p. 117) are used and it may be necessary to issue a subpoena[43].

There are various commercial software packages available to facilitate correlating across logs but in essence the process has to be fast as typical mail logs are very large and for the same reason, are not kept very long. It is painstaking work.

---

[43]Latin for "under penalty". It has it's roots in English Common Law although in England and Wales, it is now known rather less accurately as a "witness summons" in an effort to move from Latin to English.

4 Protection: the principles of filtering

Most people can recognise a spam message when they read it pretty quickly. However, the brain is a phenomenal pattern recognition system and it is hard to imagine that writing software to do this automatically, (known as spam filtering), is possible. In fact it's more than possible, it has been achieved and provably so as we will see later. This is excellent news as we have neither the time nor the inclination to scan everything visually so automation is essential especially given the incredible volumes at which junk is now delivered.

In essence, good filtering uses the whole message to decide whether something is junk or not. This includes the envelope (i.e. essentially the transaction between the MTAs), and the headers and body in the content. As has already been hinted at in the previous chapter, forensic patterns emerge clearly.

The goal of this and succeeding chapters is to show how to develop an environment whereby the user never sees anything they don't want to see. In other words, the infrastructure itself absorbs effectively all the junk thrown at it.

4.1 Basic filtering

In this section, I will discuss the basic properties of filtering. Perhaps the most important one is to define a reliable system of measurement to see how well we are doing. Using this system of measurement, I will then define an acceptable target and show from basic systems theory how such a target can be met. The proof of the pudding is in later sections.

Filters take many forms in different bits of mail software. In essence you tell them the kind of pattern to look for in a particular e-mail and what to do with any e-mails that match this pattern. In essence you could tell your mail software that any e-mail with the occurrence of "Medications" in the Subject: line should be placed in a Junk folder for example. This worked tolerably well fifteen years ago when junk was neither so prevalent nor so sophisticated. Sadly now it is both.

As has been seen from the relatively brief selection in the previous chapter, the sophistication of junk e-mail has in some cases kept pace with the sophistication of the people trying to block it, whereas the sheer volume has grown mightily. I have no idea what the current percentage of junk in all mail amounts to although I see figures of 80% quoted frequently. On my server, it is far, far higher than this, so I am either unrepresentative or the industry's estimates are out of date.

4.2 Measuring the effectiveness of filters

There are standardised ways of measuring the effectiveness of the kind of filtering inherent to junk mail generally but they preceded the age of junk mail and evolved before it, most notably in the world of medicine. I will introduce these first and particularly the important concepts of *False Positives* and *False Negatives* before showing how they are applied in junk mail filtering.

4.2.1 Binary classification and filter performance

In junk mail filtering, we have a stream of incoming e-mails of two kinds in an unknown ratio. The first kind is junk in it's many forms (often called *spam*) and the second kind is genuine which you want to see, (often called *ham*). In practice it is never this clear cut as will be explained later but for now we will assume it is. We are seeking to identify all the junk mail as junk and throw it away, quarantine it or whatever. The rest we will take to be genuine and which then needs to be delivered to it's intended recipient.

A relevant classification system has already evolved through extensive use in medical and other research areas. It is known as *binary classification* but first we need to explore the concepts of False Positives and False Negatives.

False Positives and False Negatives

Filtering is a careful balance between throwing away messages you want to see and allowing junk through. Clearly both should be zero in an ideal world. To this end, we define the following concepts:

- TP (True Positive): Issuing a warning when a problem exists, (i.e. a junk mail has been received and it is correctly flagged).

- FP (False Positive): Issuing a warning when no problem exists, (i.e. a valid mail has been received but it is flagged as junk - "crying wolf").

- TN (True Negative): No warning is issued when no problem exists, (i.e. a valid mail has been received and it is correctly flagged).

- FN (False Negative): No warning is issued even though a problem exists, (i.e. a junk mail has been received and it is flagged as valid).

In other words, True is good and False is bad. Positive simply means it's been flagged and Negative means it has not been flagged. From these, we define the following aggregate concepts:

- Sensitivity $= \frac{TP}{TP+FN}$. In the ideal case this has the value 1. The sensitivity is the fraction of junk messages which were correctly identified as junk. An insensitive filter lets through a lot of junk masquerading as valid messages.

- Specificity $= \frac{TN}{TN+FP}$. In the ideal case this has the value 1. The specificity is the fraction of valid messages which are correctly identified as valid. A non-specific filter incorrectly flags valid messages as junk. This is considered the cardinal sin of junk mail filtering.

- Positive predictive value $= \frac{TP}{TP+FP}$. In the ideal case, this has the value 1. The positive predictive value is a measure of the percentage of positive hits (i.e. warnings) which are correct warnings. (Abbreviated to PPV from here).

- Negative predictive value $= \frac{TN}{TN+FN}$. In the ideal case, this has the value 1. The negative predictive value is a measure of the percentage of negative hits (i.e. warnings not issued) which are correct warnings. (Abbreviated to NPV from here).

Of these, sensitivity and specificity are the most commonly used as junk mail filtering measures although not directly so as we will see shortly. Using examples from real filters taken from my university mailbox over a few months (my university address is nowhere near as ubiquitous on junk mail lists as my normal address but this will change with time), these might be displayed as follows:-

	Junk mail	Good mail	
Marked as junk	24,500	12	PPV 99.99%
Marked as good	24	440	NPV 94.83%
	Sens. 99.97%	Spec. 97.35%	

These figures are not actually very good and we can do much better than this as we will see but it serves to illustrate the measurement.

There is a trade-off of course between setting filters too tightly and throwing away good messages on the one hand (False Positive), and setting them too loosely and accepting junk messages on the other (False Negative). In a less than ideal world, we normally set our risk thermostat to favour accepting junk messages occasionally as the price for *never* throwing away good messages, but it's a sensitive tipping point.

To give you an idea of how difficult it is sometimes, my systems issued a FP just before this book went to press in summer 2011. This is a sufficiently rare occurrence, (the first time it had happened in 10 months and over 7 million junk mails) that I had to carry out full *root-cause analysis*[1] on why it happened. In essence, a close family friend sent an e-mail to us to share details of family photographs, unfortunately through a dirty server[2]. SpamAssassin was unimpressed accumulating 6.9 points with the following output[3]:-

---

[1] http://en.wikipedia.org/wiki/Root_cause_analysis
[2] A couple of weeks after the incident, it's still listed, this time on backscatterer.org.
[3] Noting that negative scores in SpamAssassin are beneficial.

SA code	Description
3.2 FH_DATE_PAST_20XX	The date is grossly in the future.
1.5 FORGED_HOTMAIL_RCVD2	hotmail.com 'From' address, but no 'Received:'
1.8 HTML_IMAGE_ONLY_32	BODY: HTML: images with 2800-3200 bytes of words
0.0 HTML_MESSAGE	BODY: HTML included in message
1.5 MIME_HTML_ONLY	BODY: Message only has text/html MIME parts
-1.1 BAYES_05	BODY: Bayesian spam probability is 1 to 5% [score: 0.0116]
-1.0 RCVD_IN_DNSWL_LOW	RBL: Sender listed at http://www.dnswl.org/, low trust [64.74.142.19 listed in list.dnswl.org]
1.1 DNS_FROM_OPENWHOIS	RBL: Envelope sender listed in bl.openwhois.org.

This just pushed it over the top as the committee of Bayesian filters I use for arbitration (see p. 235 onwards) were collectively undecided as we hadn't heard from our friends for sometime. Is this a FP ? The answer has to be yes even though the various analysis systems were doing their job. It is as if a bank wrote to you but sent it in an envelope emblazoned with details of yet another "Euro win zillions and spend the rest of your life being an idle moron" lottery. You would very likely throw it away and indeed nobody would blame you. Of course this sort of thing does not happen with postal mail[4] but in the world of e-mail, anything can happen, which is why forensics can teach us so much. What do you do about it ? Just don't use any web service that allows itself to be tainted like this.

4.2.2 Measurement in practice

In practice, although the underlying structure of binary classification is used, more intuitively appealing descriptions have evolved for use with junk mail.

There is a very good comparison of filtering systems here[5]. This is part of John Graham-Cumming's site and to understand it, you have to understand the method of filter scoring he uses. He defines the following:-

---

[4]Yet.

[5]http://www.jgc.org/astlt.html

Spam-Hit Rate This is the fraction of spams correctly identified as spam. A perfect score is 1.00. This is the same as the sensitivity on p. 82.

Ham-Strike Rate The fraction of hams incorrectly identified as spam. A perfect score is 0.00. This is the same as the (1 - specificity) on p. 82.

This is intuitively appealing and a perfectly acceptable method for classifying junk mail[6]. If you are not used to binary classification systems, this kind of classification makes good sense.

In his tables, he distinguishes the "good" filters as having a Spam-Hit Rate greater than 0.9 and a Ham-Strike Rate less than 0.1. The best shown here has a (0.9954,0.0000) paired score indicating that only 46 out of 10000 spams got through and no hams were incorrectly identified as spam. This illustrates what was possible a few years ago when this data appears to have last been changed[7].

For comparison, the mixture of multiple Bayesian and other techniques described in this book has the current equivalent figures of (0.999994,0.000000) for the most recent period, (the latter part of 2010), but more of this later on p. 252.

The Spam-Hit rate and Ham-Strike rate occur in other contexts and have been placed on strong statistical bases by Gordon Cormack and Thomas Lynam, [11] where the corresponding concepts are known as *Spam Misclassification* (1 - Spam-Hit) and *Ham Misclassification* (Ham-Strike) respectively. In this exceedingly thorough analysis[8], they compared eleven variants of six widely used open-source spam filters tested on a chronological sequence of 49,086 messages received by one individual in the August 2003 - March 2004 of which around 80% were spam[9].

I have gathered together some of their most important conclusions as follows:-

---

[6]There is a comprehensive justification of why he uses this scheme at http://www.jgc.org/antispam/11162004-baafcd719ec31936296c1fb3d74d2cbd.pdf.

[7]Although apparently pretty effective, on my server this would correspond to several hundred per day on a busy day which is nowhere near good enough.

[8]Their stated and achieved goal is "to advance the methodology, scale, realism and repeatability of spam filter evaluation".

[9]Those were the days. In 2010, I get that many in a day, around 99.9% of which are junk. I used to moan about this but it's a terrific incentive to improve, otherwise I just get overwhelmed.

- Content-based filters can eliminate 98-99% of spam while incurring around 0.1% legitimate mail loss, however the risk of loss depends on the nature of the message and those messages most likely to be lost may be those that are less critical, which is a relief.

- Their comparison of learning filters, (i.e. statistical filters) demonstrates differences which are statistically significant. This supports the methodology I describe later under parallel filtering systems, p. 238.

- They specifically discuss the trade-off between rejecting spam and rejecting ham using the concept of *ROC* (Receiver Operating Characteristic). A typical ROC graph looks something like that shown in Figure 4.1 (p. 88). The asymmetry between incorrectly rejecting good mail and incorrectly accepting bad mail is well illustrated by these but as always, the user has to decide optimally between the two risks. There are significant differences between the filters tested in their ROC performance.

As a final point, one of the most significant comments they make is that *spam accuracy*, which in essence is the percentage of messages treated correctly, conflates ham and spam and as a consequence depends on the ratio of ham to spam in any incoming stream. This ratio appears to vary widely both by recipient and in time. In my case, nearly everything is spam (junk in my general terms). They make the point strongly that the calculation of ROC curves for the individual misclassification of ham and spam avoids this problem.

The interested reader is strongly recommended to read the freely downloadable paper which can be found here[10] but be prepared for a detailed stroll through the Elysian Fields of statistical inference. It's well worth it.

4.2.3 Binary classification and multiple mail categories

Junk mail filtering is a simple application of binary classification. If something is junk, the filters should put it in the junk mail folder or trash it according to our confidence level. If it isn't junk, we deliver it to the user's

---

[10]http://plg.uwaterloo.ca/~gvcormac/spamcormack.html

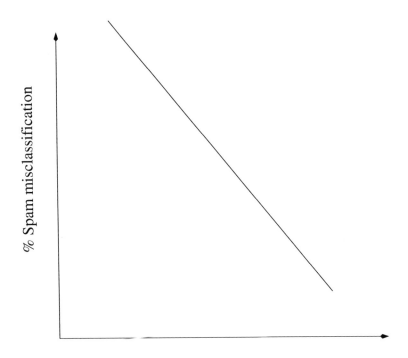

% Ham misclassification

Figure 4.1: A typical ROC diagram illustrating the trade-off between misclassification of ham and misclassification of spam. As spam misclassification is reduced, there is an increasing danger of misclassifying ham and vice versa.

inbox. So what do we mean by confidence level ? A binary classification system of course has no notion of confidence. Something is either junk or it isn't. If the filters say something is junk and it isn't, they have made a mistake we call a False Positive as above. Conversely, if they say something isn't junk and it is, they have made a mistake we call a False Negative.

The water is muddied a little further by the fact that labelling something as junk is of course subjective - one person's junk may be another person's hobby. You might argue that some messages might be junk to everyone, in other words they have an *absolute* property of junkiness, but to a security researcher like myself, they are just data and I want to see them.

The world of measurement has no place for such ambiguity. We must proceed by *defining* what we mean by junk and configuring our systems accordingly. If our systems then make a mistake, we can quantify how many mistakes they actually make using the binary classification measurements defined earlier. From time to time, we may even change our definition of junk, in which case we must restart the measurement of our binary classification system to update that performance.

Since nearly all e-mail (>99.9% on my server) is junk it would be nice to remain amenable to the measurement rigour of binary classification whilst giving the end-user more information about the content of a particular e-mail before they view it. This turns out to be entirely feasible.

The software systems I have written around my receiving MTA, currently annotate messages by inserting the following categories at the start of the Subject line, as appropriate. This is so the user has a choice as to how they wish to filter incoming mails. E-mails considered genuine, i.e. not in any of the following categories, are not annotated.

INFO: Likely bulk mail ... . This is mail about products which the user from previous choice to be interested in. Some people find that any such mail is anathema but I have a healthy respect for anybody genuinely trying to sell something they think is a good product. I might not be interested but if they respect my unsubscribe action, that's fine by me[11].

---

[11]Some authorities suggest that you never unsubscribe because this just tells the sender

WARN: Probable backscatter ... . This was mentioned earlier on p. 42. Backscatter is the mail you get returned to you as non-delivered because somebody has spoofed your address and you never sent it in the first place. These tend to occur in bursts when your mail address suddenly becomes flavour of the month and you might get several thousand of these for a few days. In extreme cases, you might have to direct these into a separate folder using this message tag and even bin them directly.

INFO: via dodgy route ... . This simply detects whether an e-mail originates from or has passed through a country with a poor record for junk mail.

WARN: contains hidden image ... . This is bulk mail which also contains a web bug (p. 310), a hidden image intended solely to discover whether you open an e-mail or not. I may be a bit of a purist but this seems to me to step over the mark. I tolerate bulk mail for reasons mentioned elsewhere in this book but I draw the line at receiving unsolicited stuff with hidden images intended to measure my reaction without my realising it.

WARN: Likely spam ... . This is mail which the filtering system decides is spam. It might be the usual body part stuff, (which is pretty low grade spam and is usually lost long before this), or sophisticated messages carefully designed to get under your mail radar such as image spam.

WARN: Spam with spyware ... . This is basically spam which also contains hidden images. I definitely draw the line at this.

DANGER: Likely scam ... . These are separately tagged. Although spam, their semantic content is some kind of deal, 100% of which are intended, not to put too fine a point on it, to screw you.

DANGER: Executable content ... . These contain executable content such as certain kinds of Javascript or perhaps have executable attachments.

---

that you exist and they can then send you more. To researchers like myself, this is great. I *want* them to send me more so I can best figure out how to stop them attacking anybody else, me included. The reason my filters are so good now is that so much crap has been thrown at them. When I started, they were very much less efficient and let in around 1,000 times more junk than they do now, so I was basically drowning in it.

90

To use binary classification, all that remains to do is to assign each category as either junk or not junk. The data shown later in this book used the following definitions:

Category	Binary category
Not annotated	not junk
INFO: Likely Bulk Mail	not junk
INFO: via dodgy route	not junk
WARN: Probable backscatter	JUNK
WARN: Contains hidden image	JUNK
WARN: Likely spam	JUNK
WARN: Spam with spyware	JUNK
DANGER: Likely scam	JUNK
DANGER: Executable content	JUNK

Table 4.2.3: Mail categories and their generic type in this book.

Note that these categories are in increasing order of severity. For example, if a message contains a hidden image and is identified as a likely scam, then it is annotated with the higher severity message that it is a scam.

4.3 Know your regular expressions

I won't say too much about these at this point but you will hear a lot about them in data mining circles in general and in mail filtering in particular. It may even be that your mail software (MUA) actually uses the term.

They have been around since the 1950s and the term was probably first used by the American mathematician and logician Stephen Kleene. For an iconoclastic Who's Who of regular expressions, check here[12].

Here is a regular expression written in English:-

"Zero or more non-vowels followed by the letter 'a', followed by zero or more non-vowels, followed by the the letter 'e', followed by zero or more non-vowels, followed by the the letter 'i', followed by zero or more non-vowels, followed by the the letter

---

[12]http://blog.stevenlevithan.com/archives/regex-legends

'o', followed by zero or more non-vowels, followed by the the letter 'u'.

We might use such a pattern to find all words in the English dictionary which have exactly one occurrence of each vowel in the order 'aeiou'. It's quite a formidable undertaking but is breathtakingly simple in the arcane world of regular expressions. It can be achieved by:-

```
# egrep \
 "\b[^aeiou]*a[^aeiou]*e[^aeiou]*i[^aeiou]*o[^aeiou]*u[^aeiou]*\b"
 < /usr/share/dict/words
```

This lists all English words (actually all words in the freely distributed list of words on Linux which lives at /usr/share/dict/words) which have all the vowels in the prescribed order. The result on my machine is:-

```
abstemious
abstemiously
abstentious
arsenious
facetious
facetiously
parecious
```

It may not be your cup of tea looking for obscure letter alignments in dictionaries, (although everybody needs a hobby), but they turn out to be extremely useful searching for sub-string occurrences in any string.

One very good example is to be found in *gene sequencing* whereby human DNA is made up of extremely long strings of just 4 nucleobases, represented by G (Guanine), T (Thiamine), A (Adenine) and C (Cytosine). Huntington's disease[13] is caused by a gene on chromosome 4 and the probability of it developing increases from zero to one as the count of consecutive occurrences of the trinucleotide sequence CAG ranges from 26 to 40. All you need to do to detect this is the regular expression

```
# egrep "(CAG){26,}" < chromosome_4_listing
```

If it finds anything, there is non-zero probability of developing the disease, an astonishingly useful piece of information to be revealed by a *one-liner*[14].

---

[13]I got this from http://introcs.cs.princeton.edu/java/72regular/

[14]One-liners enjoy exalted status in the world of computing because they cram complexity into one eye-watering line. This has unfortunately led on to the concept that

Not all is wine and roses as they are rendered in slightly different ways in different environments but they are astonishingly powerful. For now, all you need to know is that they exist and they are staggeringly effective in pulling interesting patterns out of texts very rapidly indeed[15]. This of course is just what we need in forensic work.

4.4 Reject as cheaply as you can

The simple rationale behind this is that it costs time and money to reject unwanted mail. The longer it takes to identify it as unwanted, the more it costs in server processing power and bandwidth. With today's volumes of unwanted mail, this can make a very big difference. If you are a normal mail user, you simply fire up your mail software - Outlook, the Mac Mail program, kmail or whatever - and then download your mail. If your ISP is pretty good at filtering mail, then you don't receive much unwanted mail. However, this came at a processing and bandwidth cost to them. The ISP is probably throwing away 999 out of every 1000 mails on your (and it's other users') behalf. If the ISP is not so good, a fair amount may leak through to your mailbox but the ISP is still throwing away a huge amount.

In order to deal with this vast volume of junk, throwing away early and quietly (more shortly), makes very good sense. Note however that throwing away cheaply is not exactly the same as throwing away early. For example, if a junk mail can be identified as junk in several different ways, it may well be that you can throw away earlier with an expensive check or later with a cheaper check. It's best to delay to the cheaper check in this case provided of course you are sure of picking it up. An example of this arises when throwing away junk mails based on the IP address of the sending MTA.

For example, just consider the conversation in Figure 2.2.2 (p. 22). The receiving MTA actually knows the IP address of the sending MTA immediately on connection and could block it then before even the HELO stage. for example, by looking this address up in one of the blacklists to see if it is tainted. However, this is an expensive check and a very expensive time to do this (every mail message reaches this far by definition), so usually very little is done here and checks are applied in the stages which follow.

---

people who write whole programs in amazingly complex ways just because they can be so written, are in some way to be venerated, rather than say, fired, as 30 years of experience trying to manage the resulting software defect fall-out would dictate.

[15]The dictionary search took less than a second on my Linux desktop.

Referring back to the conversation with a mail server shown in Figure 2.2.2 (p. 22), the receiving MTA then has an opportunity to respond to each of your queries - HELO, MAIL FROM:, RCPT TO: and so on. Fortunately, many junk messages can be rejected at these slightly later stages without having to do anything elaborate at all.

In order of earliest opportunity, the next stages are:-

HELO When we said HELO identifying ourselves as mail.send.com, the receiving MTA has the opportunity to check this before bothering to answer. There is a standard format for this described in RFC 822 but a surprisingly large amount of junk comes from people who do not do this properly, saying things like "HELO itsmeagain" or something equally inane[16]. Messages can be safely rejected immediately for not saying HELO properly and the check is local to the receiving MTA (it doesn't have to ask anybody else) and therefore cheap to apply. This alone can get rid of more than half of all junk.

Suppose that the junk mailer does do this proPerly[17]. The receiving MTA can then go and look this up using the DNS system as described on page 18. In other words, this is a non-local check - the receiving MTA has to ask other machines. The result is the IP address (the xxx.xxx.xxx.xxx number) of the sending MTA. If this is a junk mailer, this may be a false name (it looks OK but does not correspond to any legal IP address), so this lookup will often fail with junk. If it does, it can and should be rejected[18].

Some receiving MTAs go even further. They do a forward DNS lookup to get the xxx.xxx.xxx.xxx number and then a reverse DNS lookup to get back to the original name. If it is not the same, then it may be rejected. (Unfortunately some legitimate mail servers are set up incorrectly for this so it is perfectly possible you will throw away good mails if you do this). Fortunately in good MTAs such as Postfix discussed later, this can be set up as a warning without

---

[16]This eventually led me to the belief that nearly all spammers must be teenage males because they can't say HELO properly

[17]They will eventually because of the adaptive nature of the arms race between the junk mailers and the junk preventers, so you may as well prepare for it.

[18]A little care is necessary as legitimate lookups can fail when things are busy. (For maximum performance, DNS lookups normally use the UDP protocol for short responses which is faster than TCP but not guaranteed to complete.)

rejection so you can measure the extent to which this happens. In my experience, it happens often enough that you should probably not do reverse DNS checking currently, but this situation should be reviewed as the tsunami of junk leads to increasingly strict checking in receiving MTAs.

Supposing the forward DNS has indeed revealed a valid number yyy.yyy.yyy.yyy. As has been noted, the receiving MTA has yet another opportunity to junk this by looking it up on various databases which are held around the world containing the IP addresses of mail servers which are currently[19] registered as sending junk mail. (These are called Real-time Black Lists or RBLs). This however can be an expensive check and is often deferred until later in the mail processing when you have got rid of as much junk as possible by cheaper means.

MAIL FROM: This line tells the receiving MTA who is sending the mail. The receiving MTA could (and should) check that the domain name of the purported sender actually exists. Junk mailers often use false domain names which are in some sense evocative of the scam they are trying to accomplish, for example, what-me-a-scammer.hsbc.co.uk hoping that the user will think it's genuine.

RCPT TO: This line tells the receiving MTA who should be receiving the mail. There are lots of checks which can be implemented here, the most important of which is does this recipient actually exist.

DATA One check which can be implemented here is to make sure that pipelining[20] is only allowed if the sending MTA checks that it is supported correctly. This is a little arcane and nothing further will be said.

If everything is acceptable up to the DATA command, the sending MTA is permitted to send the message which will consist of message headers followed by the message body. These are then subject to *Content checking*. More of this shortly.

---

[19] These listings change dynamically on a very short time-scale reflecting the extraordinarily volatile internet spam environment

[20] Multiple SMTP requests to speed up bulk mail deliveries

4.5 Reject or Discard ?

When a message is received it can be treated in lots of different ways by mail software. In an ideal world, the heavy-lifting part of this should be done in the MTA by your ever-willing ISP. In my view, having to set up exotic filters in your favourite mailing software, be it Outlook or whatever, is simply too late and the average user should not have to do this. It is the responsibility of the receiving MTA to break the back of the work. They should have the technical resources.

4.5.1 Disposal in the MTA

The receiving MTA in Figure 2.1 (p. 19) has the best opportunity to dispose of junk cheaply. It used to be a matter of mail protocol that messages which could not be delivered by the sending MTA to the receiving MUA (i.e. the recipient sitting there with Outlook or whatever), would be returned. This means that the sending MTA is informed by the receiving MTA in Figure 2.1 (p. 19) that delivery was not possible, for example if no such person existed. The sending MTA then reports back to the original sending MUA that delivery failed. This will take the form of a Mail Delivery failure something like that in Figure 3.3 (p. 42). This mechanism is known as "bouncing".

Bouncing and finger trouble

This was all very well in the days when a misdirected mail (for example sending to jhon@receiver.com instead of john@receiver.com) was in all likelihood genuine. Indeed most mail servers then (and too many now) have their mail systems set up to receive *anything* sent to @receiver.com, a junk mailer's dream, leading to those wonderfully exotic addresses such as ericthederangedgerbil@receiver.com which you get unless you close this route off. Unfortunately today, the very large majority of misdirected mails ($> 99\%$) are spam and have spoofed the sender's address. If these were all bounced back to the spoofed senders, those unfortunates would find their mailboxes filled with bounced messages they never sent[21]. To make this somewhat worse, there is no real standard format for bounced messages making them somewhat difficult to detect automatically.

---

[21]Which has already happened to many people who have had their mail addresses a comparatively long time as I have. When this happened to one of my colleagues recently, they had several thousand bounces over a weekend leading to a very messy cleaning up job on the Monday morning because my University mail filtering service failed to pick it up.

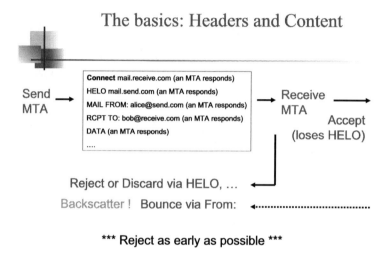

The basics: Headers and Content

Send MTA →

Connect mail.receive.com (an MTA responds)
HELO mail.send.com (an MTA responds)
MAIL FROM: alice@send.com (an MTA responds)
RCPT TO: bob@receive.com (an MTA responds)
DATA (an MTA responds)
....

→ Receive MTA →

Accept
(loses HELO)

Reject or Discard via HELO, ...

Backscatter ! Bounce via From:

*** Reject as early as possible ***

Figure 4.2: Indicating how a spam message can be bounced through a server to an innocent party. The spam message is hi-jacking some of the properties of the genuine server to deliver it's payload.

It has therefore become recent[22] standard policy to discard such messages. When an MTA *discards* a message it is basically silently throwing it away. The sending MTA thinks it has been delivered successfully as does the original sender but the receiving MTA just bins it without passing it on to the receiving MUA. The only evidence that it ever existed is to be found in the mail logs of the receiving MTA, (discussed later).

One logistical implication of this is that in order to be able to discard messages, the receiving MTA has to know what the valid e-mail addresses are. If it doesn't know, it has to try to deliver them on to the network which does know. If they are then rejected as being undeliverable, they have to be bounced back through the receiving MTA as shown in Figure 4.2 (p. 97). It is much better to lose them at the receiving MTA in the initial SMTP transaction.

Of course this has the real danger that a genuinely misdirected message will just be lost but on the experiments carried out on the MTA reported later, it turns out to negligibly small but you still may have concerns in which case you can do one of three things.

- When you define the list of e-mail addresses which can be accepted at a certain domain, you can also define slight permutations corresponding to popular finger-trouble. For example for my address lesh@oakcomp.co.uk, I might add
  - lesho@oakcomp.co.uk (next letter along)
  - leshi@oakcomp.co.uk (next letter along)
  - les@oakcomp.co.uk (dropped letter)
  - lesph@oakcomp.co.uk (transpose)
  - ... and so on.

- If you have got zillions of users at your domain, you can use an address comparator which measures the closeness of two names and define how close you think something should be for you to accept it. There's a

---

[22]This is a significant step. One of the defining characteristics of e-mail has always been that a mail should either be delivered or the sender informed that such delivery cannot take place for some reason. This is exactly analogous to the status of normal posted mail - you would not expect the postman to throw away mail he thinks is junk. Sadly this trust model has been completely undermined by junk mail to such an extent that discard has become the only option. Indeed receiving MTA's which bounce this kind of junk may themselves be blacklisted.

pretty fast one (you will need it), written in C in the Appendices on
p. 296.

- A mixture of both. Some people have e-mail addresses almost destined
  for finger-trouble so you might specify a few alternatives for them and
  discard anything else.

This may be overkill though. Currently on my server, such finger-trouble
appears to be rarer than my target quality level of six sigma[23] but it never
hurts to have things up your sleeve for when the threat landscape changes.

Another advantage of course of discarding junk is that the perpetrator of
that junk is unaware that they are being immediately binned and continues
to sell on the failed addresses to other junk mailers leaving them relatively
easy to process in the future. This is part of a general policy of denying
any useful feedback to a junk mailer.

Generic bouncing

Before leaving this topic, it should be emphasized that certain kinds of
filtering method must lead to a bounce and not a discard. For example,
many users might share an IP address on a particular machine. If just one
of them is spamming, then a discard based on the IP address punishes all
the people sharing that IP address. It is therefore convention to bounce any
blacklisted IP address with a message explaining where more information
can be found to allow the administrator of that IP address to jettison the
spammer and de-list themselves.

Here is a recent example of a blacklist rejection on my mail server. This
is the raw data taken from the mail logs, (more on the pulchritude of mail
logs later).

```
Jul 29 04:35:27 localhost postfix/smtpd[4775]: NOQUEUE: reject:
RCPT from mix.mmi.pub.ro[141.85.255.152]: 554 5.7.1 Service unavailable;
Client host [141.85.255.152] blocked using bl.spamcop.net;
Blocked - see http://www.spamcop.net/bl.shtml?141.85.255.152;
from=<webmail@onlinehsbc.co.uk> to=<lesh@oakcomp.co.uk> proto=ESMTP
helo=<mix.mmi.pub.ro>
```

---

[23] A statistical measure explained in much more detail later from p. 232.

In this case, a mail server in Romania[24], (per capita hacking capital of the world as shown in Table 5.2.3 (p. 123)) is responsible. This log entry identifies the sending MTA as mix.mmi.pub.ro with an IP address of 141.85.255.152. It is quite slick and says HELO properly and is an obvious scam as it claims to be from webmail@onlinehsbc.co.uk. Unfortunately for them, they have allowed themselves to be blacklisted on the spamcop blacklist, a reliable and well-run list. Postfix by default bounces this e-mail with the message

```
''Blocked - see http://www.spamcop.net/bl.shtml?141.85.255.152''.
```

This allows the administrator of this machine to look themselves up, check their own mail logs to find the perpetrator, turn up in the middle of the night at their front door and confiscate all copies of Paul and Ovi's masterpiece or possibly make them listen to it all night. Sorry, I'm fantasising but you get the picture.

This and other rich potential functionality merely hints at what can be achieved by the MTA along with sophisticated supporting pieces of software. As will be seen, the functionality is necessary to provide adequate protection from junk.

4.5.2 Disposal in the MUA

In a less than ideal world, you aren't prepared to pay for dedicated services and your ISP is not very good. In that case, the following section will help.

4.6 Setting up filters in the receiving MUA

Even if the receiving MTA does a good job, it can never be sure in all cases that a particular message is junk and must in those cases deliver it and leave it up to the recipient to decide.

This is a fine line to get right. If the MTA is too generous, the recipient finds a mailbox full of junk which the MTA wasn't sure about. At the other extreme, if the MTA is too stringent, there remains the chance of it binning something which the recipient would really like to see.

---

[24]For those of you who slumped into unconsciousness before the Eurovision 'Song' contest even started this year, the Romanian entry was Paul Seling and Ovi's unforgettable "Playing with Fire" which seems somewhat appropriate. No I didn't vote for it.

As a result, the receiving MTA will tag messages[25]. Normally, this is only an indication of whether a message is spam or not. For example in the estimable SpamAssassin[26], the injected text is user-programmable but usually looks like:-

```
Subject: [SPAM]/_12.5_/ ...
...
```

This means that SpamAssassin has decided that the message is spam based on a score of 12.5, (the minimum default for spam is 5.0[27] but this can be changed according to your junk sensitivity).

If you are a real nerd as I am, your mind might idly wonder just how big a score spammers have managed to hit. A little hard research reveals a phenomenal score of 131.20 back in 2003[28]. Moving forward, we are down to the 70s in 2007[29] and the best I can manage in recent times is a miserly 49.0 submitted by my "Spam Clown of the Year" last year, (Appendix p. 317).

MUAs vary very considerably in the mail filtering functionality they offer to the user. Each MUA tends to reflect the philosophy of the company supplying it as we will now see. Just to cement whereabouts this appears in the chain of filtering, refer to Figure 4.3 (p. 102).

4.6.1 kmail (Linux)

In kmail, in traditional Linux fashion, you are offered a formidable set of tools if you are er, something of a nerd. If you are, it's the most powerful of any MUA in my opinion and can do almost as much as a well-configured MTA. If you are not, it offers little protection out of the box so you will have to rely on your MTA to do the heavy lifting for you, although if the MTA is set up as described later, you will see almost no junk at all.

---

[25] Usually by adding something to the subject line which is therefore clearly visible in all views normally offered by the MUA software running on your Blackberry, PC or whatever. For my systems I tag with the annotations shown on p. 89.

[26] http://www.spamassassin.org/

[27] As is discussed elsewhere in this book, junk mailers use SpamAssassin to tailor their junk accordingly. As a result, most reasonably sophisticated junk these days comes in at around 4.5, just under the default radar, whilst the most sophisticated stuff, usually incoming from a botnet will be between -1.0 and +1.0 and be indistinguishable from valid mail on this criterion.

[28] http://www.wired.com/culture/lifestyle/news/2003/08/59859

[29] http://www.redhat.com/archives/rhl-list/2007-January/msg04520.html

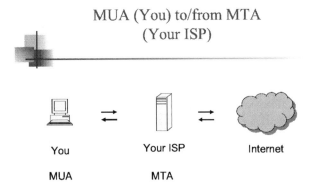

Figure 4.3: A simple view of you, your ISP and the great dark cloud of the Internet from which issues forth abundant offers of interesting ways to interfere with your body chemistry, heart-rending pleas from semi-literate 419ers and all the rest. Between you and your ISP, you have to get rid of all this. How you share it between you depends entirely on your ISP unless you have your own MTA as I do.

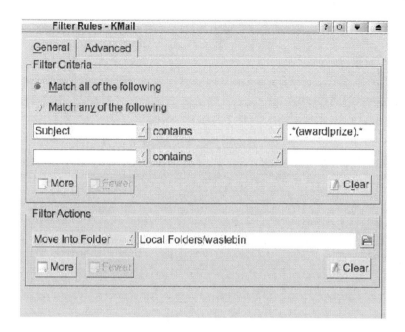

Figure 4.4: A screen shot of a regular expression based filter set up on the Subject: field from within kmail.

As a fully fledged nerd however, you are allowed to set up everything from your own regular expressions, (c.f. Figure 4.4 (p. 103)), to built-in bogofilter (see p. 150) and SpamAssassin use. If you use the configuration information provided later for these latter filters, you can set up a pretty robust MUA solution and it won't really matter if your ISP is poor at setting up it's MTAs.

4.6.2 Thunderbird (all)

Thunderbird is a sister product to the redoubtable Firefox, arguably the best cross-platform browser available[30]. On my university Windows machine, it appears to offer simple filtering options comparable to kmail although it does not appear as though I can link in SpamAssassin or bogofilter although no doubt somebody will tell me how to do it.

---

[30]I don't wish to be judgemental here as there are other excellent browsers including Opera but on general functionality, robustness and popularity, it's hard to beat Firefox.

There is little more to say really. I have used it only occasionally and whilst competent, it would not be very good unless the supplying MTA were up to scratch.

4.6.3 Windows Outlook

On first viewing of Outlook 2007, it looks as though they have got a good balance between functionality and ease of use to inexperienced users. The basic interface is shown in Figure 4.5 (p. 105).

As can be seen, they offer different levels of filtering protection and also options to disable links and other active functionaltiy in phishing messages as well as warning about suspicious links. The other tabs allow automatic white-listing and the ability to block specific named senders and also country codes[31] and international character sets like Chinese Traditional.

Well, that's the good news. The bad news is that it misses an average of 2 spams and scams per day and it junks about the same number of valid e-mails so I am forced to rummage in the Junk Mail folder from time to time. Although I am set at the high setting and it does actually warn me about this, at the time of writing this bit (14-Jul-2010), 13/29 of the e-mails placed in Junk were not Junk, so this is a pretty average performance given what can be achieved as I describe later. At this level of coarseness, the Junk folder is promoted into a sort of squiffy Inbox necessitating regular inspection. *That* is *not* good filtering.

Useful rules

You will have to experiment to see what works and what doesn't. I don't really approve of things that sound good and don't work properly.

4.6.4 Mail (OS X)

In contrast the Mac OS X Mail appears to rely on a hidden implementation of SpamAssassin (please correct me if I'm wrong) which automatically places things into a Junk folder for you. Of course if the supplying MTA doesn't do it's job, this just gets overwhelmed, and although admirable, something like SpamAssassin isn't good enough on it's own. As can be seen in Figure 4.6 (p. 107), the Apple mailer does allow you to use a Bayesian training option

---

[31]The two-letter international codes for countries - see later.

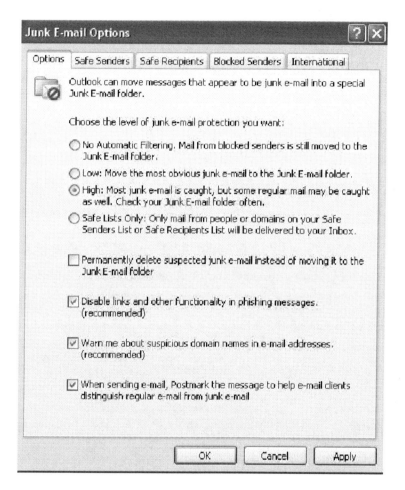

Figure 4.5: A screen shot of the Outlook 2007 junk mail filtering options.

but this puts quite a lot of onus on a possibly inexperienced user who would wonder what on earth this meant. Whilst laudable, and it certainly works better out of the box than the Outlook 2007 equivalent described above[32], this approach has real drawbacks when things go wrong and whilst the interfaces are pleasant to look at and remarkably untaxing on the cerebral processes, some of them are opaque to say the least[33].

4.6.5 Squirrelmail (webmail)

This is my preferred web-mailer. There are lots of others but Squirrelmail is solid, simple and reasonably full-featured. If you have a well-figured MTA, you need do nothing. If it's not so well-figured then through a rich set of available plug-ins, it can access both SpamAssassin and separate Bayesian filtering options as can be seen by consulting it's main web page[34].

4.6.6 Eudora (OS X and Windows)

I haven't used Eudora for some time. I used to use it on Windows when I was considering Windows as an option for my main computing needs some years ago and it was OK although at the time, the bar was not set very high. Today, it's junk mail filtering options are confused by it's payment model. As I write this, it has three modes on it's site[35] - Paid, Sponsored and Lite. It then goes on to say that the Paid mode is no longer available. When you download it, it explains that the Über-Ultra Quantum Electrodynamic Spam filtering[36] is only available in the Paid mode. Sigh. I used to live on

---

[32] Admittedly this does not set the bar very high.

[33] Lest I sound uninformed here, my wife has a Power Mac G5. Whilst most of the time, it runs swimmingly, every now and then it simply refuses to do things with no explanation whatsoever. For example, it occasionally loses it's wireless connection. To reinstate it as far as I can see requires the various devices to be turned off and on according to some obscure cabalistic ritual. It usually reluctantly decides to play on the fourth or fifth attempt with no explanation. Even worse, about 6 months ago, it invited me to update the operating system for some vital new security fix. I did and no printer I connect to it has worked since. It claims they are not there but teasingly, can measure their ink levels. The forums are full of complaints but Apple have done nothing. It appears that if I want to fix it, I have to reload my original operating system and then allow it to update up to the one where it failed, just the kind of thing the average user would like to contemplate. There was a time when I compared OS X very favourably in comparison with Windows offerings but I have come to dislike Apple intensely for it's appalling laissez-faire attitude. Arrogance tends not to have much longevity as a business model. There, I feel better already.

[34] http://squirrelmail.org/plugins_category.php?category_id=3

[35] http://www.eudora.com/

[36] Alright, I made this bit up. It's called, rather less originally I feel, SpamWatch. More intriguingly, this mystical version has something called BossWatch. Goodness knows

Figure 4.6: A screen shot of the Junk mail filtering options of Mac OSX Mail.

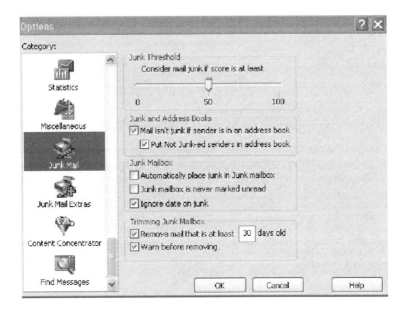

Figure 4.7: A screen shot of the Eudora mail filtering options.

a planet where English-speaking people spoke English in ways that other English-speaking people were able to understand. If I had to describe the 21st century so far as a historian far in the future is concerned, I would use the single word "Sloppy".

Be that as it may, the version I did manage to install has the options shown in Figure 4.7 (p. 108). As such, it is a bit feeble. Make that a lot feeble[37].

4.6.7 Blackberry (proprietary)

The Blackberry cannot perform filtering directly. Rather you have to log on to the Blackberry Internet Service (BIS) and decide which messages should be pushed to your Blackberry by setting up filters which seem to be pretty naive. It looks very much like you would need to buy a commercial service (see below) to do anything effective with this device. After watching people

---

what that is supposed to do.

[37] It reminds me of the control panel in "Plan 9 from Outer Space", which incidentally, you *have* to see owing to it's repeatedly voted status as the worst film ever made.

blunder into trees and generally staggering down the street trying to send e-mails on their handheld, I have opted to receive no junk on my Blackberry by the simple expedient of not owning one. Works for me.

4.7 Commercial and non-commercial services

4.7.1 Commercial systems

There are lots and lots of commercial services who will offer everything from basic mail filtering where they will intercept all your e-mails, sanitise them and pass them on to you, all the way to full mail filtering, archival and the works. It is an easy solution, (i.e. you throw money at the problem) but your mileage may vary as they say, (your money may miss). My own experiences with them are mixed. My university uses a big name in the area and it is only average in my opinion and certainly not worth the very considerable amount of money it costs.

4.7.2 Open systems

There are a number of full or partial solutions available with differing implications for how much of your own time you need to invest.

Probably the best known full system is Julian Field's Mailscanner, [15] which has an excellent reputation. If I had known about it when I started researching this area, I might just have used that instead, although then I would not have had the opportunity to learn about it the hard way. Mailscanner allows you to integrate lots of tools and methods into a single infrastructure which works alongside the most commonly used MTAs. The number of configuration options is pretty breathtaking as can be seen by studying [15].

There are also much less sophisticated ways of glueing together different filtering methods but if you are going to go this full integrated route, I would recommend MailScanner.

Another open source effort worth a mention is hMailServer[38] which is available for Windows-based computers. Although I have not used it, this includes many of the junk mail defense techniques mentioned later such as SPF (p. 170) and greylisting (p. 139) and looks to be well worth a try.

---

[38]http://www.hmailserver.com/

4 Protection: the principles of filtering

5 Going deeper: setting up a mail server

To provide adequate protection against incoming junk mail, there has to be a high quality measurement-based infrastructure present in the receiving MTA. Once mail passes through the MTA to the recipients MUA, the options to reject it are considerably diminished. If you do not have access to the MTA, as is the case with most users, you rely on whoever does have access to provide an adequate environment. This is often your ISP. Unfortunately, ISPs must err on the side of caution. They deal with perhaps thousands of users and many millions of e-mails a day and they cannot afford to throw away genuine mail. Understandably, this is usually taken to extremes so that far too much junk is let through. In some cases, the ISP simply does not provide a sufficiently high quality mail environment or they may sell it to you as a value-added service. Even then, your mileage may vary as they say in the business.

If you do not have access to the MTA, then you are restricted to whatever you are able to achieve in your MUA. Again, your options may be very limited here. Some MUAs do not provide much in the way of filtering, making the assumption that the heavy work has already been done. Other MUAs, such as the excellent open source Squirrelmail[1], provide lots of plug-ins capable of applying many advanced techniques.

So, if you feel you are up to the challenge of running your own server, read on.

For many people, this is probably not an option as there are minimum technical knowledge requirements. These are not particularly taxing but nevertheless it is not a decision to be taken lightly. Having said that, junk mailers are definitely keeping ahead of the average ISP and/or third-party mail filtering services, so the benefits are definitely worth having and the

---

[1] http://www.squirrelmail.org/

information provided generally in this book and specifically in this chapter should allow spam to be effectively eliminated for the present.

The chapter starts with a general introduction to setting up a server and the different kinds of checking which can be done. Following that, I will switch specifically to setting up Postfix and will intersperse that commentary with measurements as to how effective a particular filtering principle is.

As I have noted previously, measurement is the essence of forensics. For each of the rules I will show measurements of the effectiveness of a particular filtering method averaged over long-term use on my own server. It should be noted that such measurements are very sensitive to where the filtering method appears in the filtering chain. In the early days of experimentation, I continually changed this order trying to optimise the maximum number of junk messages which could be detected for the cheapest method. The current order of filtering has not changed substantially for a long time and seems close to optimal. The measurements I will present are based on this stable ordering.

5.1 Acquiring a server

What you are looking for is a dedicated server with *root access*. Dedicated means that you don't share it with anybody else and if you don't know what root access[2] means, stop reading now and experiment more with the chapter covering filtering in your MUA.

The low end dedicated servers, (which are perfectly adequate to run a serious mail server), currently cost around GBP 30-100 pounds a month. They come with a bare bones operating system which may or may not have mail server software pre-installed. Linux based ones are the cheapest and are absolutely rock solid in my experience, (mine has gone down once in three years I suspect because the suppliers mucked up a reverse DNS record I requested). I use Centos which is a derivative of the well-known Red Hat distribution, although there are lots of choices. You can of course get Windows but I won't cover that in this book.

---

[2]You can do anything you want, including untold damage.

Linux servers come in various stages of preparation. The really cheap ones require you to install mail, web and other servers yourself. This is not hard although the installation method depends on the version of Linux you use. On my Centos servers, the installation method is *yum*[3] which I have to say is excellent. For example, to install web software on mine is done simply by the incantation

```
# yum install httpd
```

All the necessary dependencies are handled invisibly by yum. Please note that I don't carry this kind of stuff around in my head. There is ample excellent advice on this topic plastered all over the web. In these days of soul-destroying telephone menu support systems, "customer support executives" who wouldn't know a mail server if one crashed through the ceiling, and impossibly difficult access to anyone who appears to know what they are doing, this is a great relief[4].

The slightly more expensive ones come ready to go. They all have some form of web interface to access your server but unless you use something like Webmin[5], you will probably have to use the command line to do stuff. Again this is not too taxing but with root access on a command line, you can do an awful lot of damage. In the first week in spite of my years of experience, I managed to screw the file permissions up so badly, I had to request a re-imaging of the server, (the supplier has to reload the operating system from scratch). It didn't cost anything other than a very large portion of humble pie but this is how you learn.

In my case, the server was ready to go and already had a mail server installed, in this case Postfix[6]. Postfix was originally written by Wietser Venema at the IBM T.J. Watson research centre. You can always tell when a piece of software is well-designed and well-built because the longer you use it, the more comfortable it feels, like an old and favoured pair of shoes. Postfix is very well-designed and implemented and I have had absolutely

---

[3]http://en.wikipedia.org/wiki/Yellowdog_Updater,_Modified, accessed 11-Aug-2011.

[4]Lest you think I am exaggerating, have a look at some of the war-stories on http://www.leshatton.org/. Today, shortly before I sat down to write this, I tried to access my O2 mobile phone provider to pick up my voice-mail. The disembodied voice announced that I had to change my PIN "for security reasons" and asked me to enter my new PIN number. Notice that they didn't ask me to confirm the old one first in case my phone had been picked up by somebody else. Sigh.

[5]http://webmin.org/.

[6]www.postfix.org.

no problems with it. Furthermore, it was designed around the principles of security and filtering and provides arguably the best environment of all in which to implement what we need to do to stem the flood of junk.

So amongst the myriads of options, how do you set yourself up with a good basic filtering system ? The best MTAs all allow you to do multiple filtering actions at each stage of their negotiation with the sending MTA about whether or not they should accept an incoming mail. This is what you do with Postfix and with the current sophistication levels of some spam, you need to.

First note that most filtering actions can be applied at most stages. This is not intuitively obvious but the fact that something is called a recipient check does not mean that it cannot be applied at the sender checking stage. It may indeed have a relevance there and should be applied. For example, it is possible that it is more efficient at removing certain kinds of junk than other methods applied at that stage. If this all sounds a bit opaque, I will return to it in the commentary which follows but you are reading the results of nearly three years of experimentation.

5.2 Blacklists and whitelists

Blacklists and whitelists work very simply. Each is a list of IP addresses xxx.xxx.xxx.xxx or domain names or individual mail addresses. IP addresses usually appear in externally (i.e. external to the MTA) checked lists, whereas internally checked lists are usually domain names or individual mail addresses. If the IP address of a sending MTA or a domain name or individual address is on a blacklist, it is usually summarily rejected. If it is on a whitelist, it is either accepted unconditionally or more likely, passed on to the next check as much junk emanates from computers which are normally OK but have been compromised.

I have to confess that in filtering terms, I am a purist. External blacklists or whitelists are fine. Somebody else is doing the heavy-lifting for you and some of them are extremely effective although you have to choose carefully to find one with an excellent record for accuracy. On the other hand, internal blacklists and whitelists of exceptions are by definition, maintained by the administrator of the server. They can rapidly get out of hand and a large internal whitelist is usually a sign that you are not treating incoming junk very efficiently: your rules do not match the threats well.

In an ideal world, there would be no exceptions and all junk would be recognised as such and non-junk left in the bottom of the sieves. It is not an ideal world, but you can get surprisingly close. There are relatively few exceptions necessary in what will follow and very, very little that I don't want gets through it.

On a final note, there are one or two cases when you might want to use a whitelist to restrict even valid mails, for example if your child has an e-mail address and you want to define who is allowed to send e-mail.

5.2.1 External Whitelists

External whitelists are basically reputation based. If your server meets or exceeds various (not particularly well-defined) spamming standards, you can apply to have your IP address added to the whitelist. The benefit of this is that appearance on such lists is measurable by spam checking products such as SpamAssassin which associates an increasingly negative score depending on how good you are. Such negative scores of course will offset any positive scores you pick up making delivery of your mail more likely.

Some mail servers will give an automatic pass based on the presence of the IP address of the sending MTA in such a list.

dnswl.org

One of the most commonly used ones is dnswl.org[7]. The site itself has this to say

> *dnswl.org assigns all "good mailservers" into one of four trust levels: none, low, medium and high trust. Higher trust levels are the result of how a mailserver and the network are operated, how spam coming from these sources is contained and similar factors. Trust is gained over time[8] and the levels are explicitly recognised by SpamAssassin as indicated below.*

---

[7]http://www.dnswl.org/

[8]This has a slight downside in that you can get locked in to a particular dedicated server and it's IP address because you have built up trust. If you find a better deal on a server, which of course will have a different IP address, you basically have to start the trust clock again.

The trust levels are defined as:

High Never sends spam. Spam filtering need not be done for such servers. SpamAssassin code is RCVD_IN_DNSWL_HI, scoring -5.0[9].

Medium Spam is an extremely rare occurrence and any transgressions are corrected promptly. Spam filtering need not be done for such servers. SpamAssassin code is RCVD_IN_DNSWL_MED, scoring -2.3.

Low Occasional spam outbreaks not perhaps corrected so promptly. This is the normal default. SpamAssassin code is RCVD_IN_DNSWL_LOW, scoring -0.7. Should not be blacklisted or greylisted[10].

None Legitimate server but may also send spam. This is the default for bulk mailers. Should not be blacklisted or greylisted. SpamAssassin code is RCVD_IN_DNSWL_NONE, scoring -0.0001.

My own experiences with this listing organisation are very positive and I can recommend them and recommend being involved with them in some capacity. Although free for non-profit access up to 100,000 DNS lookups a day, as of November 2010, they have moved to a pricing model similar to that of spamhaus.org where an annual usage-based fee is charged for commercial use.

There are other whitelists but they all seem to be commercial and will charge you a variable fee to be included. I have no idea how much they vet a server's history before accepting it nor the amount of value it brings so your mileage may vary although the model seems to be that they will negotiate with big ISPs to accept mail emanating from their members as a matter of greater priority than the hoi polloi. There are cheaper ways of reaching trusted status as we will see.

5.2.2 External Blacklists

These have flourished in recent years in response to the rapidly increasing wave of junk. As forensic analysis becomes more sophisticated, more and more ways of distinguishing junk mail from ordinary mail become available and detection tends towards perfection. It turns out that there are many patterns of use of IP addresses which help to distinguish junk.

---

[9]Default in version 3.2.1
[10]p. 139

Here is a brief description of some of the better known blacklists and the particular patterns of IP address abuse encoded in each list. These are publicly available lists which a receiving MTA (or even a MUA) can access free of charge or relatively cheaply[11].

Spamhaus Spamhaus is one of the best of the listing organisations. Professionally run, in my experience it has registered no false positives in the three years I have been using it and every MTA should use it, (I will show you how later). One small note of caution is that it is free for use for only small mail loadings and if you exceed it you are summarily blocked from using it in future. There is no warning. This actually happened to me because I placed this block too early in my filtering chain in my inexperienced days and too many hits were registered. In the end, I forked out the normal subscription of USD 250[12], to pay for professional access. On it's own, it's not that big a contribution to the filtering quality but I think it's an organisation worth supporting.

Spamhaus run multiple lists described as follows.

- SBL: A block list of IP addresses from which Spamhaus recommend no mail should be accepted.
- XBL: To quote from the Spamhaus site[13], "the Spamhaus Exploits Block List (XBL) is a realtime database of IP addresses of hijacked PCs infected by illegal 3rd party exploits, including open proxies (HTTP, socks, AnalogX, wingate, etc), worms/viruses with built-in spam engines, and other types of trojan-horse exploits.". XBL is a slightly adjusted version of the CBL[14] and the NJABL Open Proxy IPs list[15]. Open proxy computers are computers which communicate on behalf of other computers. They can be used to hide the real source of a particular message so are popular with junk mailers. If a junk mailer sends a mail through

---

[11] Note that most if not all of these are connected inside SpamAssassin. However some of them have been 100% accurate so can be brought forward in the filtering chain to live inside the MTA where they are used to reject mail from servers which appear on these lists. In spamAssassin of course, they only accumulate a positive penalty, (which can nevertheless be a large one).

[12] At the time of writing. Note that this is a footnote not a power in case you were worried about the expense.

[13] http://www.spamhaus.org/, accessed 10-Aug-2010.

[14] (Composite Block List) from cbl.abuseat.org

[15] www.njabl.org

a proxy, they can destroy the traces pointing back to their own machine. If the proxy happens to be in a country with a relaxed attitude to junk mail, it can be very difficult to get them to peruse their logs, even in criminal cases in some regimes.

- PBL: A DNSBL[16] These normally include listings of the addresses of zombie computers or other machines being used to send spam. Such lists might also include addresses of ISPs who willingly host spammers, or even listing addresses which have sent spam to a honeypot system, (p. 181).

- Zen: Simply a combination of SBL, XBL and PBL and the normal way Spamhaus lists are accessed.

- DBL: This is different from the other lists in that it is a list of domain names which are commonly embedded in the body of a junk mail rather than IP addresses. It also includes domain names which might occur in From: fields. Given that these are invariably spoofed, this aspect might not be so useful[17].

Spamcop A competent DNSBL. If you use Spamhaus, it doesn't add very much, (typically less than 1%). Remember however, that even at this level, it could be a few a month. These might well slip through the rest of your defences and scam one of your users. This is a cheap check compared with the advanced content filtering necessary later in the filter chain so use whatever facilities you trust. You will need them. It is however worthwhile checking the logs on a regular basis to make sure that your trust in them is justified.

psbl.surriel.com . I use this blocklist in my own server. I have had no false positives and it is at least as good as Spamcop (above). In essence, an IP address gets added to the PSBL when it sends email to a spamtrap, that email is not identified as non-spam and the IP address is not a known mail server. A very useful bit of software called Spamikaze is available from the same site to help you build your own lists which I will probably do at some stage with my hack list.

rfc-ignorant.org These are not block lists but they simply list those mail servers which appear to depart from web mail standards for some reason. This site maintains a number of lists described as follows.

- dsn.rfc-ignorant.org: Listed if the publicly listed MX record for a domain refuses to accept mail with an originator given as <>.

---

[16]DNS-based blacklist
[17]Also known as a RHSBL or Right Hand Side Block List

The domain will then be considered a viable candidate for inclusion in the zone.

- abuse.rfc-ignorant.org: the listing criterion is that any domain for which abuse@domain is rejected, times-out, or for any other reason cannot be delivered, shall be considered grounds for listing.

- postmaster.rfc-ignorant.org: If the right-hand-side of an address doesn't have a postmaster address (e.g., given an address of foo@example.tld, if "postmaster@example.tld" bounces as non-existent (on any of the valid MX servers for 'example.tld'), then example.tld would be listed.

- bogusmx.rfc-ignorant.org: If any publicly listed MX record for a domain contains a hostname which points to bogus IP address space, such as those documented in RFC 3330, or IPv6 reservations detailed in RFCs 3879, 4048, 4193, and 4291 or if the domain contains an MX RR that points to an IP address, in violation of RFC 1035 or if the domain has MX RRs which point to hostnames which themselves do not have an associated A record (including MXs which return an NXDOMAIN, or which are CNAMEs)

- whois.rfc-ignorant.org: A variety of ways of mis-stating the required WHOIS information. RFC 1032 specifies the following

  > *The reply from WHOIS will supply the following: the name and address of the organization "owning" the domain; the name of the domain; it's administrative, technical, and zone contacts; the host names and network addresses of sites providing name service for the domain.*

  If you don't, you are likely to be listed.

njabl.org This site[18] maintains a list of known and potential spam sources consisting of open relays, open proxies, open form to mail HTTP gateways, dynamic IP pools and direct spammers. In my experience, this should not be used to block mail directly but is well worth using as part of an escalating policy, (it is connected inside SpamAssassin).

uribl.com This lists domains which appear in the body of e-mails. There are several. The wording is taken directly from the site as of 20th Dec 2010 give or take a few spelling corrections.

---

[18]NJABL is short for Not Just Another Bogus List

- black.uribl.com - This list contains domain names belonging to and used by spammers, including but not restricted to those that appear in URIs found in Unsolicited Bulk and/or Commercial Email (UBE/UCE). This list has a goal of zero False Positives. This zone rebuilds frequently as new data is added.

- grey.uribl.com - This list contains domains found in UBE/UCE, and possibly honour opt-out requests. It may include ESPs which allow customers to import their recipient lists and may have no control over the subscription methods. This list can and probably will cause False Positives depending on your definition of UBE/UCE. This zone rebuilds several times a day as necessary.

- red.uribl.com - This list contains domains that actively show up in mail flow, are not listed on URIBL black, and are either: being monitored, very young (domain age via whois), or use whois privacy features to protect their identity. This list is automated in nature, so should be used at the user's risk.

- white.uribl.com - This list contains legitimate domain names that we do not want to show up on any other URIBL lists. This list is pretty static, with only a handful of changes per day. URIBL white is not currently bitmasked into multi.uribl.com. To query it, a separate query should be sent. This zone rebuilds as needed.

- multi.uribl.com - This zone contains domains which appear on any of the above lists. This zone rebuilds if any of the above zones are rebuilt, with the exception of white.

When you are still learning, you may get caught out by one of the junk mailers and get yourself blacklisted. This happened to me very early on when I unknowingly put up a website containing the FormMail injection bug(s)[19]. This allowed junk mailers to relay their stuff through forms on my web-site without me even realising it. The first thing I knew was when I was blacklisted.

After removing the FormMail script and replacing it with my own, I was then able to contact the blacklist on which I appeared and request removal. *Do not request removal from a blacklist without resolving the problem first !* This might seem a trifle obvious but if you offend again immediately after being taken off, it's often much harder to get off the second time.

---

[19]http://www.monkeys.com/anti-spam/formmail-advisory.pdf

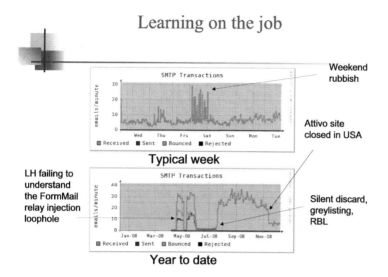

Figure 5.1: Amongst other things, this shows the dramatic effect on mail throughput on a dedicated server before and after I removed the FormMail injection problem.

You can see the effect on the mail volumes of my server in Figure 5.1 (p. 121). This figure also shows a number of other effects.

First of all, note the significantly increased activity at the weekend in the week view in the top part of the figure. The bottom part of the figure shows the year to date view at the time, (in 2008), with a number of significant events annotated including my little contretemps with the FormMail problem.

5.2.3 Personal hate lists

You don't have to be involved in mail filtering for very long before you start building personal hate lists. There is a rich source to assimilate.

Third-party bulk mailers

For example, third-party bulk-mailers handle mail on the behalf of many companies, particularly the smaller ones. Unfortunately, if you get on the

121

list of one of the smaller companies for products you are interested in, the bulk-mailing companies have a tendency to migrate you on to the lists of other companies which they handle, (see my earlier comments about transitive relationships on p. 77). The end result is that having signed up to receive information about guitar amplifiers, you suddenly start receiving e-mail about holidays in Tierra del Fuego, which then have the cheek to say something like "You are receiving this mail because you subscribed ...". What they really mean of course is "You are receiving this mail because we might get away with it."

They don't. Faced with this I add the embedded link from the third-party bulk mailer to a personal hate list and whitelist the guitar amplifier supplier directly[20]. This doesn't happen very often so there are only 10 or so after couple of years of operating a server but forensically, this is easy because third-party bulk mailers stuff their e-mails with links, (web bugs as described on p. 310) which accumulate clicks to tell them how well they are doing.

Hackers

One of the other things you notice about running your own server is that somebody tries a secure shell illegal login by password guessing every few minutes. Modern operating systems keep a complete trail of these attacks in the form of logs which can be read through to understand their nature as discussed shortly. Logs are your friend as we will see shortly.

From very early on, I wrote Perl scripts to scan these logs and accumulate information about the IP addresses from which these attacks were emanating[21]. In the three years since I have been doing this, the list of IP addresses from which somebody has tried to hack into my server has grown to over 37,200 and it's growing at several hundred a month. I keep this list as a SQLite database, updated daily and accessible to a supporting script on the mail server which tags any e-mails emanating from one of these servers or containing embedded links to them as tainted. When I have a bit of time, I will make this list available in some form.

---

[20]This is an open invitation to send me mails from guitar shops by the way. It's lesh@oakcomp.co.uk and I have a soft-spot for Fenders, Gibsons and Marshall stacks. I am however prepared to consider PRS, Steinberger and Humble amps. Basically anything loud is OK and the band I play in is at http://www.juniperhillblues.co.uk/ and we are available for major rock and blues festivals. End of advert.

[21]In Centos-based Linux systems as my server uses, the log is called /var/log/secure.

Let's name and shame. Table 5.2.3 (p. 123) contains a list of the top twenty countries from which illegal secure shell login attempts have been launched so far. The twenty countries account for around 80% of all attacks. Let us be clear about this. There is nothing soft and fluffy about hackers. These are in the main, determined criminal attempts by people who are exploiting their skills to attack others for financial benefit. They should be treated as if they are trying to sledgehammer your front door down.

Number of attacking servers	Country
4773	India
3369	Romania
1978	Russia
1976	China
1191	Morocco
884	Brazil
828	South Korea
775	Algeria
727	Germany
591	Kazakhstan
562	Turkey
357	Bulgaria
331	United States
324	Belarus
275	Indonesia
268	Austria
252	Vietnam
220	Ukraine
212	Italy

Table 5.2.3: Number of distinct servers from which illegal secure shell login access emanated compared with country of origin.

A glance through this list compared with populations[22] reveals that Romania is by far and away the per capita hacking centre of the world, unless they are taking it out on me for not voting for them in the Eurovision song contest.

---

[22]http://en.wikipedia.org/wiki/List_of_countries_by_population

Opinions seem divided on this but if you employ strong passwords on your server, (*minimum* 10 non-dictionary related characters, upper and lower case, numbers and punctuation), the entire hacking population of Romania beavering away for the rest of the lifetime of the galaxy wouldn't crack it[23]. It is however slightly annoying to read through the logs and see them banging away so after a while you get fed up with it.

There is a very nice little trick called *iptable throttling* you can do on modern Linux systems using iptables[24] which essentially gives people three failed attempts and then kicks them off for some long period, (the example below shows 30 minutes but you can make it a lot longer).

```
#!/bin/bash
#
#       Block repeated attempts on ssh.
#
#       Revision:       $Revision: 1.24 $
#       Date:    $Date: 2011/08/25 15:12:18 $
#----------------------------------------------------------------
#
#       Because of inserts at the head (-I), these are in
#       reverse order.
#
#       Update the entry and if there are more than 4 hits in
#       30 minutes, just drop the packet.  The insert (-I) is
#       necessary as there is a default rule to accept all
#       port 22 traffic so an append (-A) would just put it
#       after it has already been accepted.
#
iptables -I INPUT -p tcp --dport 22 \
        -m state --state NEW \
        -m recent --update --seconds 1800 --hitcount 4 \
        -j DROP
#
#       Insert above that a rule to set the new
#       incoming IP address in the recent queue.
#
iptables -I INPUT -p tcp --dport 22 \
        -m state --state NEW -m recent --set
```

---

[23] Although they are clearly not going to let this knowledge stop them.
[24] http://www.netfilter.org/projects/iptables/index.html

```
#
#         Insert above that, a rule to make sure my local machine
#         is not stopped, (because I issue multiple sudos in backup
#         scripts).  My local machine is xxx.xxx.xxx.xxx
#
iptables -I INPUT -p tcp --dport 22 -s xxx.xxx.xxx.xxx -j ACCEPT
```

I hope I don't need to remind you to be careful doing things with iptables because if you screw it up, you can lock yourself out or let everybody in. This is the front door we are talking about.

Throttling works like a charm. Very few people come back but one or two determined people will keep trying randomly over several days or even weeks. I used to set trip-wires to watch people doing this to watch how the attacks develop and what techniques are used. They tend to be very similar now so if anybody does this for more than say two sequences of attempts, I block the subnet automatically and permanently by adding an iptable lockout rule such as

```
#
#         This Dar es Salaam subnet banged away for weeks in early
#         2010.
#
iptables -A INPUT -s 196.41.57.0/255.255.255.0 -j DROP
```

For anybody who doubts the global nature of IT threats, all you need to do is try to run a server for a few weeks or have a read of [1] and you will be left in no doubt that the world is at digital war. So long as it remains digital, that's fine with me, but you can never relax and forensic skills need to be continually honed[25].

5.3 A little on proxies

A proxy server is simply one which stands in between a client and some other server and acts on behalf of the client. The client is typically you or

---

[25]I could block all subnets permanently other than the ones I use for secure login but this then deprives me of the ability to collect statistics on this kind of hacking. Never stop measuring - it's the only way you can keep up with the threats.

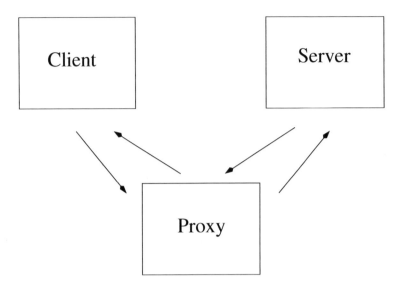

Figure 5.2: A proxy server acting on behalf of a client in it's transactions with another server. Note that it is normal to chain proxies, i.e. have several where one is shown here, all linked in series.

me requiring some kind of service. It's role is illustrated in Figure 5.2 of p. 126.

Proxies take on all kinds of useful roles, particularly in improving the performance of the web by caching web pages, (i.e. storing commonly accessed pages locally). The book by [55] is highly recommended if you want to get into this.

However proxy usefulness, like everything else, also extends to the dark side and their primary use here is to remove the traces of criminal activity using something called an anonymising proxy server. In Figure 5.2, if the proxy server is an anonymising server, it presents it's own credentials to the destination server on the right, hiding the original client's details. Of course the anonymising server knows who the client is so a trust relationship has to exist between the client and the proxy server. Proxy servers normally serve a specific subnet (i.e. subset) of the web however, there are also *open proxy servers*. These are open to anybody on the internet.

The use of an open anonymising server to conceal the IP address of the client is not necessarily a symptom of criminal activity. They are also used by freedom activists to evade detection in repressive regimes which exercise unreasonable censorship.

In terms of spamming and scamming, they are used to hide the origin of the sender of junk mail. However, such open anonymising servers are generally known on the web and lists of them are kept as DNSBL (Domain Name System Block Lists), to allow a receiving MTA to look up the sending MTA address to see if it is listed as an open proxy. If so, you have the choice of blocking it, (there is a very low chance of it being genuine) or just tagging it with a black mark to be added up later with any other evidence.

For a forensic scientist, open proxies can be used for probing dark side servers without revealing your own IP address. An excellent example of an open source proxy application is *proxychains*[26]. Using it simply involves setting up it's configuration file proxychains.conf and then using it to control some other application for example

```
# proxychains telnet targethost.com
```

will run telnet on the site targethost.com through proxies defined in proxychains.conf. The proxylist defined in proxychains.conf has the proxies listed one per line in the following format. Under option, these proxies can be taken in order, randomised or subsetted.

```
type(socks4|socks5|http)  hostname  portnumber [user pass]
```

To find open proxies (the list changes all the time), just Google for them.

To run firefox by proxy you would do the following

```
# proxychains firefox targethost.com
```

This is as much as we need to know here.

5.4 Configuring Postfix

So we come to configuring the MTA Postfix. For this, you should read [12] from the excellent O'Reilly stable, it's a very good reference.

---

[26]http://proxychains.sourceforge.net/. A roughly equivalent Windows version is called Sockschain and is available from http://www.ufasoft.com/.

Layered protection and Postfix

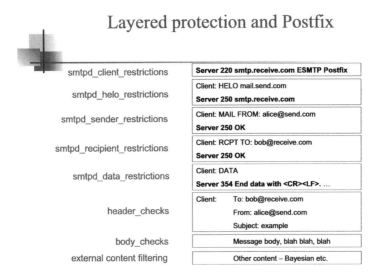

Figure 5.3: The layered nature of Postfix with the Postfix categories on the left hand side and the SMTP conversation between the sending and receiving MTAs on the right hand side.

The stages at which filtering is done in Postfix are shown in Figure 5.3 (p. 128). This figure shows the Postfix categories on the left compared with an example SMTP conversation on the right between the sending MTA and the receiving MTA. The figure is worth some study to understand what follows.

Postfix has two principle configuration files, *main.cf* and *master.cf*. main.cf sets rules for treating mail at the various stages whereas master.cf is more concerned with other issues such as the paths those mails can follow through the mail infrastructure.

I will now compare the contents of a typical main.cf (very close to my current one), against each of these stages where they are relevant to junk mail rejection. There are other rules associated with authentication and so on which are not shown here.

Each step is accompanied by average measurements of volume rejected from my own server over a typical week, in which around 590,000 mails were received altogether. These measurements appear in boxes.

Note also that each stage may contain multiple rules, each of which can have multiple parameters as shown below. To make sure that you don't get lost in what follows, note the following nomenclature:-

Stages Recipient check.

    Rules *reject_rbl_client=*

        parameters *bl.spamcop.net, zen.spamhaus.org*

With reference to this hierarchy, Postfix, gives the following options for action to take with a received e-mail.

REJECT The message is immediately rejected and the sending MTA told that the message can't be delivered. By default Postfix waits until after the RCPT TO: command is received before doing this because like nerds, some sending MTAs don't like rejection during a transaction and keep jabbering away until they pause for breath.

OK Accept the item. Processing for the current rule stops and continues with the next rule.

DUNNO Don't know. Pass it on to the next parameter in the current rule.

FILTER (Additional option in access map). Pass it on to some other kind of filter.

HOLD (Additional option in access map). Place it in the hold queue.

DISCARD (Additional option in access map). Tell the sending MTA that everything is fine and then lose it. As was discussed above, this is a dangerous step because of the chance of losing genuine messages but the statistics strongly support it as will be seen.

So a single rejection from any parameter is all that is required to reject a mail but all tested parameters must say OK or DUNNO for it to be accepted. The difference between DUNNO and OK is when a DUNNO is encountered, Postfix just carries on with the next *parameter*. When an OK is found, Postfix carries on with the next *rule*.

The description of the whole sequence which follows with examples should make this clear[27].

In particular, do NOT say OK when you really mean DUNNO ! OK means that you trust this particular e-mail with your 1959 Gibson Les Paul Standard. Greater love hath no man.

5.4.1 Client checks

These are checks which can be done on the sending MTA's IP address on connection. Whilst this is a seemingly attractive place to ditch junk mail using the "earliest is best" rule, in practice, IP address checks can be expensive, particularly blacklist checking as they normally require DNS lookups. Remember that *every* e-mail makes it this far. A vast percentage of these are such puerile nonsense that they can be rejected more cheaply later. Also, they may even pass at this stage anyway in the situation where an unsophisticated spammer such as a 419'er has bought time on the botnet of a sophisticated botmaster so the sending MTAs are clean whilst the content of the e-mail would not fool anything higher up the evolutionary ladder than a deranged hamster. Postfix provides reject_rbl_client=, reject_rhsbl_client= and reject_unknown_client= parameters at this stage but I don't use any for the above reasons.

```
main.cf entry:
```

```
smtpd_client_restrictions=
```

Percent rejected by client restrictions: 0% {0/590,000 - not implemented}

5.4.2 Helo checks: yes that's spelt helo

The relevant entry for the next stage of checking, (the HELO stage in the transaction shown in Figure 5.3 (p. 128)) is shown below.

```
main.cf entry:
```

---

[27] It certainly wasn't clear to me for a while when I started. On one occasion, I used OK in an early parameter instead of DUNNO and inadvertently bypassed a whole pile of other parameters in the same rule including greylisting. I only found out when I discovered greylisting didn't seem to be greylisting anything. Two weeks of junk later, I finally figured it out. Happy days.

```
smtpd_helo_required = yes
smtpd_helo_restrictions =
    permit_mynetworks,
    check_helo_access hash:/etc/postfix/self_helo,
    check_sender_access hash:/etc/postfix/sender_whitelist,
    reject_non_fqdn_hostname,
    reject_invalid_hostname,
    permit
```

The smtpd_helo_required=yes requires the sending MTA to say HELO. The rest do the following.

permit_mynetworks Allows my own networks to participate.

check_helo_access hash:/etc/postfix/self_helo This stops the sending MTA pretending to be me when it says HELO. The hash: bit simply tells Postfix that the list has been turned into a special format called Berkeley DB database format. There is nothing special about this. Postfix provides a utility called *postmap* to make these format files from your list. They can then be accessed a lot faster.

A couple of words of explanation should be given here. The self_helo file is just a list of the ways in which my receiving MTA identifies itself. For example mine originally contained amongst other things:-

```
oakcomp.co.uk    REJECT  You cannot be SERIOUS
88.208.247.158   REJECT  You cannot be SERIOUS
```

When I first started doing this in mid 2010, only a relatively small percentage of junk masqueraded using self-helo as shown below.

Percent rejected by self_helo restrictions: 0.7% {4,031/590,000}

Since then, at the time of writing, although the total junk load is down to about 25% of it's mid 2010 level, the self-helo masquerade has shot up to 20% of this figure so it is obviously considered a successful way of delivering[28].

---

[28]An impact test to mitigate this recent increase is described on p. 262

check_sender_access In spite of your best efforts, it will turn out that one of your customers or best friends will happen to use a mailer which either does not do the SMTP transaction proPerly[29] or sends and receives on dynamically rapidly changing IP addresses[30]. For these you have to whitelist them. I have about 30 entries in mine about half of which are because the ISP concerned is sloppy. Hopefully, this will reduce over time. An example of one follows, (although I don't actually use this).

```
tiscali.co.uk                    OK
```

Percent allowed by white-listing: Unknown but very small.

reject_non_fqdn_hostname, reject_invalid_hostname An astonishingly effective measure. Quite a lot of junk mail is *really* sloppy and can't say HELO properly which requires a fully-qualified valid hostname. Here's a recent example from my logs:-

```
Aug  8 04:03:45 localhost postfix/smtpd[30565]: NOQUEUE: reject:
RCPT from unknown[189.216.190.174]: 504 5.5.2 <EKORWTKOCQ>:
Helo command rejected: need fully-qualified hostname;
from=<solemnlypk8@remaxtalk.com> to=<peirce@oakcomp.co.uk>
proto=ESMTP helo=<EKORWTKOCQ>
```

As can be seen, this junkie tries to say HELO EKORWTKOCQ in the SMTP transaction. Naughty.

Percent rejected by reject_non_fqdn_hostname: 50.2% {295,997/590,000}

This statistic is the origin of my earlier comment that most junk mailers are teenage males because they can't say HELO properly, although in actuality, the principle source of this surly behaviour is junk mail emanating from botnets under the control of botmasters.

---

[29]This is just sloppy.

[30]Big ISPs have to do this for load balancing of the truly gigantic number of e-mails they handle a day

5.4.3 Sender checks

So we come to the next stage, (the MAIL FROM: stage in the transaction shown in Figure 5.3 (p. 128)).

`main.cf` entry:

```
smtpd_sender_restrictions =
    permit_mynetworks,
    reject_non_fqdn_sender,
    reject_unknown_sender_domain,
    check_sender_access hash:/etc/postfix/sender_reject,
    permit
```

The pattern here is very similar to the HELO checks with the first three entries allowing my own networks to send and then forcing any sender to talk properly.

check_sender_access There will be times when one particular domain is hijacked by spammers and you (or any of your users) have no particular interest in that domain. Alternatively, it's a persistent marketing company who take no notice of your unsubscribe requests, (if you submit any), or perhaps a scammer using a bank domain which you know will never send you legitimate e-mail. In this case you make up a hash: format file called sender_reject say with entries like:-

```
wowgao.com            REJECT ACE20081125 Known spammer
barclays.com          REJECT ACE20081013 e-mail never sent
```

The first one is a serial junk mailer and the second is a very widely used address by scammers trying to extract your bank details. The ACEYYYYMMDD code is my own to allow me to extract this rule from the mail logs using a Perl reporting program. You have to build these files up dynamically based on the junk sent to your own servers. Mine are merely shown for example but represent live rules which although not frequently hit are of value. The following shows a recent hit of the second of these two rules by an ever-optimistic parasite probably from Peru, (the sending MTA is client-200.121.29.171.speedy.net.pe).

```
Jul 26 18:45:58 localhost postfix/smtpd[5493]: NOQUEUE: reject:
RCPT from unknown[200.121.29.171]: 554 5.7.1
<crew@marinefinance.barclays.com>:Sender address rejected:
```

```
ACE20081013 e-mail never sent;
from=<crew@marinefinance.barclays.com>
to=<shermanpearsonbahama@oakcomp.co.uk>
proto=ESMTP helo=<client-200.121.29.171.speedy.net.pe>
```

If it hadn't have been stopped here, it would have been stopped later
by virtue of the stupid to=<shermanpearsonbahama@oakcomp.co.uk>address.
Note also that marinefinance.barclays.com is currently a widely used
spoof address by scammers but will disappear for a while before re-
emerging again as is often the way with these things.

Percent rejected by reject_non_fqdn_hostname: .001% {5/590,000}

This doesn't catch many but the ones it catches are nasty and it's a
cheap check so it's worthwhile.

5.4.4 Recipient checks

So we come to the next stage, (the RCPT TO: stage in the transaction
shown in Figure 5.3 (p. 128)).

main.cf entry:

```
smtpd_restriction_classes = check_bounce_recipient
check_bounce_recipient =
    check_recipient_access hash:/etc/postfix/non-sending_recipients

smtpd_recipient_restrictions =
    reject_invalid_hostname,
    reject_non_fqdn_recipient,
    reject_unknown_sender_domain,
    reject_unknown_recipient_domain,
    permit_mynetworks,
    reject_unauth_destination,
    check_sender_access hash:/etc/postfix/sender_whitelist,
    check_recipient_access hash:/etc/postfix/recipient_access,
    check_sender_access hash:/etc/postfix/check_bounce_sender,
    reject_rbl_client                 zen.spamhaus.org,
    warn_if_reject  reject_rbl_client  bl.spamcop.net,
    warn_if_reject  reject_rbl_client  psbl.surriel.com,
```

```
warn_if_reject  reject_rbl_client   dnsbl-1.uceprotect.net,
warn_if_reject  reject_rbl_client   dnsbl-2.uceprotect.net,
warn_if_reject  reject_rbl_client   dnsbl-3.uceprotect.net,
warn_if_reject  reject_rhsbl_sender dsn.rfc-ignorant.org
check_policy_service unix:postgrey/socket,
permit
```

As we will see from the measurements, some real heavy lifting has to go on here.

The first four entries under smtpd_recipient_restrictions make sure the transaction is sane and well-formatted as already described. The fifth, permit_mynetworks allows e-mail from my own networks to be received. This defaults to the machine that Postfix is running on but you can add networks by class or individual IP address if you wish so that they are considered as local also.

The rest are described in more detail below.

reject_unauth_destination *This must appear immediately after permit_mynetworks or you will allow the bad guys to relay e-mail through your server.* To see an example of an attempt to do a relay through a mail server, see the appendices, p. 300.

A recent example is shown here:-

```
Aug  8 22:03:18 localhost postfix/smtpd[11908]: NOQUEUE: reject:
RCPT from unknown[187.21.52.216]: 554 5.7.1 <zzzz@kcl.ac.uk>:
Relay access denied; from=<xxxx.zzzz@balitribune.com>
to=<zzzz@kcl.ac.uk> proto=SMTP helo=<bb1534d8.virtua.com.br>
```

This shows a sending MTA based in Brazil, a very vigorous country in the junk mail world, trying to relay messages to addresses at kcl.ac.uk claiming to be from somebody at balitribune.com. I've replaced the names in case they are real.

Percent rejected by reject_unauth_destination: .2% {1378/590,000}

check_sender_access sender_whitelist: It is important to note that when this is done in the HELO check stage earlier, friendly senders are only

135

passed for that stage. They need to be fast-tracked again here since some of the parameters which follow in this stage might also reject them.

check_recipient_access Another very heavy lifting rule and an essential part of any serious attempt to reject junk. Junk mailers often do dictionary attacks on domain names, (aaaaaaa@target.com through to zzzzzzz@receive.com) in the hope of finding a name which is valid. *It is very important to restrict the receiving MTA to recognise only those users with valid e-mail addresses, iamvalid@receive.com.*

This is achieved using the check_recipient_access rule. The rule points to a hash: format file recipient_access containing entries like this:-

```
...
lesh@oakcomp.co.uk          DUNNO
oakcomp.co.uk               DISCARD CATCH-ALL DISCARD
```

Any e-mails received for lesh@oakcomp.co.uk are passed onto the next parameter in this rule or if none, the next rule. Any mails for anybody.else@oakcomp.co.uk are immediately discarded. Note DIS-CARD and not REJECT. The sending MTA thinks it has been delivered OK and the spammer is none the wiser. Furthermore I avoid sending a bounce to an innocent user.

This sieves out loads of messages. Here is an example from the logs.

```
Aug  8 04:03:19 localhost postfix/smtpd[30567]: NOQUEUE: discard:
RCPT from unknown[122.161.35.236]: <dkarevigian@oakcomp.co.uk>:
Recipient address CATCH-ALL DISCARD;
from=<icevysiw9089@airtelbroadband.in>
to=<dkarevigian@oakcomp.co.uk>
proto=ESMTP helo=<airtelbroadband.in>
```

This junkie from India is discarded since dkarevigian@oakcomp.co.uk is not a valid address at oakcomp.co.uk.

Percent rejected by check_recipient_access:	45.9%
{270,812/590,000}	

The observant reader will note that this rule and the HELO verifiers reject or discard over 96% of all e-mails. That's the current state of the internet - an ocean of junk with a bit of flotsam corresponding to valid e-mails which we have to carefully scoop out of the mire. When industry commentators or solution providers tell you that it's at least 80%, they are either guessing or they are missing another 19% or so.

check_sender_access check_bounce_sender: As has been discussed previously, sometimes, the bad guys get hold of your e-mail address and send their junk to somebody else in your name. The first you know of this is that you start receiving messages bounced back to you which you never actually sent. This rule is triggered by entries like this in the file check_bounce_sender:

```
<>                              check_bounce_recipient
<MAILER-DAEMON>                 check_bounce_recipient
```

Mail from these causes postfix to execute the check_bounce_recipient above check_recipient_access. This in turn points to a list, non-sending_recipients, which lists users which never send mail as shown here.

```
...
abuse@oakcomp.co.uk            REJECT Address never sends mail.
```

In other words if anybody tries to spoof one of these, the resulting bounces will be themselves bounced, (and then lost). If of course somebody spoofs an address which does send mail, then different measures have to be taken as discussed later when I discuss backscattered junk on p. 183.

Percent rejected by check_bounce_sender: 0% {0/590,000 in this period.}[a]

---

[a]It's never more than a handful but it just happened to be zero for this period.

---

reject_rbl_client This is where we ask Postfix to check if the sending MTA is on any specified blacklists. These have been discussed before but it should be noted that blacklists are of somewhat variable quality. Some lead to a high rate of false positives - flagging valid items as spam, whilst others are of exceptional quality like Spamhaus, which has never given a false positive in my experience. I experiment with these. As you can see above, four of them have the prefix warn_if_reject. In this case, Postfix places a warning in the log but still passes the mail on to the next parameter or rule. Here's an example from the dnsbl-1.uceprotect.net blacklist.

```
Aug 12 05:01:25 localhost postfix/smtpd[21679]:
NOQUEUE: reject_warning: RCPT from
outgoing.hosting.tp.pl[193.110.120.20]:
554 5.7.1 Service unavailable;
Client host [193.110.120.20]
blocked using dnsbl-1.uceprotect.net;
IP 193.110.120.20 is UCEPROTECT-Level 1 listed. See
http://www.uceprotect.net/rblcheck.php?ipr=193.110.120.20;
from=<chemetlipsko@neostrada.pl> to=<lesh@leshatton.org>
proto=ESMTP helo=<mta7.hosting.tp.pl>
```

In most cases these are valid but every now and then one of the big ISPs gets a server on one of the uceprotect lists which leads to false positives which is why I keep them as warn_if_reject and monitor them regularly. Note however, that the overall hit rate of blacklisting compared with the total amount of junk mail or some of the really successful rules is pretty small. Note also that of the 833 blocked in this period by blacklist checking, 810 were detected by Spamhaus. A further 67 were flagged by the experimental warn_if_reject blacklists of which a couple were false positives, (one to ntl.com and one to btconnect.com), so these would be considered persuasive but not perfect.

In short you have to have full confidence in the blacklists you reject on if you wish to meet the exacting goals for junk mail rejection accuracy described later. *It is probably worth noting before continuing that for very high accuracy systems, there is a case for not rejecting on any blacklist and accumulating scores later using the SpamAssassin method of doing things, deciding on which to reject on aggregate performance alongside other filtering technologies as described later. This will certainly be the case when a blacklist is less reliable than the goal you are trying to reach.* At the moment, with the three I use, they have not compromised the desired accuracy but vigilance is increasingly necessary as my own systems become more accurate.

> Percent rejected by check_bounce_sender: 0.14% {833/590,000 in this period.}

check_policy_service After running the gauntlet of the blacklists, our heroic e-mail is now plunged into the marshlands of greylisting. This is extraordinarily effective on the spam that makes it this far, although by now there shouldn't be much left because from now on, it starts to get expensive. I will explain this next.

> Percent rejected by check_policy_service: 0.02% {126/590,000 in this period.}

Greylisting

I like greylisting. It's a very neat idea and attacks one of the foundations of successful junk mailing, notably the need to get millions of messages out there as quickly as possible and move on. It appears to have originated with a white paper by Evan Harris in 2003[31].

In essence, Greylisting[32] places some fly-paper in the receiving MTA into which messages plunge and then have to wriggle free but only if they get a bit of help from their sending MTA. The way it works is that the receiving MTA always rejects an e-mail from a previously unknown address and tells the sending MTA to try again later, (something the SMTP protocol is set up for because of possible transmission problems with genuine e-mail because servers may be temporarily busy and all genuine MTAs must retry according to RFC 821[33]). However it records the first attempt in a simple database with a record structure similar to the following

IP-address	Sender	Recipient	Time-stamp ...

The sending MTA is supposed to try again later and when it does, the greylisting software retrieves the first attempt from it's database and provided a (configurable) amount of time has elapsed since the first attempt, allows the retry and passes it through, (i.e. digs it out of the fly-paper

---

[31] http://projects.puremagic.com/greylisting/whitepaper.html, accessed 11-Jan-2011.
[32] http://en.wikipedia.org/wiki/Greylisting, http://www.greylisting.org/
[33] There are actually one or two deranged but genuine systems which don't do this properly so good greylisting systems have to have small whitelists at the moment. It is hoped that these rogue implementations will gradually disappear.

and accepts it). Junk mailers generally do not retry because they have to get zillions of e-mails out quickly before they get closed down by various co-operating internet mechanisms like blacklists. Consequently, they tend to leave the glued messages to their fate and move on.

There is a very good open implementation of this called postgrey[34]. Postgrey is around 1000 lines of Perl and has been very robust indeed on my server, requiring no maintenance or updating. Once a week, it automatically scrapes the fly-paper clean of everything left to it's fate and starts again. On my server, there are perhaps 30 or so still wriggling around in there by the end of the week.

Once messages have been successfully extricated, repeat messages from the same source are not grey-listed unless they are sent sufficiently infrequently, (defined by another configuration parameter). There are lots of other things which you can configure the software to do but I haven't needed. If you exposed it to higher volumes of e-mail, you would probably have to tune it but there is no need to because so much junk can be thrown away cheaply. If you do need to handle a higher volume, or junk mailers become increasingly wise, there are much faster implementations written in C and C++[35].

To summarise, it is an extraordinarily effective procedure although it is a little more expensive to apply and the junk mail needs to have been pretty successfully culled before you get this far or your server will whinge a little. It is less effective against zombie machines which are probably set up to handle the forced delay correctly but the extra delay is often enough for the zombie to get flagged on one of the real-time blacklists so you can catch it by other means. On a practical note, on my own server, the greylisting volume has remained virtually identical over three years with no signs of it becoming stressed and it appears to represent therefore a successful and semi-permanent solution, at least as anything else is in such a rapidly changing environment. I highly recommend it and it is tightly coupled with Postfix and trivial to implement, (see Appendix p. 301 where you will also find a couple of things you need to keep an eye out for and which I had to learn the hard way).

---

[34] http://postgrey.schweikert.ch/.
[35] http://greylisting.org/implementations/postfix.shtml

There are some interesting additional features which could easily be added such as consulting external resources for inoculation feedback (p. 243), RBLs (p. 116) or co-operating spam databases such as Vipul's razor (p. 215), and these may need to be added in future as zombie use and the associated RFC compliant response to temporary delays increases. For reference, an example of an extended implementation which includes HELO/EHLO checking (p. 21), SPF checking (p. 170) and greylisting can be found here[36]. I have not personally used this but it illustrates some of what might be done.

Before leaving this, I will just summarise the advantages and disadvantages:-

Advantages of grey-listing

- A very simple concept built around something for which the SMTP protocol is already designed to handle.

- It's adaptive

- Many viruses and worms use hand-crafted SMTP code which does not retry

- It occurs very early in the transaction and can be rejected cheaply as junk mail which does not retry is never accepted.

Disadvantages of grey-listing

- Genuine mail which the grey-listing software has not seen before will be delayed by up to a few hours. (In practice it's rarely more than about 15 minutes these days and has not disrupted even time critical things like airline booking or support requests in my case).

- One or two legitimate mailers for example from the big ISPs load balance and may switch IP addresses for the retry, so that every retry looks new. In practice, good grey-listing software allows for this by permitting banks of IP addresses to be grouped to appear as one.

- You have to be administrator or know the administrator very well. However, grey-listing is so effective that many ISPs already implement a form of it.

---

[36]http://www.policyd.org/.

- As mentioned above, it is undermined by botnets to a certain extent as they retry correctly but this would still require the junk mailer to be fairly sophisticated and track which piece of junk went through which slave computer in a botnet and when. In practice, this is a bridge too far if the mailer is trying to get a million pieces of junk out before collaborative internet protection systems shut them down.

5.4.5 Data checks

The next stage is DATA checks as shown in Figure 5.3 (p. 128)). This is a small part of the proceedings and the only thing we do is to prevent pipelining which is a technique intended to facilitate bulk mailing. The relevant configuration parameter in Postfix is shown next.

```
smtpd_data_restrictions =
    reject_unauth_pipelining,
    permit
```

> Percent rejected by reject_unauth_pipelining: Unknown but not seen yet.

5.4.6 Content: Header checks

So we come to the next stage, (the header check stage in the transaction shown in Figure 5.3 (p. 128)). This is where we begin to use Postfix features to identify junk mail from it's content - headers and body. These are implemented in Postfix by the following lines in the main.cf configuration file.

```
header_checks = pcre:/etc/postfix/header_checks
body_checks = pcre:/etc/postfix/body_checks
```

The pcre: here tells Postfix that these files contain Perl format regular expressions for the patterns to be matched and the actions to be taken.

There is lots of advice on this on the web[37]. One particular area which is useful to include are checks to block certain kinds of attachment, for example Windows executable files, which have a suffix .exe. This can be done by checks like the following embedded in the header_checks file[38]. Please refer to Jim Seymour's site for much more on this.

---

[37]See for example, Jim Seymour's excellent comprehensive notes on this at http://wwwjimsun.linxnet.com/misc/header_checks.txt, accessed 12-Aug-2010.

[38]Note that I have put newlines in so it appears properly

```
/^Content-(Disposition|Type):\s+.+?(?:file)?name="?.+?\.
(386|ad[ept]|app|cvp|dll|dot|drv|ex[_e]|fon|fxp|hlp|
ht[ar]|in[fips]|isp|jar|jse?|keyreg|ksh|
... and many more ...
pif|p[lm]|pot|pps|prg|reg|sc[rt]|sh[bs]?|slb|smm|sw[ft]
|sys|url|vb[esx]?|vir|vmx|vxd|wm[ds]|ws[cfh]|xms|
\{[\da-f]{8}(?:-[\da-f]{4}){3}-[\da-f]{12}\})\b/
         REJECT Sorry, attached files of type ".$2"
              are not accepted
```

You will find this reads much better after a large gin and tonic. After two, you can produce this kind of thing with your eyes closed. After three, you begin to talk like this and people will move away. It is an eye-watering example of the genre. The expression picks out the "Content-Disposition" and "Content-Type" headers and extracts the suffix of any attachments before comparing it to this list. You need to experiment a bit with these before going live as Perl regular expressions rarely do what you expect them to do the first 37 times. Then you go into a bit of a decline.

Since phishers *must* use an attractive and credible looking bank From: address as a hook to get your attention, (this is one of their Achilles' heels), this is a very good place to intercept them. You can either reject them as I usually do or you can re-direct them through another filtering system which you might want to do either for forensic purposes or because your bank is daft enough to send you legitimate e-mails.

Here are a selection which are useful for UK banks. You will need to add new ones from time to time and no doubt any junk mailer reading this will want to invent new ones but they *have* to be sufficiently like the real ones or you will ignore them, so their hands are a little tied. (See also the later discussion on impact analysis on p. 264.)

```
if /^From:/
#--------------------
# Phishing from mock bank or credit card From addresses should
# always be rejected as banks say they will not contact people
# like this.
#
# Try to catch base addresses and sub-domains.
#
/.*.365online/              REJECT KSP20081222J Phishing
```

```
/.*.abbey.co/                REJECT KSP20081222C Phishing
/.*.abbeybank.co/            REJECT KSP20090109B Phishing
/.*.abbeynational.co/        REJECT KSP20090107A Phishing
/.*.aibgb.co/                REJECT KSP20081222K Phishing
/.*.alliance-leicester.c/    REJECT KSP20090112A Phishing
/.*.askbm.co/                REJECT KSP20081223B Phishing
/.*.bankofscotland.co/       REJECT KSP20081222I Phishing
/.*.barclays.co.uk/          REJECT KSP20081222G Phishing
/.*.barclays-online.co/      REJECT KSP20090204A Phishing
/.*.bradford-bingley.co/     REJECT KSP20081223A Phishing
/.*.cahoot.co/               REJECT KSP20090223A Phishing
/.*.esavingsaccount.co/      WARN   KSP20081223C NO email please.
/.*.firstdirect.co/          REJECT KSP20090101A Phishing
/.*.halifax-online.co.uk/    REJECT KSP20090801A Phishing
/.*.halifax_update.co.uk/    REJECT KSP20081222D Phishing
/.*.halifax.co/              REJECT KSP20081222H Phishing
/.*.hsbc.co/                 REJECT KSP20081013A Phishing
/.*@leicester.co.uk/         REJECT KSP20090831H Phishing
/.*.lloydstsb.co/            REJECT KSP20081222E Phishing
/.*.lloyds.co.uk/            REJECT KSP20090104A Phishing
/.*.mint.co.uk/              REJECT KSP20090109A Phishing
/.*@new.egg.com/             REJECT KSP20090511A Phishing
/.*.nationwide.co.uk/        REJECT KSP20090104A Phishing
/.*.natwest.co/              REJECT KSP20090117B Phishing
/.*.nwolb.co/                REJECT KSP20081222F Phishing
/.*.ybonline.co.uk/          REJECT KSP20081222B Phishing
#--------------------
endif
```

If you wish to re-direct these to a purpose built filter, then you replace the REJECT keyword with a FILTER transport:nexthop. Refer to the Postfix documentation for this or a discussion in [12]. Note that the text after REJECT appears in the log and is also sent back to the sender. I usually auto-trace these but the REJECT gives a genuine sender the chance to contact you by old-fashioned and more reliable means such as writing to you. The KSPXXXXX code simply allows me to measure their quantities in the log.

If your bank does send you genuine e-mails and you want to accept them, you will need to find patterns which will get through (see the WARN one in the list above) whilst still identifying the scammed ones for rejection. It could be argued that you should let these through on the grounds that one might be genuine. Against this is the fact that this is a major scamming vector which catches people out all the time.

Finally, you can also check for the presence of foreign character sets in the Subject: or other lines. Here's an example of the detection of a Russian character set in the Content-type header:-

```
/^(Content-Type:.*|\s+)charset\s*=\s*"?(koi8)"?/
        WARN FLH20090720A Allowed foreign character set.
```

> Percent rejected by header_checks: 0.003% {24/590,000 in this period.}

Content: Nested header checks

I don't use these but they can be used for handling attachments used to forward copies of junk[39]. Nested headers occur for example when a message is bounced and the bouncing system is kind enough to include at least some of the headers of the message which is being bounced. Sadly, there is no standard for this so I tend to treat them later in the flow where I have more flexibility in how I deal with them.

Content: Mime header checks

I don't use this either because I deal with MIME messages in a much more sophisticated detail in the chapter on advanced content filtering by parsing the MIME structure in full using a Perl program. However, it's worthwhile noting that this mechanism can be very useful in some cases. For example it can be used to do generic checking for dangerous attachments including the SOBIG.F virus using the following patterns shown at Ralf Hildebrandt's homepage[40].

main.cf ...

```
mime_header_checks =
    regexp:/etc/postfix/mime_header_checks.regexp
```

body_checks.regexp ...

---

[39]See discussion at http://readlist.com/lists/postfix.org/postfix-users/0/1161.html, accessed 12-Aug-2010.

[40]http://www.arschkrebs.de/postfix/postfix_sobigf.shtml, accessed 12-Aug-2010.

```
/filename=\"?(.*)\.(bat|chm|cmd|com|do|exe|hta|jse|
rm|scr|pif|vbe|vbs|vxd|xl)\"?$/
      REJECT Frequently insecure attachment type
```

Other sources on the internet[41] include patterns for other virus strains such as Bagle, Netsky and Sober. Again I haven't tried these so your mileage may vary. In the setup described here, very few get this far so I can keep these up my sleeve for later.

5.4.7 Content: Body checks

Body checks work in exactly the same way as Header checks in Postfix. Again, a very good reference for what might go in here can be found at Jim Seymour's site[42].

Here, checks for embedded executables, images, scripts and other dodgy stuff can be carried out. Here's a simple example placed in the file body_checks.

```
#
# A particularly nasty embedded .exe file.
#
/href=\"https?:\/\/(\S+\.exe\/?)/
      REJECT RCR20081102A Embedded executable "$1"
```

Percent rejected by body_checks: 0.02% {154/590,000 in this period.}

5.4.8 Enabling other checking systems

Postfix provides a very simple environment whereby other kinds of content filtering can be esily combined. Well-known spam filters such as SpamAssassin can be directly configured in the master.cf configuration file of Postfix as for example:-

```
spamassassin unix  -  n  n  -  -  pipe
   flags=Rq user=suser argv=/usr/bin/spamc -f -u suser
   -e /usr/lib/sendmail -oi -f ${sender} ${recipient}
```

---

[41] http://www.posluns.com/files/mime_header_checks, accessed 12-Aug-2010
[42] http://wwwjimsun.linxnet.com/misc/body_checks.txt, accessed 12-Aug-2010.

In this book, I will be combining numerous techniques alongside each other so I choose to place them altogether in one place (allcontent.sh) and access them through a single script as follows:-

```
smtp   inet   n   -   n   -   100   smtpd
       -o content_filter=mycontent:

mycontent   unix   -   n   n   -   -   pipe
    flags=Rq user=suser argv=/var/spool/spam/allcontent.sh
      -f ${sender} ${recipient}
```

Before describing the script allcontent.sh (below on p. 153), let's have a look at some of the third-party tools that it might reference.

Including SpamAssassin

SpamAssassin is probably the world's most popular anti-spam filter[43]. It is open source, very highly configurable (almost too configurable) and pretty fast. It is written in Perl but even so is a large and very complex program. It is expertly described in [32] and has moved on considerably since then.

It can be installed in the MTA or the MUA or even both and many organisations heavily depend on it. This can also be claimed to be a disadvantage because it also available to junk mailers who use it to craft their junk to fly under the SpamAssassin radar. In spite of this it remains a formidable barrier to the junk mailer and is testament to the idea that revealing details to all, including the junk mailers, is beneficial rather than detrimental.

If you are using it on your personal MUA, you can afford to tailor it specifically to your needs. If you are using it on a mailserving MTA serving many users, it is better to be generic, although it can be individually configured in that enviroment also.

Simple configuration   The most important thing to understand when configuring SpamAssassin is where and in which order it looks for it's configuration files. The order in decreasing preference is this:-

1. /usr/share/spamassassin. (Don't touch anything in here, it's volatile with version).

---

[43]http://spamassassin.sourceforge.net, accessed 12-Aug-2010

2. /etc/mail/spamassassin/local.cf (System wide)

3. ⌐user/.spamassassin/user_prefs (per user preferences).

I am not a fan of per-user preferences because I'm a bit of a purist and feel that junk mail should be rejected using generic properties wherever possible otherwise it becomes very difficult to manage. As a result I only use configuration files in /etc/mail/spamassassin and you can use several because it searches them all.

Basic configuration is easy and you can even get automated help[44].

How it works   SpamAssassin works by applying many, many checks to an incoming message and scoring a specified amount for each one that occurs. The scores are positive for spamminess and negative for hamminess. At the end, it adds up all the scores and if this exceeds some value that you set personally, the e-mail is marked as spam and disposed of as you see fit.

Using third-party rule sites   I would caution against this generally. The junk mail a particular server receives might not have the same profile as another server. In addition, sometimes one user's notion of junk is rather different than another's. Having said that, some of the rule sets you can download contain very useful patterns and save you having to debug them after writing them yourself, (particularly if you get deeply into the dreaded regular expressions). A glance round the web reveals lots of people willing to share their rulesets[45].

Adding your own rules   This is fun for a while but you can get bored with it because the threat landscape changes so quickly. I personally believe this is better handled by Bayesian filtering but there remains a place for home-rolled rules as there is always a personal flavour to junk mail. It's very easy to add rules. The following is an example of some I have used. In each case, I tell it the rule, where to apply it, how to score it and a bit of commentary to remind me.

The hard bit is the regular expression between the /../ on the first line. For example, the LOCAL_BUSP rule says if the word "business" separated by a space then 0 up to 5 more spaces followed by the word "proposal"

---

[44]http://www.yrex.com/spam/spamconfig.php
[45]http://www.rulesemporium.com/rules.htm

occurs in the body of an e-mail then add 1.0 to the accumulating score. The little "i" at the end of the first line tells SpamAssassin to ignore the case of the words so any mixture of uppercase and lowercase is fine.

```
###################
body        LOCAL_BUSP          /\bbusiness .{0,5}proposal\b/i
score       LOCAL_BUSP          1.0
describe    LOCAL_BUSP          Business proposal - very likely junk.
###################
body        LOCAL_SMONKEY       /surveymonkey/i
score       LOCAL_SMONKEY       2.0
describe    LOCAL_SMONKEY       Another bloody marketing survey.
###################
body        LOCAL_LOANAPP       /\bloan .{0,5}application\b/i
score       LOCAL_LOANAPP       1.0
describe    LOCAL_LOANAPP       Business proposal - very likely junk.
###################
body        LOCAL_COMPLIMENTS   /compliments of the day/i
score       LOCAL_COMPLIMENTS   1.0
describe    LOCAL_COMPLIMENTS   Compliments of the day - it's junk
###################
body        LOCAL_GMAIL         /\@gmail\.com/i
score       LOCAL_GMAIL         1.0
describe    LOCAL_GMAIL         embedded gmail address - often junk.
###################
body        __Survey1           /\bentered .{0,5}into\b/i
body        __Survey2           /\bindependent survey\b/i
body        __Survey3           /\b(survey|raffle)\b/i
meta        LOCAL_SURVEY        ((__Survey1+__Survey2+__Survey3) > 1)
score       LOCAL_SURVEY        2.0
describe    LOCAL_SURVEY        Another sodding survey
###################
```

The last rule LOCAL_SURVEY above is worthy of a bit more comment. It describes three patterns: the word "entered" followed by up to 6 spaces followed by the word "into"; the phrase "independent survey"; and finally the appearance of the words "survey" or "raffle". The meta rule says that if at least two of these occur, then the rule should trigger and add 2.0 to the accumulating score.

I used to spend a fair bit of time crafting these but in the end, I haven't really needed to. The variety of forensic techniques described in this book together effectively eliminate junk mail without any signs of FP (false positives).

As a final important reminder, if you do monkey around with SpamAssassin in this way, make sure your rules are syntactically correct by issuing:-

```
% spamassassin --lint
```

SpamAssassin will then tell you if it's happy.

Including bogofilter

I really like bogofilter[46] in spite of only discovering it's charms relatively recently. A central theme of this book is that successful junk mail detection requires multiple tools acting in parallel each using different techniques. We can then rely on the power of statistics to combine the various checks to allow optimal identification of junk. There is an excellent and compelling paper on the practical deployment of bogofilter in a large-scale environment by Blosser and Josephsen, [4].

bogofilter is a vocabulary based filtering system written in C so it's very fast. It was originally written by Eric Raymond, the author of the well-known open-source essay "The Cathedral and the Bazaar". Latterly, it has been further developed by David Relson, Matthias Andree, Greg Louis, and a group of open source volunteers.

You train it on spam and non-spam messages, typically around a few hundred of each, and it uses a form of Bayes theorem and the Fisher inverse chi-square technique as described by Paul Graham in "a plan for spam"[47]. As an independent look at a suspect e-mail it is absolutely indispensable. Bayesian filtering is discussed in considerable detail in a later section, (see p. (195)).

Training bogofilter from your own mail examples is very simple as shown by the following two Bourne shell scripts. The first tells bogofilter that the e-mail is not spam (-n flag). The -d flag tells bogofilter to use the database kept in a .bogofilter sub-directory of the current directory.

---

[46]http://bogofilter.sourceforge.net/, accessed 12-Aug-2010.
[47]http://www.paulgraham.com/spam.html, accessed 23-Aug-2010.

```
for file in SPAM_EXAMPLES/ham*
do
     bogofilter -t -n -d ./.bogofilter < $file
done
```

The following script tells bogofilter that the e-mail is spam (-s flag).

```
for file in SPAM_EXAMPLES/spam*
do
     bogofilter -t -s -d ./.bogofilter < $file
done
```

That's all there is to it. The result of these is a database file wordlist.db in the sub-directory .bogofilter which can then be accessed with new e-mails to determine whether bogofilter thinks they are junk or not. This can be done as follows:-

```
% bogofilter -d./.bogofilter -t < SPAM_EXAMPLES/spam43.txt
```

which produces the output:-

```
S 1.000000
```

This is the terse (-t) output. The S means it has been identified as spam and the 1.000000 means it's certain. The return code of bogofilter can also be tested (0=spam, 1=non-spam, 2=unsure, 3=error).

Alternatively, if it is being used as one of a number of parallel methods, the -p option outputs the entire message with an added header which might look like:-

```
X-Bogosity: Spam, tests=bogofilter, spamicity=1.000000,
     version=1.1.1
```

This header can easily be parsed out along with any other headers (for example the SpamAssassin header) and other special purpose information to produce a combined assessment of the likelihood of a message being junk, (see for example the advanced content filter skeleton described in the Appendix on p. 285).

Including ClamAV

ClamAV[48] is a well-known open source virus database. In essence, it contains "signatures" of observed viruses, worms, trojans, phishing scams and all the usual paraphernalia. The idea is that you take any attachments included with a suspect e-mail and pass them through the Clam Anti-Virus engine which will detect if it's signature matches anything in it's current database. At the time of writing, there were over 800,000 signatures of viruses in the wild with an alarming set of statistics presented[49].

In practice, as will be seen later, if all the other checks described in this book are applied, very few viruses ever make it as far as ClamAV checking. In the first 7 months of 2010, only 6 were recorded out of a total of around 21 million messages received altogether. All the rest had something else wrong with them which other rules were able to reject more cheaply. So this isn't a question of effectiveness of virus filtering - most e-mails containing viruses are flawed in more obvious ways. When I first starting putting together this infrastructure I was filled with thoughts of integrating some of the many anti-virus products or at least the free ones. It has proved unnecessary.

Having said that, ClamAV is free, stable, well supported and worth having on the principle of defence in depth, however it makes very clear the relative importance of keeping them off your systems in the first place by blocking the threat vector rather than checking your system after you have already got one.

If you have to use a Windows machine, having a virus scanner installed is mandatory and I can recommend the free for non-commercial use one produced by AVG[50].

Combining content filters

Although there are a number of ways of combining filters together, some far more efficient than the shell implementation described below, it doesn't really matter and ease of change can be very important when the threat landscape changes as quickly as it does with junk mail.

---

[48] http://www.clamav.org/
[49] http://www.clamav.net/lang/en/download/cvd/malware-stats/
[50] http://www.avg.com/

The following is an annotated Bourne shell script, allcontent.sh, driven by Postfix at the end of it's chain of other filters as referenced in it's master.cf file shown on p. 147. In practice I use a different form based on the discussions around Figure 6.8 (p. 235) but this will do for illustration. First we set up the parameters and return codes.

```sh
#!/bin/sh
#       Content filtering script.
#
#       This should be invoked as:-
#               allcontent.sh -f [sender] [recipient(s)] ...
#
#       Revision: $Revision: 1.24 $
#       Date:       $Date: 2011/08/25 15:12:18 $
#------------------------------------------------------------
BASE=/var/spool/spam
MSG=$BASE/$$.message
TMSG=$BASE/$$.tmp
FMSG=$BASE/$$.flt
LOG=$BASE/$$.log
SENDMAIL="/usr/sbin/sendmail -G -i"
WONDERHEADER="X-WonderFiltered: Yes"
#
#       EX_TEMPFAIL     - try again later.
#       EX_UNAVAILABLE  - return to sender
#
EX_TEMPFAIL=75
EX_UNAVAILABLE=69
EX_DISCARD=0
EX_OK=0

trap "rm -rf $MSG $FMSG $TMSG $LOG.spm $LOG.scn" 0 1 2 3 15
#
#       Retrieve arguments
#
shift
SENDER="$1"
shift
RECIPIENT="$@"
FIRSTREC="$1"
```

```
THEDATE=`date --rfc-3339=seconds`
#
#    Make sure it's OK.
#
if [ -z "$RECIPIENT" ]
then
    echo "Filtering for unknown recipient"
    exit $EX_UNAVAILABLE
fi
```

The next section first enters and stores the e-mail message returning an appropriate code to Postfix if it fails. After this it records the e-mail in the file users.alg.

```
cd $BASE        || { echo "Cannot enter $BASE"; \
                     exit $EX_TEMPFAIL; }
cat > $MSG      || { echo "Cannot store message"; \
                     exit $EX_TEMPFAIL; }
#
#    Record to measure volumes.
#
echo "$THEDATE,$RECIPIENT,$SENDER" >> $BASE/users.alg
```

The message is now in $MSG and we are ready to go. First of all do a cheap check on whether there is an attachment before deciding to run virus filtering as it is expensive.

```
egrep -q "^Content-Type: application" < $MSG
ziphit=$?

if test "$ziphit" -eq "0"
then
#    Attachment found.  Run a virus scan.
#
    /usr/bin/clamscan $MSG > $LOG.scn 2>$1
    clamhit=$?

    if test "$clamhit" -ne "0"
    then
#        We have a virus.  Just log and lose it.
#        It could be quarantined.
#
```

```
        echo "$THEDATE,$FIRSTREC,virus,$SENDER" \
          >> $BASE/users.vlg
        exit $EX_DISCARD
    fi
fi
```

Here, either there is no attachment or it passed the virus checking. Now use SpamAssassin.

```
/usr/bin/spamc -E < $MSG > $FMSG 2>$LOG.spm
spamhit=$?

if test "$spamhit" -ne "0"
then
#       SpamAssassin triggered.
#       Log and keep a copy for training.
#
        echo "$THEDATE,$FIRSTREC,spam,$SENDER"  \
          >> $BASE/users.slg
        cp $FMSG  $BASE/SPAM
else
#       SpamAssassin did not trigger.  Run bogofilter.
#
        /usr/bin/bogofilter -p -d $BASE/.bogofilter  \
          < $FMSG         > $TMSG
        mv $TMSG  $FMSG
```

Both SpamAssassin and bogofilter will have added headers to the mail in $FMSG. We now move to our research filtering represented here by the Perl script combine.pl to combine them along with any other patterns. This can be based on the template script shown in the Appendix (p. 285) with whatever additional algorithms you wish to experiment with as I will discuss shortly. In this case, combine.pl outputs a text addition such as "[WARNING: Likely scam]" to be placed in the Subject line to alert the user and also an exit code to allow the shell script to behave correctly.

```
        spamcause=`$BASE/combine.pl -m $FMSG -ilz`
        domhit=$?
        if test "$domhit" -ne "0"
        then
            isspam=1
        else
```

```
                isspam=0
                spamcause="-"
        fi
```

Now test if combine.pl triggered. If it did, the rest of this section simply decides on how to add the returned text addition, (the message may or may not contain a Subject line on which to insert it). If there is no Subject line, we must create one. We also use this opportunity to log the message in the file users.slg.

```
#
        if test "$isspam" -eq "1"
        then
#               It's been flagged.
#               See if there is a subject line.
#
                egrep -q "^Subject:" < $FMSG
                subhit=$?

                if test "$subhit" -eq "0"
                then
#                       Subject already present, treat as usual.
#
                        cat $FMSG \
                                | sed "s/^Subject:/Subject: $spamcause /" \
                                > $TMSG
                else
#                       No subject at all.  Add one.
#
                        echo "Subject: $spamcause"        >       $TMSG
                        cat $FMSG                         >>      $TMSG
                fi

                mv  $TMSG $FMSG

                echo "$THEDATE,$FIRSTREC,$spamcause,$SENDER"          \
                        >> $BASE/users.slg
        else
                spamcause="sa_dom_ok"
                echo "$THEDATE,$FIRSTREC,$spamcause,$SENDER"          \
                        >> $BASE/users.slg
        fi
```

```
fi
```

Almost finished. We now feed the annotated message back into Postfix. This also gives you a chance to add in your own header so that the recipient can tell that it has been legitimately filtered[51].

Finally, remember that this shell script processes both incoming and outgoing mail so you might want to do something different based on the contents of $SENDER and $RECIPIENT. For example earlier on p. 4, we saw three rules proposed by [48] to help reduce internal e-mail pollution. The place to apply them is here. All that is necessary is to check that $SENDER and $RECIPIENT are both internal, count the number of recipients in $RECIPIENT and respond accordingly.

```
#
#    Pass the annotated message back into Postfix.
#

{ echo "$WONDERHEADER"; cat $FMSG; } | \
    $SENDMAIL -f $SENDER $RECIPIENT
exit $EX_OK
```

That's it.

5.4.9 Demands on the server

As has been repeated on a number of occasions, checks gradually get more expensive as e-mails gradually go through the filtering pipeline. However, if they are carefully ordered in the manner described above, the effect on the server is pretty slight.

Figure 5.4 (p. 158) shows the load on the CPUs of a dedicated server running an MTA with all the e-mail checks described in this section. As can be seen, the hit on the server is very slight. Similarly, Figure 5.5 (p. 158) shows the load on the memory allocation. Again, nothing special is observed compared to when the server is unloaded.

---

[51]This stops skullduggery whereby the junk mailer bypasses the DNS system and talks directly to the IP address of the receiving MTA.

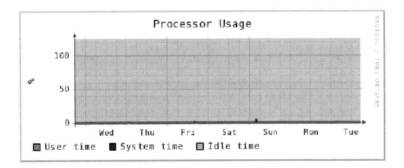

Figure 5.4: The CPU load of a dedicated server running all the e-mail checks described in the text.

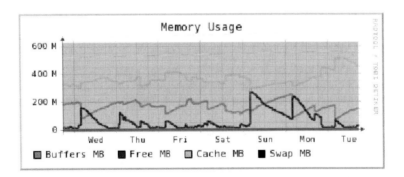

Figure 5.5: The memory load of a dedicated server running all the e-mail checks described in the text.

This is actually very good news for forensic analysts and very bad news for junk mailers. It means that a typical low-end server has a huge amount of CPU power left over for ever more sophisticated filtering. It's worthwhile noting that even at 590,000 e-mails a week, that's only around 1 per second. A modern CPU can do an awful lot of processing in one second.

5.5 Rummaging around in logs

I like logs but then I am an unreconstructed nerd. You will learn to love logs when you administer your own server. You will also learn to love Perl[52] whose otherworldly incantations are necessary to turn the megabytes of gobbledygook in your logs into something on which you can act.

First it should be noted that all operating systems keep logs of activities, whether it be e-mail, web or whatever. Usually, the logs are human-readable in an ASCII format. This doesn't mean they are the kind of thing you would browse through while waiting for your take-away but they can be read if you know what to look for. It is however much simpler to write simple tools using Perl and that's what we will do here with both Linux logs and also Windows logs.

5.5.1 Logs on Centos Linux

There are lots of logs in Linux and they usually live in /var/log. As far as I know, they are all in ASCII so a tiny bit of Perl hacking can glean all kinds of useful information from them. Here's an example of a log entry from the main current mail log file, /var/log/maillog[53].

```
Aug 28 17:29:05 localhost postfix/smtpd[8583]:
  NOQUEUE: discard: RCPT from unknown[188.3.50.150]:
  <gguereca@oakcomp.co.uk>: Recipient address
  CATCH-ALL DISCARD; from=<gguereca@oakcomp.co.uk>
```

---

[52]http://www.Perl.org/. The masters of this genre collect at http://www.Perlmonks.org/. I've never got into it at this level - you know you are in trouble when it's denizens say things like "it's obvious" and give a code example which looks like you have painted the feet of a small bird and then let it hop around on your screen. In a previous life, I got quite good at C (http://www.saferc.com/) but Perl is a different beast. Perlmonks is a formidably good source of information though.

[53]Linux systems keep the last month or so, week by week in compressed format in the same place called maillog.1.gz - maillog.4.gz.

```
to=<gguereca@oakcomp.co.uk> proto=ESMTP
helo=<[188.3.50.150]>
```

This is a bit dense but reading along, it first of all says "RCPT from
unknown[188.3.50.150]". This is the IP address of the sending MTA. Although it can be proxied, proxies are often flagged as dirty, so it is usually
pretty reliable. Continuing, the log entry goes on to give the MAIL FROM:
address as gguereca@oakcomp.co.uk and the RCPT TO: address, which is
the same here. It finally says that the sending MTA said HELO by giving
it's IP address.

If you issue a

```
% whois 188.3.50.150
```

You find it's in Turkey, an up and coming star in the junk mail league.
This hopeful is trying to pretend he or she is somebody at my domain
sending to themselves and has been plunged into a digital black-hole for
their trouble, one of 26,637 others so far today (and it's only 5pm). Bit of
a quiet day really.

Having looked it up, I could now send a copy of the offending log entry
above to the abuse address at this provider (it's abuse@koc.net). In theory,
they can then check their own logs to see where it's coming from. In practice,
very few can be bothered because there is so much of it, so the junk mailers
keep banging away. If it's a criminal investigation, it would be more likely
to be pursued.

Perl program to scan mail logs

One of the things you certainly might want to do is to find out all the
messages sent to a particular address in a certain period which were rejected
or discarded. Remember that rejecting or discarding legitimate messages
is the ultimate sin in junk mail filtering so every now and then you might
need to make sure you haven't trashed one by being over-enthusiastic. A
simple program, fromtospec.pl to do this follows.

First the header, the necessary package, the declarations and a single
option giving the "to" address.

```
#!/usr/bin/Perl
#
#       Print out all rejects or discards for a
#       particular address.
#
#       Revision: $Revision: 1.24 $
#       Date:       $Date: 2011/08/25 15:12:18 $
#-----------------------------------------------------
#
use strict;
use Getopt::Std;

my      (@partsfrom,@partsto);
my      ($action,$process,%opt);

getopts('t:', \%opt);
die("-t email is a required option\n") unless $opt{t};
my      $to = $opt{t};
```

Print a header and then troll through the input.

```
printf "%18.18s %35.35s\n","time","from";
printf "%18.18s %35.35s\n","----","----";

while (<>)
{
        $process  = 0;
        if ( /reject:/ )      { $action = "r"; $process = 1; }
        elsif ( /discard:/ ) { $action = "d"; $process = 1; }
```

We are going to process this so extract the relevant fields. Note that you will have to join the regular expression together - I split it to fit it on the line. Don't include any extra spaces.

```
        if ( $process == 1 )
        {
#
#               Extract the time, from and to fields.
#
                /^(\S+\s+[0-9]+\s+[0-9]+:[0-9]+:[0-9]+).*
                    from=\<(\S+@\S+)\>.*to=\<(\S+@\S+)\>/;
```

161

```
            @partsfrom    = split( /@/, $2 );
            @partsto      = split( /@/, $3);

            if ( $3 eq $to )
            {
                printf "%2s %16.16s %35.35s\n",$action,$1,$2;
            }
        }
    }
}

exit(0);
```

If this is now invoked like this:-

`% fromtospec.pl -t lesh@oakcomp.co.uk < /var/log/maillog`

The following output results (actually I am only showing a small part of the incredible amount of junk I receive).

```
               time                                   from
               ----                                   ----
r   Aug 22 04:27:52         kcwuybihieohby@pafac.org
r   Aug 22 04:37:34  pluralizingmo3@responsiveweb.com
r   Aug 22 04:59:57               lesh@oakcomp.co.uk
r   Aug 22 06:02:14            feebleAo@sofitel.com
r   Aug 22 06:34:14         chicfj83@privatedebit.com
r   Aug 22 06:35:10   jimmiedwtsb1@overtone-flute.com
r   Aug 22 07:20:19      housecoats19@800findarc.com
r   Aug 22 07:29:34        static5u@museumsnett.no
r   Aug 22 08:41:38           ferventIX@reuters.com
r   Aug 22 09:16:37      beltem8277@7marestur.com
r   Aug 22 11:14:09           info@lloydstsb.co.uk
r   Aug 22 11:23:55           info@lloydstsb.co.uk
r   Aug 22 12:47:00       aviatrix6@relianceinfo.com
r   Aug 22 12:47:58         oustingk63@rotarycc.com
...  and about a zillion others.
```

You can see that this is a nice cross-section of people pretending to be me: scammers, (the lloydstsb ones) and the spammers, (the largely idiotic addresses).

Knocking together Perl scripts to troll through logs like this is part of the job of forensics. Here's another one to check on who is trying to break the back door down using secure root logins trying to guess the password.

Perl program to scan security logs

The log detailing attempts to hack in is at /var/log/secure on Centos systems. A typical entry might look this:

```
Dec 20 13:22:46 localhost sshd[308]: pam_unix(sshd:auth):
 authentication failure; logname= uid=0 euid=0 tty=ssh
 ruser= rhost=120.138.96.21  user=root
```

This shows a failed root login from India.

The following little Perl program countHackerIPs.pl shows just how much can be done in just a few lines using associative arrays, [54].

```perl
#!/usr/bin/Perl
#
#       Analyse System logs to extract IP addresses
#       of hackers.
#
#       Revision:       $Revision: 1.24 $
#       Date:   $Date: 2011/08/25 15:12:18 $
#-------------------------------------------------------
#
use strict;

my      ($hackip);
my      (%rcrhackerIP);

while (<>)
{
#       Look for login rule in the correct format
#
        if ( /Failed password for (\S+) from ([0-9\.]+)/ )
        {
                ++$rcrhackerIP{$2};
        }
}
```

```
foreach  $hackip (sort keys(%rcrhackerIP) )
{
        printf "%d %s\n",$rcrhackerIP{$hackip},$hackip;
}
```

```
exit(0);
```

This can be run as follows, sorting and counting the output using the estimable Linux utility, *sort*.

```
countHackerIPs.pl < /var/log/secure | sort -nr
```

This yields this weeks international crop.

```
6 119.145.109.202          <- China
3 80.191.214.7             <- Iran
3 68.234.15.46             <- Florida, USA
3 212.150.176.98           <- Israel
3 148.204.124.99           <- Mexico
2 222.73.161.149           <- China (again)
2 211.154.167.23           <- and again ...
2 122.194.21.12            <- and again ...
1 202.108.145.191          <- ... and again
```

Some of these made further attempts but were throttled, (c.f. p. 124). There was a time when you might have laughed at this as it was probably a few students having a bit of fun. Not any more. This is the visible signs of continual and increasingly frequent criminal attempts to break into other people's property for profit. There's a lot of money to be made in this by the unscrupulous.

5.5.2 Logs in Windows

Not all logs in Windows are human-readable. For efficiency's sake, some logs must be binary and unless there is some available API[54] that you can use or possibly a third-party tool to turn them into ASCII[55], you are stuck.

---

[54] Applications Programming Interface. This is a set of functions or methods you can call from a high-level language like Java, C++, C, Perl and many others which provide the information you need without ever having to know the format of the file.

[55] This is the approach used by Mike Andrews when a PhD student at the University of Kent, http://www.mikeandrews.com/projects/signpost/thesis.pdf.

Fortunately, Windows mail logs are available in a variety of formats including several ASCII ones (which you can choose) and can be easily analysed by Perl programs. An example of a W3C format SMTP log follows[56]. Before we get to the gobbledygook, each of the fields is explained in the log header[57] as:-

```
#Fields: date time c-ip cs-username s-sitename s-computername
s-ip s-port cs-method cs-uri-stem cs-uri-query sc-status
sc-win32-status sc-bytes cs-bytes time-taken cs-version
cs-host cs(User-Agent) cs(Cookie) cs(Referer)
```

Here we see each stage of the SMTP conversation between the sending and receiving MTAs. First we have the initial contact.

```
2010-04-29 06:05:54 xxx.208.247.yyy OutboundConnectionResponse
SMTPSVC1 zzzzzz-WWW1 - 25 - -
220+localhost.oakcomp.com+ESMTP+Postfix
0 0 39 0 156 SMTP - - - -
```

You don't have to know what all this stuff means but the date, time and receiving MTA (slightly edited) are obvious. The returned SMTP code (220) by the receiving MTA is also shown at the front of the 220+localhost.xxxxxxx.com bit. This is the code sent when the receiving MTA is ready, (a list of important SMTP codes appears in the Appendix on p. 302).

A little further down the log, (the log contains a record of all the transactions going on so you get overlaps of different bits of SMTP conversations), we see

```
2010-04-29 06:05:54 xxx.208.247.yyy OutboundConnectionResponse
SMTPSVC1 zzzzzz-WWW1 - 25 - - 250-localhost.xxxxxxx.com
0 0 25 0 281 SMTP - - - -
```

This was the 250 (received OK) response. Finally, we have the RCPT TO: part below.

```
2010-04-29 06:05:54 xxx.208.247.yyy OutboundConnectionCommand
SMTPSVC1 zzzzzz-WWW1 - 25 RCPT - TO:<lesh@oakcomp.co.uk>
0 0 4 0 390 SMTP - - - -
```

---

[56]These can be found at *%windir%\system32\logfiles\SMTPSVC1∗* and one a day is typically produced.

[57]The prefixes mean c- (client), s- (server), cs- (client-server) and sc- (server-client).

Perl program to analyse Windows mail logs

We might for example be interested in analysing these logs for problematic mails, in which case we are looking for response codes like 450, 550, 553 and 554. The following simple Perl program which we will call wlog.pl, will analyse such a log on it's standard input, extract relevant messages, parse them and then output them in an HTML formatted report.

First, the header and declarations.

```perl
#!/usr/bin/Perl
#
#    Author:    Les Hatton 2009-.
#    Revision: $Revision: 1.24 $
#    Date:      $Date: 2011/08/25 15:12:18 $
#-------------------------------------------------------------
#
use strict;

my    ($email,$cs_uri_query,$smtp_code,$receiving_ip,$ip);
my    (%unknown_emails);
my    (%cs_uri_query_553, %ip_count_553);
my    (%cs_uri_query_554, %ip_count_554);
my    (@fields,@subfields);
```

Now we loop on all the lines in the input log file.

```perl
while (<>)
{
#    Split the record on spaces, (MS SMTP log format).
     @fields  = split( / /, $_ );
#
#    cs_uri_query is the MS name for the main response
#    from the receiving MTA.
     $cs_uri_query   =    @fields[10];
     $cs_uri_query  =~    s/\+/ /g;              # '+' -> ' '
     $receiving_ip   =    @fields[2];
#
#    Further split on spaces to get the SMTP code which
#    is the first sub-field in the cs_uri_query field.
```

```
@subfields    = split( / /, $cs_uri_query);
$smtp_code    = @subfields[0];
```

Having split out the bits we are interested in, we now check for the offending codes and fill up various data-structures.

```
      if ( $smtp_code =~ /450/ || $smtp_code =~ /550/ )
      {
#           Mailbox undeliverable.  Extract an e-mail address
#           if we can.
            if ( $cs_uri_query =~ /([a-z.0-9-]+@[a-z.0-9-]+)/ )
            {
                  $unknown_emails{$1} = $receiving_ip;
            }
      }
      elsif ( $smtp_code =~ /553/ )
      {
#           Attempted relaying.
            $cs_uri_query_553{$receiving_ip} = $cs_uri_query;
            ++$ip_count_553{$receiving_ip};
      }
      elsif ( $smtp_code =~ /554/ )
      {
#           Identified as spam by the receiving MTA.
            $cs_uri_query_554{$receiving_ip} = $cs_uri_query;
            ++$ip_count_554{$receiving_ip};
      }
}
#     Summarise.
```

Finally we print them out wrapped in HTML codes to produce a nice
report.

```
      printf "<H3>Broken addresses</H3>\n\n";
      printf "<TABLE WIDTH=100%% BORDER=1>\n";
      printf "<TH>Number of occurrences</TH>\n";
      printf "<TH>IP address</TH>\n";
      printf "<TH>Receiving MTA response</TH>\n";
      foreach  $ip (sort keys(%cs_uri_query_553) )
      {
            printf "<TR>\n";
            printf "<TD WIDTH=10%% ALIGN=CENTER>\n";
```

```
        printf "%d\n",$ip_count_553{$ip};
        printf "</TD>\n";
        printf "<TD WIDTH=10%%>\n";
        printf "%s\n",$ip;
        printf "</TD>\n";
        printf "<TD>\n";
        printf "%s\n",$cs_uri_query_553{$ip};
        printf "</TD>\n";
        printf "</TR>\n";
    }
    printf "</TABLE>\n";
```

The code is the same for the 554s.

... same thing for %cs_uri_query_553 and $ip_count_553{$ip}

and finally, print out unknown e-mail addresses.

```
    printf("<H3>Unknown recipients</H3>\n\n");
    printf "<TABLE WIDTH=100%% BORDER=1>\n";
    printf "<TH>e-mail address</TH>\n";
    foreach $email (sort keys(%unknown_emails) )
    {
        printf "<TR><TD ALIGN=CENTER>\n";
        printf "%s\n",$email;
        printf "</TD></TR>\n";
    }
    printf "</TABLE>\n";
```

```
exit(0);
```

To run this program, all you need to do is to type

```
% wlog.pl < ex100829.log
```

This ploughs through logs pretty fast even though they are usually voluminous - a couple of hundred megabytes for a typical server per day[58].

---

[58]There was some discussion in UK government circles a while ago by a
particularly ill-informed group of unnamed civil servants and politicians
(http://news.bbc.co.uk/1/hi/uk/7819230.stm) that legislation would be forthcoming
to make *everybody* yield copies of their mail server logs for storage and analysis for

5.6 Outgoing mail

Your server sends mail as well as receives it. Much of this book is concerned with protecting yourself from the enormous volume of junk which is directed at every mail server. However, this is only half the battle. Your mail server sends mail on your behalf and you would like it to be delivered. Furthermore, normal users would not like their mail server to be responsible for sending junk. This is a major concern for ISPs who have to deal with thousands of users, some of whom might be from the dark side.

In general, for a legitimate user using one of the giants - gmail, yahoo and so on, this is simply not an issue unless somebody cracks your password and starts using your account. This has happened to a number of friends of mine with various forms of Yahoo! accounts, (see p. 278 for more detail) and Yahoo seem useless at sorting this kind of thing out. I have yet to encounter it with gmail but this of course does not mean that it will not.

For a small business or a single user with your own domain name and therefore a measure of independence, it can very easily become an issue, particularly if your machine is contaminated.

5.6.1 Contaminated machines

The first thing is to make sure then that your machine is not contaminated. For Windows machines, this is an enduring problem and you will have to sweep it with one of the many Windows support packages on a regular basis. My personal favourite is AVG, which is free for personal use[59]. I am also a fan of ZoneAlarm,[60] and Firefox[61]. These latter three very effectively

---

security reasons. Clearly this group had difficulty understanding the incredible volumes involved. A single server will produce around 200Mb per day, that's around 75Gb a year. There are quite a lot of servers in the UK. Let's take a jump in the dark and assume there are about 100,000. That would mean around 7.5Pb (petabytes or 10^{15} bytes per year). Some 99.9% of this would be copies of the same junk mail. The mind boggles at the idea of storing around a petabyte of Viagra adverts in the name of security. It's gone a bit quiet now so I'm not sure if the penny has dropped or whether it's because we are now officially broke, but I don't think we have to do it anymore. Well, not yet anyway. I can't wait for the next instalment of white-hot digital Government.

[59] www.avg.com
[60] www.zonelabs.com
[61] www.mozilla.com/firefox/

protect a Windows machine and I have never experienced a problem[62].

An even better way of protecting yourself is to use some flavour of Linux which is what I do most of the time[63]

One other piece of advice I will give is to get into good habits with your passwords. Nobody can remember the kind of thing which web hosting companies send you - Xa87dgYhr4 - but it's easy to come up with some kind of scheme which you can remember and is still secure. For goodness sake, don't use your pet horse's name 'sid' or whatever and try to avoid sticking a post-it note to your machine in plain sight of everybody with it written down[64].

You must make sure your machine is clean. Every other piece of advice in this book is a complete waste of time if you find yourself an unwitting contributor to a botnet.

5.6.2 Sender verification

SPF

Sender verification is one of those big ideas which was intended to help stamp out the disease of junk mail. It's very simple in principle. We have already seen that nearly everything about an e-mail can be spoofed, (p. 29). Wouldn't it be nice then if there was something which couldn't be spoofed which announced to the receiver that a message was really sent by whoever is claiming to send it.

---

[62]If you want a bit more detail on how to set these up, have a look at http://www.leshatton.org/basic_security_for_pc_users_2008.html. It's not exactly rocket science but even this will make a very substantial improvement in your basic PC security. You can also have a look at http://blog.zonealarm.com/blog/2010/10/how-to-get-basic-internet-security-for-free-.html.

[63]I remember the last time I bought two new servers for my office - nice little Acers with big disks, big memory, dual core and cheap as chips. As I marched to the door with a salesperson hanging onto each leg trying to sell me something to "make my PC secure", I informed them gently that I was intending to install the ultimate anti-virus software - Linux.

[64]One of the central techniques of ethical (and unethical) hacking is to walk into companies and read passwords written on post-it notes, stuck on machines in reception. This saves the hacker an awful lot of time researching pet names and so on. Don't do it.

There are a whole bunch of these. One of the best known is SPF (Sender Policy Framework) originally described by Meng Weng Wong[65]. The idea is very simple. The whole internet depends on the sanctity of the DNS as we have already seen on p. 30. The idea of SPF is to add simple TXT records to the DNS entry for a domain to tell the world which mail servers are entitled to act for it. That's it. An example of an SPF record for a BIND[66] server follows:-

```
example.com. IN TXT "v=spf1 a mx -all"
```

This simple version simply says that only the DNS A record and MX record for example.com may be used for sending e-mail for this domain. There is a very neat utility to build these interactively on http://www.openspf.org/. You just paste these into your BIND records (or whatever DNS system you are using), and since you are the only one who can do this, this has the effect of verifying you as the sender as intended[67].

It's very simple and effective and is explicitly implemented in the very widely used SpamAssassin with the following defaults:-

```
score SPF_PASS -0.001
score SPF_HELO_PASS -0.001
# <gen:mutable>
score SPF_FAIL 0 0.919 0 0.001 # n=0 n=2
score SPF_HELO_FAIL 0 0.001 0 0.001 # n=0 n=2
score SPF_HELO_NEUTRAL 0 0.001 0 0.112 # n=0 n=2
score SPF_HELO_SOFTFAIL 0 0.896 0 0.732 # n=0 n=2
score SPF_NEUTRAL 0 0.652 0 0.779 # n=0 n=2
score SPF_SOFTFAIL 0 0.972 0 0.665 # n=0 n=2
```

---

[65]http://www.openspf.org/blobs/sender-authentication-whitepaper.pdf

[66]http://en.wikipedia.org/wiki/BIND, accessed 11-Aug-2011.

[67]Actually, messing around with BIND records is not for the faint-hearted and I strongly recommend you read [30] before doing this. Don't be put off, but do be careful. A knowledge of how the DNS works is indispensable if you are managing a dedicated server.

Having said all this, the benefit of doing this is currently set very low[68]. On the other hand, the penalty of doing it and getting it wrong is pretty high. The argument offered is that spammers will quickly rush to do it anyway. The bottom line seems to be not to bother at the moment. If you screw it up, you get penalised. Given that spammers are adroit at taking over machines and you currently get hardly any benefit, then it seems a dubious benefit to say the least. This may change if it becomes more widely acceptable. Just as a final note on this, even with the help of Internet sites like http://www.openspf.org/, I had problems figuring out if the changes were actually functioning properly so there follows a simple Perl *spf.pl* script to check.

```perl
#!/usr/bin/Perl
#
#     spf.pl: Perform a SPF query.
#
#     Revision: $Revision: 1.24 $
#     Date:     $Date: 2011/08/25 15:12:18 $
#-------------------------------------------------
#
use strict;
use Getopt::Std;
use Mail::SPF;

my    (%opt);

getopts('m:i:h:', \%opt);

if ( ! defined $opt{m} )
      { die "-m [mail address] is required\n"; }
if ( ! defined $opt{i} )
      { die "-i [ip address] is required\n"; }
if ( ! defined $opt{h} )
      { die "-h [helo identity] is required\n"; }

my    $mailaddress    = $opt{m};
my    $ipaddress      = $opt{i};
my    $heloidentity   = $opt{h};
```

---

[68] It is in SpamAssassin but that does not mean that other checking systems do not rate highly.

```perl
my    $spf_server   = Mail::SPF::Server->new();

my    $request      = Mail::SPF::Request->new(
# optional
      versions        => [1, 2],
# or 'helo', 'pra'
      scope           => 'mfrom',
      identity        => $mailaddress,
      ip_address      => $ipaddress,
# optional, for %{h} macro expansion
      helo_identity   => $heloidentity
);

my    $result       = $spf_server->process($request);

# 'pass', 'fail', etc.
my    $result_code  = $result->code;
my    $local_exp    = $result->local_explanation;
my    $spf_header   = $result->received_spf_header;

print "result:      $result\n\n";
print "result_code: $result_code\n\n";
print "local_exp:   $local_exp\n\n";
print "spf_header:  $spf_header\n\n";

exit(0);
```

You may have to install the Perl module Mail::SPF first by issuing the following incantation

```
% sudo cpan -i Mail::SPF
```

Usage is then very simple:-

```
% spf.pl -m sender@sender.com -i 111.112.113.114
      -h localhost.sender.com
```

This will check if e-mails from sender@sender.com can be sent from a machine with ip address 111.112.113.114 whose HELO name is localhost.sender.com.

DomainKeys

DomainKeys Identified Mail (*DKIM*) is a method for associating a domain name with an e-mail. In essence the sender adds headers containing details of the e-mail and the originating domain signed using *asymmetric cryptography* as described in more detail in the next section. The receiver then accesses the corresponding *public key* of the sender by looking it up using the Domain Name System and uses it to verify that the e-mail actually originated from them. Since the private and public keys are uniquely associated and effectively un-crackable at the current state of knowledge provided they are sufficiently long, this uniquely associates the sender with the e-mail.

It is an unquestionably beneficial technique but as with all sender verification techniques, it is undermined if spammers gain control of a protected machine and use it for relaying spam.

5.6.3 Notional payment

This seems a bit more promising although take up has been poor. Again, it's a very simple idea built around the economics of sending vast amounts of mail. As was described earlier, the essence of junk mailing is to deliver as many messages as possible in as short a time as possible to get people to respond before internet protection systems such as RBLs kick in. At various stages, people have suggested that an e-mail should cost a small amount of money to send so that occasional senders (the vast majority), pay next to nothing whilst a spammer would pay a lot, perhaps destroying the economic base for doing it at all.

There are two fundamental arguments against this.

- List managers would get badly hit.

- Who would receive the money ? In a global market where mails randomly track across the internet possibly passing through several countries in the process, this is far from clear.

As a result of this, the idea of paying *notional* money arose. This was originally suggested by Dwork and Naor [13] as long ago as 1992 and as with DKIM, described above, is based on principles embedded in asymmetric cryptography, ([51] is a very good general reference). The essence of asymmetric cryptography as used to secure all modern financial transactions is to find an operation which is fast in one direction and very, *very* slow in the other. In the case of RSA public-key cryptography[69], multiplying two large prime numbers together is very fast but factoring the result back into it's prime factors is extremely slow.

Dwork and Naor's idea was named HashCash. The idea was to perform some significant calculation, perhaps a few seconds in duration and add the details of this calculation to the mail header. Crucially, the calculation could not be forged and also it can be very quickly checked. In other words, it's slow to compute but quick to verify. The idea of adding a few seconds of computation to the average user's e-mail is nothing but it completely destroys the economics of junk mailing because a separate computation has to be carried out for each constituent e-mail since it involves the address of the intended recipient. In essence you are telling the recipient that you have donated a significant amount of time (at least in server-speak) to the e-mail you have sent and therefore cannot be sending piles of junk.

As a measure for suppressing the total amount of junk floating round the web, this has been criticised for example by [29] using realworld data from a large ISP, who showed that significant numbers of senders of legitimate e-mail would be unable to continue their current levels of activity. Like SpamAssassin, it is also undermined by junk mailers who transmit through botnets, (although they will need a significantly bigger botnet to devote the necessary virtual cash resources to their junk). However, it is implemented in SpamAssassin with the current weightings

```
score HASHCASH_20 -0.5
score HASHCASH_21 -0.7
score HASHCASH_22 -1.0
score HASHCASH_23 -2.0
score HASHCASH_24 -3.0
score HASHCASH_25 -4.0
score HASHCASH_HIGH -5.0
score HASHCASH_2SPEND 0.1
```

The number on the end of HASHCASH refers to the number of 0s to appear in the generated hash key. The more there are, the longer it takes to compute and the more credit you get from SpamAssassin. To give an idea of timings, a 24x0 version gives a -3.0 benefit in SpamAssassin but only takes around a few seconds on average to compute on a typical mail server. For comparison, this is more than being medium-rated on the well-known

---

[69]http://en.wikipedia.org/wiki/RSA

whitelist dnswl.org which only gives -2.3 credit. All that needs to be done after downloading and building the application[70], is to add the line produced by the following command to the headers of your e-mail message a

```
% hashcash -m -b 24 -r lesh@oakcomp.co.uk | sed 's/^/X-Hashcash: /'
```

which will give something like the following line (which I have split to fit).

```
X-Hashcash:1:24:101221:lesh@oakcomp.co.uk:
 :NSZm/SDJpq/4UlpP:0000000000000000000000000000000000000001Lzg8
```

This will be parsed by SpamAssassin automatically at the recipient end and ignored by other mail software.

It therefore represents an easy way of improving the chances of e-mail being accepted even by a very stringent SpamAssassin configuration. (It also helps in detecting backscattered junk) as I discuss on p. 182. This seems well worthwhile in spite of the drawbacks highlighted by [29] and the botnet issue described above. However, whilst people persist in leaving their machines vulnerable, this latter will be an enduring problem as it undermines a number of the techniques described in this book as summarised in the last chapter.

---

[70]http://www.hashcash.org/

6 Advanced content filtering

Even with a sophisticated MTA like Postfix, you can only do a certain amount with the transaction between the sending and receiving MTA displayed in Figure 2.1 (p. 19). Granted, it is sufficient to sieve out the majority of the junk, but that's the easy stuff. The stuff that gets through these defences can be very sophisticated and to protect the intended recipient, you need the whole e-mail message, envelope, headers and content and a whole army of techniques to analyse for forensic patterns of junk.

Although there are good commercial products out there, the open source world has responded magnificently to the challenges presented so far to the extent that currently, if you use them well, you can get rid of nearly everything. Indeed, in my view, as with a number of other key infrastructural areas, the open-source community is largely responsible for the effectiveness of anti-junk techniques.

Returning briefly to my comments in the Preface, I quoted Ross Anderson to the extent that an open knowledge of these techniques benefits the junk mailers also. Yes indeed, but it remains true that in spite of these techniques being open, *if you use them as described in this book*, you can shut the junk tap off almost completely. In other words, right now, we are keeping abreast of it. This emphatically does *not* mean that we can relax. The science of Forensics is a dynamic one, continually adapting to the threat environment which can change daily and in a digitally lubricated world, a new threat can sweep round the globe in a matter of minutes.

One last thing I should emphasise before launching into this is so important that I will put it in one of those cute little boxes I have discovered LaTeX can do.

> To really get to the top of your game in junk mail filtering, you have to be a good tool builder. This is the essence of forensics. When you have no (or little) control over the structure of data, then we are not talking about *data mining*, we are talking about *data rummaging* - the art of spotting patterns and then constructing tools to exploit them.

6.1 Simple text patterns

By simple text patterns, we merely mean recognising words of phrases which are commonly used in junk mail such as Viagra or V1agra or the many other ways it is commonly obfuscated, (although of course, in some environments such as the hospital system I discuss later by [4], it may be entirely legitimate). We have seen how this is done in SpamAssassin for fairly simple rules but regular expressions allow you to recognise much more complicated patterns.

6.1.1 More on regular expressions

Regular expressions were once a major research area as previously alluded to on p. 91 and there are numerous implementations of them including as we have seen, simple ones in MUAs like the Linux-based kmail which are generally based on the Perl dialect.

Perl regular expressions

In junk mail filtering, arguably the dominant implementation for regular expression parsing is that embedded within Perl itself. It is phenomenally powerful and an afternoon with it will leave you whimpering for your mother or a priest.

To keep the flow of this narrative going, I won't digress at this point but I have included the bare bones of regular expressions in the Appendix on p. 309.

6.2 Advanced text patterns

6.2.1 Perl and rolling your own

In order to get at the envelope, headers and content, including any attachments, you have to fight your way through the standard formats in which e-mail is distributed. The most important ones currently are:-

Character sets e-mail is a global phenomenon and must and does support the character sets of every nation. It is inclusive.

HTML formatting Humans like pretty things. The old days in which e-mails were simple text with lots of nerdy stuff in them have gone. e-mail is now for everybody and there is an overwhelming need to supply *rich content* in the forms of images, formatting, text highlighting and linking on to other interesting and related material and so on.

MIME structure e-mail designers realised this and produced the MIME (Multipurpose Internet Mail Extensions) format. This format allows rich content to be provided.

This rich content has been instrumental in e-mail becoming the most potent form of communication there has ever been. However, from the point of view of a junk mailer, it gives countless opportunities for slipping something toxic through to the recipient whilst making it difficult to get off the starting line to search for new forensic patterns.

SpamAssassin as we have already seen does this for you and gives you the opportunity to add rules of your own. However, sometimes you need more. To this end, a working Perl program[1] is supplied here which can act as a testbed in which to embed your own forensic techniques. It provides a good forensic framework and as it took me a fair while to put together and test, it can be found in full in the appendices on p. 285. As usual, I don't guarantee perfection, so if you have an improvement to suggest, have a look at the companion site for this book, http://www.emailforensics.org/.

---

[1] Based on the previous work of many contributors starting from Luis Munoz' excellent article at http://www.ddj.com/web-development/184415983 but I must also mention the work of Sean Burke [6] and Gisle Aas on LWP, a superb Perl harness which hides all the complexity. An online version of Sean's book on LWP and Perl can be found at http://lwp.interglacial.com/index.html.

Variants of this program can be easily added to the chain of content filters - SpamAssassin, bogofilter and so on to add state of the art content checking to the Postfix environment as was shown by the combine.pl filter included in the allcontents.sh shell script on p. 153.

One other thing which took me a little while to figure out is how to check an IP address against a published RBL which is one of the things you might like to do when you analyse the links in the above program. The following Perl fragments show how to query a well-known RBL, multi.surbl.org[2].

```
#----------------------------------------------------------
#       This subroutine calculates the target to query in
#       the expected reverse format.
#
sub     calculateQueryTarget
{
        die q[usage: calculate_query_target($addr, $zone)]
                unless (@_ == 2);

        my($addr, $zone) = @_;
#
#       Make sure there's a dot on the end.
#
        $zone .= "."
                unless ($zone =~ /\.$/);
#
#       Extract numeric fields from the address.
#
        $addr =~ /^(\d+)\.(\d+)\.(\d+)\.(\d+)$/
                or die "$0: bad address \"$addr\"\n";

        return "$4.$3.$2.$1.$zone";
}
#----------------------------------------------------------
```

This might be used as follows.

---

[2]http://www.surbl.org/. Please note and respect that this is free to use only for low-volume sites. See the site for usage criteria.

```
$qtarget = calculateQueryTarget($ip_address, 'multi.surbl.org');
$indnsbl = gethostbyname($qtarget);
if ( defined $indnsbl )
{
    printf "    DOMAIN %s IN DNSBL %s\n", $domname,$qtarget;
}
```

Such searches sometimes fail and this can be done in a more sophisticated manner but this simple approach works in the vast majority of cases.

6.3 The role of honeypots

Honeypots are simply e-mail addresses which you spread around the web by posting on forums or hiding on web-sites[3]. The idea is that you never use these for normal mail so that everything that gets sent to them is junk. Note that they are also called spamtraps. I have avoided that use here as we are trying to attract all kinds of insect into our trap.

The format of the e-mail addresses should be such that there is *never* any chance that it will be associated with a real person. One technique I use is to have a reasonable sounding name followed by a date code as to when it became live, for example, mrgibson20100824-1745@oakcomp.co.uk indicating that it came into use at 1745 on the 24th August, 2010. There is no evidence that junk mailers are put off by these addresses, (some proponents advocate lots of random letters but these might provoke suspicion). These can then be used for analysis or comparison with e-mails sent to legitimate addresses.

A simple way of adding them to a web-site is to use hidden fields so that normal users can't see them. For example, by adding the following "hidden" style definition to an HTML document

```
<HEAD>
<STYLE type="text/css">
.hidden
{
  position: absolute;
```

---

[3]There are a number of ways of doing this which render them hidden to a human but so that they can still be seen by the automated scraping which spammers carry out looking for e-mail addresses using bits of software called web spiders)

```
    left: 0px;
    top: -100px;
    width:1px;
    height:1px;
    overflow:hidden;
}
</STYLE>
```

To use this, somewhere in the body of your HTML document, you might add

```
<BODY>
<DIV class="hidden">
<A HREF="mailto:mrgibson20100824-17:45@oakcomp.co.uk">
Please do not use this address</A>
</DIV>
```

The accompanying warning might be shown in browsers for the partially sighted so needs to be shown. In normal circumstances, it remains completely invisible although a junk mailer's web crawler will no doubt experience a tiny frisson of digital excitement as it recognises a legitimately formatted e-mail message to plunder for it's master.

As a final point, you might like to consider joining Project Honeypot, http://www.projecthoneypot.org/, a centralised project monitoring vast numbers of honeypots.

6.4 Dealing with backscatter

I discussed mail bouncing back on p. 96 as part of a general appraisal of whether to reject or discard mail. It remains a significant problem, so here I will be more explicit as to how you deal with it.

6.4.1 Third-party backscatter

A legitimate e-mail might be bounced because of a little finger-trouble - perhaps a transposed letter or somebody moves their e-mail address and forgets to tell everybody so that all e-mails to the old address are returned undelivered, (i.e. bounced). In contrast, backscatter is deliberate and is what happens when a junk mailer spoofs your address as the sender of their junk and then sends it to somebody whose mailer then rejects it as junk.

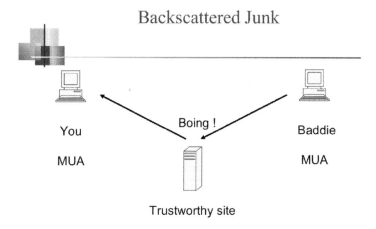

Figure 6.1: Illustrating the basic principle of backscattering junk. It might be more appropriately called reflected junk. It is quite deliberate.

Because you are down as the sender, the mail is rejected and bounced back to you even though you had nothing to do with it. This is very irritating and is rather clumsy as I commented on earlier.

In spite of the variability of the format of the bounced responses as we saw, this can be dealt with pretty effectively in the receiving MTA as described in the section on Postfix set up on p. 137 where you simply define addresses which never send. This is OK provided the junk mailer is using an address which you do not use for sending e-mail such as abuse@ or info@, which are usually reserved for incoming e-mail only. The following example however is backscattered junk which is sent to my main address which of course does send, so it demands a more sophisticated approach.

6.4.2 Personal backscatter

The principle is the same as seen in Figure 6.1 on p. 183 but there are various ways to do it.

- The junk mailer hunts around for a mailbox set to auto-reply, (in other words it's user is away and just wants to tell legitimate senders that they are away or busy for the moment).

- The junk mailer finds a receiving MTA that rejects rather than discards non-existent addresses.

- The junk mailer sends it to a false address on a mailing list.

- The junk mailer sends it to a mailbox known to be full.

When they have found one of these on a reputable system, they then spoof your address on an e-mail containing the junk they want to send to you and instead of sending it direct to you and having your junk filters reject it, they bounce it off one of the above. However, since these are reputable sites, your junk filters detect that the bounce is coming from a trustworthy place and let it through. Most bounced responses are allowed through because of this. In other words, you get your junk neatly wrapped in a bounce wrapper from the trustworthy site which, with a bit of creative formatting on behalf of the junk mailer, arrives in your mailbox with the payload easily readable.

There's an example of this in Figure 3.3 on p. 42 and is one of several received at the time of writing, taking advantage of the Xmas shopping season:-

```
...
Received:   from  zen.co.uk  (212.23.3.9)  by  remote.ck-ind.com
(10.0.0.101)
with  Microsoft  SMTP  Server  id  8.1.436.0;  Fri,  10  Dec  2010
14:05:21 +0000
Return-Path: <lesh@oakcomp.co.uk>
Received: from mail.dunainfo.net ([80.95.70.173])
by bastion03.mail.zen.net.uk
with smtp (Exim 4.69) (envelope-from <lesh@oakcomp.co.uk>)
id
1PR35b-0007GC-C1 for deraelhubq@ck-ind.com;
Fri, 10 Dec 2010 13:32:47 +0000
Date: Fri, 10 Dec 2010 14:51:39 +0000
From:            "order-update@amazon.com"          <order-
update@amazon.com>
Reply-To:          "order-update@amazon.com"          <order-
update@amazon.com>
To: "deraelhubq@ck-ind.com" <deraelhubq@ck-ind.com>
Message-ID: <9697282.49937949461285617763.JavaMail.correios@na-
mm-relay.
amazon.com>
Subject:  Amazon.com - Waiting  Confirmation  (1273-21342186-
474554)
...
```

As can be seen the mail headers reveal an e-mail pretending to be an Amazon update confirmation. This is sent to a non-existent user at the ck-ind.com domain with the Return-Path set to me. The receiving MTA duly returns this back to me. It shouldn't. Amazon are not in the habit of sending out order confirmations with me as the return address.

...

Order #1273-21342186-474554 placed on December 10, 2010.

Status: WAITING CONFIRMATION

A communal
By: Blodwen Wilson

Sold by: Amazon.com, LLC

Order details:
<a href="http://laureana.net/realizably.html">
#1273-21342186-474554</a>

Because you only pay for items when we ship them to you,
you won't be charged for any items that you cancel.

Thank you for visiting Amazon.com!

Amazon.com
Earth's Biggest Selection
<a href="http://www.amazon.com">http://www.amazon.com</a>
...

The body as seen above is a spoof of an Amazon confirmation from which
I have removed some of the formatting so you can see it more clearly. Right
in the middle is a dirty link to laureana.net, (I bold-faced it so you can see
it clearly). This resolves to 94.102.216.213 which is registered in Germany
which transfers to http://femalerxtabletsfitness.com/ which is registered in
Russia as 88.255.78.111. Guess what this sells.

So how do you protect yourself against this ? Well, it's not that hard
and there is already a mechanism at hand which we have discussed earlier
and goes a long way towards eliminating the problem. Although there
are implementation-defined limits, the bouncing mechanism should always
include the original headers of the message being bounced[4]. Note the use
of "should" here - in standard-speak, this means that it isn't forced but is
strongly recommended. In practice, all the ones I have seen return at least

---

[4]RFC 3461, section 6.2

the headers. Now earlier on, I talked about Hashcash, (p. 174). Hashcash can be used to add a header to all the outgoing mail from your server (or even your MUA if you embed it as a signature in your e-mail). As described earlier, the point of this is that it increases the acceptability of your message because it declares you have invested a significant amount of CPU time, (i.e. "money") in preparing and sending the message which you would not do if you were a junk mailer in general. However, the bouncing mail server will dutifully return the original headers. If you find a valid hashcash there, then it is very, very likely indeed that it came from you. If there isn't, it's backscatter and can go in the bin[5].

On a final note, if you must use the auto-reply in your mailer, attracting backscattered junk as described above, make sure you are sitting behind a pretty good junk mail filtering system so very little gets to you, because as you can see from the example above, a fair amount of heavy lifting and careful thought is required to deflect them. You should also bear in mind that you may be bouncing the junk onto an entirely innocent party.

6.4.3 A final note on auto-responders

Just as a note in passing, in the later stages of my experiences of detecting junk, the lack of standardisation of bounced messages and auto-responders provided most of the difficulties in reaching six sigma performance. As can be seen above, bounced messages were eventually dealt with satisfactorily because all the ones I have seen contain all the original headers, including my validation headers if I sent it. SMTP bounce messages have an empty envelope sender address <> known as the null sender address and usually a From: address of MAILER-DAEMON. They should also contain codes indicating why the mail was not delivered[6]

In contrast auto-responders usually contain none of the original e-mail other than a non-standard acknowledgement that it was received. RFC 3834 recommends that they contain an "Auto-submitted: auto-replied" header

---

[5]You can of course be really sophisticated and cryptographically sign all your e-mail. Few organisations do but it is remotely possible that junk mailers will go to the expense of reducing the efficiency of their botnets and computing hashcash signatures. When you are trying to operate at very high levels of efficiency, cryptographic signing is probably worthwhile and since January 2011 I do this as I discuss on p. 253.

[6]These are the remit of RFC 3463, an example of which is code 5.1.1 which corresponds to an unknown user.

Figure 6.2: The message is pure HTML as indicated by the embedded message from kmail, my MUA, warning me of this.

but they often don't. The Reply-To: header should be sane if set but is often set to MAILER-DAEMON.

The bottom line is that anything with MAILER-DAEMON in Reply-To: or From: needs to be fairly carefully analysed to avoid issuing a false backscatter message.

6.5 Dealing with image spam

One of the tricks which spammers try to use is to get their message through your defences expressed as an image.

An example of this is shown as Figure 6.2 (p. 188). which is an example of a 419 scam, (p.53). In this case, the message is and simply fetches a JPG image which contains the spam which is itself shown as Figure 6.3 (p. 189).

When the JPG image is rendered it's content is the by now well-established formula of a somewhat eccentric view of the world, seen through naivety, pathos and greed.

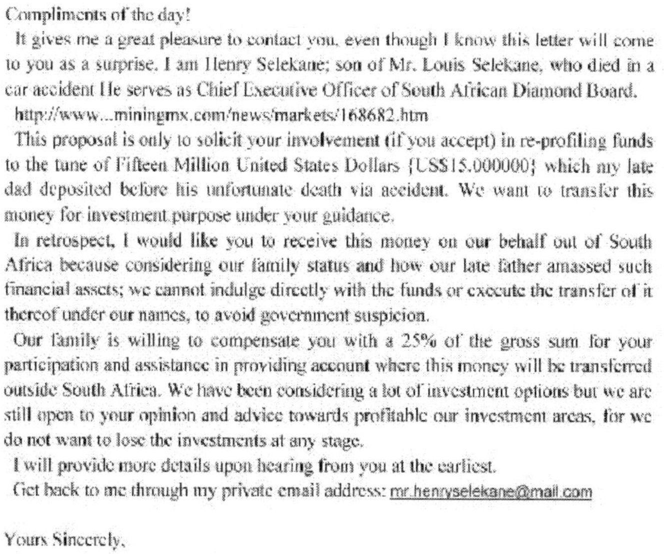

Compliments of the day!

It gives me a great pleasure to contact you, even though I know this letter will come to you as a surprise. I am Henry Selekane; son of Mr. Louis Selekane, who died in a car accident He serves as Chief Executive Officer of South African Diamond Board.

http://www...miningmx.com/news/markets/168682.htm

This proposal is only to solicit your involvement (if you accept) in re-profiling funds to the tune of Fifteen Million United States Dollars {US$15.000000} which my late dad deposited before his unfortunate death via accident. We want to transfer this money for investment purpose under your guidance.

In retrospect, I would like you to receive this money on our behalf out of South Africa because considering our family status and how our late father amassed such financial assets; we cannot indulge directly with the funds or execute the transfer of it thereof under our names, to avoid government suspicion.

Our family is willing to compensate you with a 25% of the gross sum for your participation and assistance in providing account where this money will be transferred outside South Africa. We have been considering a lot of investment options but we are still open to your opinion and advice towards profitable our investment areas, for we do not want to lose the investments at any stage.

I will provide more details upon hearing from you at the earliest.

Get back to me through my private email address: mr.henryselekane@mail.com

Yours Sincerely,

Figure 6.3: The rendered version of Figure 6.2 (p. 188). The image really is of this poor quality.

Forensically, these are a little more difficult to deal with than textual spam because of the problems of trying to assess whether an image is junk or not. In addition, this has come from a relatively trusted address, me.com which resolves to 17.250.248.152, (as you may recall, the last received address cannot be spoofed, although rarely, it has been proxied). This address is also white-listed[7]. Fortunately, the sender is an idiot like so many of them and adds a jaunty "Compliments of the day!", nothing else of note and sends it to an undisclosed list with only an image file attached. Even better, it was sent to a honeypot of mine so that the image details can be used to scan for similar mails to non-honeypot addresses. The MIME scanning Perl program referred to earlier can easily pick these up and check to see if the same file has been sent to anybody else, a dead giveaway.

You will find efforts described by anti-spam researchers in the literature to read the attached image files but this itself can be defeated by spammers

---

[7]http://www.dnswl.org/

using technology similar to that employed by Captcha[8], (the deformed letters which sites use to prevent script kiddies auto-logging in and also me, because I can't read the damn things). Fortunately, the forensic pattern of the whole package is usually a dead giveaway and my Bayesian filters are now awfully good at plucking them out of my mail stream.

6.6 Dealing with embedded links

As has been seen, one of the standard ways of categorising the legitimacy of an e-mail address is by the links it contains. We have seen some examples of toxic embedded links in earlier sections such as Figure 3.9 (p. 49). Originally MUA software did not make it easy to see these links. Instead the recipient saw the equally dangerous but superficially acceptable version in Figure 3.10 (p. 50). As MUAs have got better, the toxic link is clearly revealed for what it is - a clandestine attempt to pry information from you for criminal purposes.

Forensically, the embedded link problem can be solved reasonably successfully with a mixture of RBLs and link inconsistency with From: addresses.

However there has been a considerable recent heightened tendency[9] to use the *shortened link* services to obscure their real location from MUAs in spite of the efforts of the service providers to police this.

Shortened links might look like http://tinyurl.com/unicycles[10]. If you type this into your web-browser, you will be re-routed to:-

```
http://rover.ebay.com/rover/1/711-53200-19255-0/1?
  type=3&campid=5336224516&toolid=10001&customid=
  tiny-hp&ext=unicycle&satitle=unicycle
```

---

[8]http://www.captcha.net/
[9]http://www.pcworld.com/article/201759/shortened_url_spam_increases.html?tk=hp_new, accessed 31-Jul-2010
[10]Example shown on the tinyurl.com site, accessed 31-Jul-2010.

This of course makes it more difficult. Some browsers are beginning to supply methods of unravelling these for normal browsing but the problem remains in e-mail where the underlying link needs to be analysed to judge if it is safe.

I will now show methods for accessing these underlying links from the two main short link service providers, http://tinyurl.com/ and http://bit.ly/. Both use simple Perl scripts but will demonstrate the idea so that this can be embedded within home-spun content filtering mechanisms. The Perl programs are not paragons of style but as with everything in open source, they are there to get you started. Take it, build on it and give it back to the community.

6.6.1 TinyURL

The short Perl program below *tinyurl.pl*, illustrates how to unravel a tinyURL link. In this case, you need to parse the shortened link "http://tinyurl.com/unicycles" into "http://tinyurl.com/preview.php?num=unicycles" and then search for the string "<blockquote><b>". The link can be extracted from what follows.

```
#!/usr/bin/Perl
#
#     A demonstration script to expose short links from tinyURL.
#     Copyright: Les Hatton, 2010.
#
#     Distributed with the same conditions as Perl itself.
#
#     Revision: $Revision: 1.24 $
#     Date:     $Date: 2011/08/25 15:12:18 $
#-----------------------------------------------------------------
#
use strict;
use LWP::Simple;
use LWP::UserAgent;
use HTTP::Request;
use HTTP::Response;

my   ($turl,$contents,$browser);
```

```perl
# http://tinyurl.com/unicycles is submitted as ..
$turl     = "http://tinyurl.com/preview.php?num=unicycles";

# Make sure browser disconnects if problem.
$browser = LWP::UserAgent->new();
$browser->timeout(10);

my $request = HTTP::Request->new(GET => $turl);
my $response = $browser->request($request);
if ($response->is_error())
    {printf "Error %s\n", $response->status_line;}

# Get contents.
$contents = $response->content();

# Desired link appears as only blockquoted field.
$contents =~
    m|<blockquote><b>(http://([\w\-\.]+)([.][\w]+)).*|;

printf "Hidden link is %s\n", $1;

exit(0);
```

6.6.2 bit.ly

To access the underlying links with bit.ly, you have to append the shortened url with a "+" and then search for the string "Bitly.docurl". A bit more rummaging with the program below, *bitly.pl* and there it is.

```perl
#!/usr/bin/Perl
#
#    A demonstration script to expose short links from tinyURL.
#    Copyright: Les Hatton, 2010.
#
#    Distributed with the same conditions as Perl itself.
#
#    Revision: $Revision: 1.24 $
#    Date:     $Date: 2011/08/25 15:12:18 $
```

```
#----------------------------------------------------------------
#
use strict;
use LWP::Simple;
use LWP::UserAgent;
use HTTP::Request;
use HTTP::Response;

my    ($turl,$contents,$browser);

$turl     = "http://bit.ly/gXwbf+";

# Make sure browser disconnects if problem.
$browser = LWP::UserAgent->new();
$browser->timeout(10);

my $request = HTTP::Request->new(GET => $turl);
my $response = $browser->request($request);
if ($response->is_error())
    {printf "Error %s\n", $response->status_line;}
# Get contents.
$contents = $response->content();

# The Bitly.docurl string occurs only once,
# just before the desired link.
$contents =~
    m|Bitly\.docurl.*(http://([\w\-\.]+)([.][\w]+)).*|;

printf "Hidden link is %s\n", $1;

exit(0);
```

There are numerous other shortened link providers but this shows how the underlying links can be extracted and then subjected to the usual checks for appearance on a RBL or for mismatches with the From: address.

There is an even simpler solution.

> If you see a tinyurl or otherwise obscured link in your e-mail and it's from somebody you do not know, trash the mail and complain to the short link provider. They will be very pleased to hear from you. Nobody likes their systems to be undermined by criminals.

6.6.3 Link forensics

You have another choice. This is discussed in more detail on p. 244 where the concept of Filter Fights Back (FFB) is introduced. In essence, you issue a get on the link if you are pretty sure it's toxic, (for example, if there are other clues in the text semantics and it is the only embedded link) - it is usually pretty obvious. You then have various choices.

Shallow parsing

Shallow parsing is often enough to determine the relative toxicity of a link. For example, one ploy of junk mailers is to break into a benign system and introduce a web page which itself contains an embedded link to a toxic system. This can either be the spammer's wares all laid out for sale or it might contain toxic downloadable material to introduce some spyware onto the hapless visitor's machine. Here's an example of one sent on 13th November, 2010. It contains the single link:

```
http://litterator.fr/go.php
```

This particular piece of junk is an example of double-hacking. First the aol.com address of a friend had been broken into and used to send on this e-mail to his mailing list. Second, the embedded link itself is a benign private literary site and has also been hacked. At the time of writing, this mail excites no adverse comment from SpamAssassin and leaves Bayesian analysers which have not seen it before unsure as to it's provenance and it has a pretty good chance of making it through most filtering systems. The referenced go.php page is something else entirely however. This redirects in a time-dependent way to varying domain names such as ancient-stonetablets.net which looks fairly benign and the somewhat less benign ripcapsules.net, which turn out to have adjacent IP addresses 95.64.109.230 and 95.64.109.231 and which are in, guess what, Romania, per capita hacking capital of the world, (c.f. p. 123)). Not only that, they are on the redoubtable Spamhaus RBL.

In other words, without such exploration, it would be difficult to detect. However, a little shallow parsing has revealed an indirected link into a country with an appalling record for this kind of thing, which is also blacklisted on a reputable BL so out it goes. You would also of course train Bayesian filters on this as well. Every little helps when you are identifying junk by it's content.

Deep parsing

Shallow parsing is usually sufficient as a tie-breaker. Any e-mail whose body is simply a link to another link through the HTML Refresh mechanism is highly suspicious on it's own in my experience. Sometimes you may want to follow the refreshes and hoover out the site either as part of an FFB, (p. 244), or because you need more information to feed into the content checking. As a general rule, this latter is rarely necessary - the junk-mailer will have given themselves away before now but it's nice to have something in reserve. Since it's moderately expensive, it is done at the last possible stage in the filtering system described later.

6.7 Bayesian filtering

This is quite simply something you really need to know about whether you are a prospective junk mail filterer or not. It is based on the notions of probability.

First, let me say that a substantial percentage of the population is fundamentally crippled by failing to understand the basics of probability in general and conditional probability in particular. The usual argument is "That's mathematics and I'm no good at mathematics". If you accept that premise, you are asking to be ripped-off and you will be, repeatedly and enthusiastically by the banking fraternity amongst many others. Basic probability is not that hard and is fundamental to making rational choices in life. If you doubt me, please read the eloquent words of John Allen Paulos, [40]. It won't take you long and you will be immensely the richer for it. Let me quote you one of the many splendid examples which you will find discussed within it's pages, this time on the subject of biasing decisions by selection.

Suppose you receive 10 successive mailings from a self-styled financial guru who claims to have found a method of predicting the direction of stock movements, (i.e. betting a particular stock or index will go up or down, the basis of spread-betting. In each case, the guru correctly picks the direction and in the 11th e-mail invites you to send a pile of money in order to make you (and them rich). You do, you lose and you hear no more. How on earth could somebody who guesses correctly 10 times on the run be wrong on the 11th attempt ? A simple calculation reveals that the chances of getting 10 guesses on stock direction correct on the run is 1 in 1024, so surely this guru has indeed found a reliable predictor, (we normally think of 1 in 20 as being reasonable evidence that something unusual is happening; 1 in 1024 is almost a guarantee.).

Sadly not. This is how this very simple scam works. I contact 4,096 potential punters through the wonders of e-mail - it doesn't really cost me anything as explained throughout this book[11]. I make up two e-mails, the first says that a particular stock will go up and the other says it will go down. I split my 4,096 into two halves and send the first e-mail to the first 2,048 and the second e-mail to the second 2,048. If the stock goes up I repeat the process with the first 2,048 and forget the second 2,048 (as I was wrong). The punters do not know each other so I finish up after 10 attempts with 4 punters who think I have a divine power when it comes to picking stock directions - after all, I have been correct 10 times on the run. To each of these 4, I invite them to invest some serious money and then make off with it. Easy isn't it ! It's especially easy when it comes to using e-mail because the mechanism of doing this can be automated to the point of just pressing a button.

Baycsian filtering is simply the application of probability methods to partition junk. It's modern incarnation is due to a seminal paper written by Paul Graham [17] followed up by other work such as the article by Gary Robinson[12]. For an excellent and very detailed discussion of it's efficacy in general and it's applications to Spam filtering in particular, [56] is particularly recommended.

First I am going to introduce some simple symbols as follows:-

$P(H)$ The probability that an event H will happen. This is also known as the unconditional or prior probability. For example, if H is the event that I draw a Heart from a pack of cards, then P(H) = 13/52 = 1/4.

---

[11] In practice I would use millions but this serves to illustrate.
[12] http://www.linuxjournal.com/article/6467, accessed 11-Jan-2011.

On the other hand if H represents the event that I win the lottery, then P(H) = 0 to all intents and purposes, because you would have to be daft to bet as the odds of winning are so low[13]. Actually, that's a little cruel. At least in the case of the UK National Lottery, it's better to think of it as an expensive mechanism for giving money to worthy causes, with a tiny chance of becoming as rich as the ancient King of Lydia, Croesus, allegedly responsible for being the first to issue gold coins.

$P(H \mid J)$ The conditional probability that an event H will happen *given that event J has already happened.* It is exceedingly common for people to confuse P(H) with $P(H \mid J)$ in real life to their great detriment, as explained by Paulos in [40]. Note also that $P(H \mid J)$ **is not the same as** $P(J \mid H)$. For example, if H is the event that I pick a Heart from a pack of cards and J is the event that I pick a Jack, then $P(H \mid J)$ = 1/4 (one of the four Jacks will be a Heart) and $P(J \mid H) = 1/13$, (one of the thirteen Hearts will be a Jack).

$P(H \cap J)$ The joint probability of H **and** J occurring. Using the example above, if H is the event that I pick a Heart and J is the event that I pick a Jack then $P(H \cap J) = 1/52$ as there is only one Jack of Hearts.

You can then see the following:-

$$P(H \cap J) = P(H \mid J)P(J) \tag{6.1}$$

(The probability of drawing the Jack of Hearts is the probability of drawing a Heart given that you have already drawn a Jack. Note that (1/52) = (1/4).(1/13) which checks out.)

Now for a bit of trickery that mathematicians do all the time. I can swap the events H and J in equation (6.1) (they are only arbitrary labels after all) and that gives me

$$P(J \cap H) = P(J \mid H)P(H) \tag{6.2}$$

---

[13]Note that they prey on your gullibility by saying trite things like "If you are not in it, then you can't win it". It would be more accurate to say that "If you are not in it, then you can't win it but if you are in it, then you have about as much chance of winning as being struck by lightning on a Friday", http://www.bbc.co.uk/weather/features/understanding/lightning_strike.shtml, accessed 23-Aug-2010.

However, $P(H \cap J) = P(J \cap H)$, because the probability of having a Heart and a Jack is exactly the same as having a Jack and a Heart - they are both the same card, the Jack of Hearts. This means the left hand sides of equations (6.1) and (6.2) are the same so their right hand sides must be the same too. This then gives:-

$$P(H \mid J)P(J) = P(J \mid H)P(H) \tag{6.3}$$

and we will write this as:-

$$P(H \mid J) = \frac{P(J \mid H)P(H)}{P(J)} \tag{6.4}$$

In other words, we have now related the two conditional probabilities $P(H \mid J)$ and $P(J \mid H)$. This is known as Bayes rule after the eighteenth century English mathematician and Presbyterian minister, Thomas Bayes. Before seeing what on earth this has to do with filtering junk mail, I will develop a couple of other simple ideas.

A probability of 1 means that something is certain to happen. For example, tomorrow it will either rain where I am or it will not rain. One of these events is certain[14]. If I am picking a card then I will either pick a Heart or not pick a Heart. It is traditional in probability to represent these as the events H and H' (i.e. not H). We can then say:-

$$P(H) + P(H') = 1 \tag{6.5}$$

So H either will happen or it won't. There are no other possibilities. Logicians call this, rather delightfully I think, the *law of the excluded middle*.

I will now expand this as follows. Events usually depend on other events. Supposing we list all possible other events that a particular event J might depend on. In the simplest case I can write

$$P(J) = P(J \mid H)P(H) + P(J \mid H')P(H') \tag{6.6}$$

In other words, since by definition H and H' cover all possible things which J can depend on (because you either have H or you don't), we can then write Bayes rule in the form

$$P(H \mid J) = \frac{P(J \mid H)P(H)}{P(J \mid H)P(H) + P(J \mid H')P(H'))} \tag{6.7}$$

---

[14] Although one may be more likely than the other. For example, I was brought up in the Western Pennines in the North of England. There was a saying that if you could see the Pennines, it was going to rain. If you couldn't see them, it was already raining.

So what has this all to do with filtering junk mail ? Well, suppose a particular keyword is associated with spam, for example, "prize".

Let P(prize) be the probability of encountering the word "prize" in an e-mail. Let $P(prize \mid spam)$ be the probability of encountering "prize" *given that a message has already been identified as spam* and let $P(prize \mid ham)$ be the probability of encountering the word "prize" in *a message already identified as non-spam, widely known as ham.*

In spam filtering, we would actually like to know the inverse conditional probability $P(spam \mid prize)$, in other words the probability of a message being spam, *given that the word "prize" has been found in a particular message under scrutiny.*

We can then rewrite equation (6.7) in this context as

$$P(spam \mid prize) = \frac{P(prize \mid spam)P(spam)}{P(prize \mid spam)P(spam) + P(prize \mid ham)P(ham)} \tag{6.8}$$

However, we can calculate everything on the right hand side from a population of known spam and ham. For example, supposing now we test 1000 spam messages and find 200 contain the word "prize" and in a body of 500 ham messages, we find 10 contain the word "prize". Then equation (6.8) becomes

$$P(spam \mid prize) = \frac{(200/1000)(1000/1500)}{(200/1000)(1000/1500) + (10/500)500/1500} \simeq 0.952 \tag{6.9}$$

So the probability of a particular message being spam given that it contains the word "prize" is more than 95%. This of course is not certainty but it's pretty close.

6.7.1 Practical implementations

In practice, this is extended to lots of other words and the probabilities can then be combined using more sophisticated statistical models. We have already seen bogofilter, (p. 150), the mechanics of which are described here[15] and here[16] based on work by [17], [18] which itself refers to [39], [49].

---

[15]http://www.linuxjournal.com/article/6467, accessed 23-Aug-2010
[16]http://www.paulgraham.com/wfks.html, accessed 23-Aug-2010

An excellent description of a simple multi-category Bayesian filter is given by John Graham-Cumming at [19] along with a number of other pertinent papers.

Apart from the well-known spam filtering tools SpamAssassin (mostly written in Perl) and bogofilter, written in C , (p. 150), these include:-

- SpamBayes[17].

- SpamProbe[18].

- DSPAM[19].

- CRM114[20].

- The Bow tool kit, [31].

All of these systems are open source and there seems to be generally little to choose between them other than ease of use[21]. When trained properly, they are all very good indeed. For a far more general comparison see here[22]. The most flexible seems to be CRM114 which uses multiple methods but this comes at the price of understanding how to set it up. Given that bogofilter and SpamAssassin together get rid of most spam, the added complexity is only justified if you wish to achieve six sigma levels of accuracy. However as I argue here, the volume of spam is sufficiently high that we need to achieve this so the added complexity is indeed justified and is documented later.

6.7.2 Training Bayesian filters

Much is written on the subject of training such filters and I mentioned earlier on p. 150 how bogofilter can be trained non-interactively from an

---

[17] http://spambayes.sourceforge.net/

[18] http://spamprobe.sourceforge.net/

[19] Originally written by Jonathan A. Zdziarski, http://www.nuclearelephant.com/index.php and reportedly >99.95% accurate

[20] Written by Bill Yerazunis, http://crm114.sourceforge.net/ and a complete manual at http://crm114.sourceforge.net/docs/CRM114_Revealed_20061010.pdf. I've been around programming languages for most of my career and even designed some and I thought Perl was er, well, quintessentially opaque. It is however as diaphanous as a mayfly's wing compared with CRM114. In the right hands however, it is immensely powerful and Yerazunis reports >99.98% accuracy at identifying junk.

[21] http://kristianandmarie.com/kristian/reviews/bayesian/, accessed 23-Aug-2010.

[22] http://www.jgc.org/astlt.html, accessed 23-Aug-2010.

existing corpus of spam[23]. However, there is fairly widespread agreement that spam is not simply a generic attack and training your filters on a corpus of general spam rather than the spam you actually get sent is not so effective. I will quantify this statement shortly with my own experiences.

In essence training is simply an environment where you run a filter, it tells you what it thinks, and if you agree you don't do any more. If it's wrong however, you tell it the correct category (all statistical filters have options to tell them they are wrong), and it re-adjusts it's internal data structures (i.e. probabilities) accordingly. It is fundamentally interactive. There are however several ways of doing this with sometimes differing views on which produces the best filters. Yerazunis[24] identifies the following

TOE Train On Error. Here you only train the filter on the errors it makes.

TEFT Train Everything. Here you train the filter on everything, for example an entire corpus of spam and non-spam. The relative percentages of these are of course influential.

TUNE Train Until No Error. Here you train the filter iteratively until it makes no errors on a specific set of spam and non-spam messages. The drawback of this on big installations is that *all* mail in the growing training corpus must be kept which is impracticable when you get millions a day.

Yerazunis concludes that with statistical significance, TUNE is a bit better than TOE and both are quite a bit better than TEFT. Since TUNE is impracticable on big sites, TOE emerges as the best choice and is the one I use. Yerazunis also concludes that since spam is essentially time-variant, (I can certainly substantiate this over the three years I have spent far too much time in analysing it),

> "Forgetting old data allows the database to track evolution in spam more accurately"

Finally, Yerazunis finds that Markovian methods (i.e. Bayesian methods extended to phrases with various subtle weighting schemes), are significantly more effective before concluding amongst other things:-

---

[23]http://plg.uwaterloo.ca/ gvcormac/spam/
[24]http://crm114.sourceforge.net/docs/Plateau99.pdf

- Bayesians are very good

- Markovians are even better

- Neither by itself is sufficient

The central theme of this book is that *combinations* of these algorithms along with voting principles as discussed later, are indeed sufficient.

For reference, a couple of simple shell scripts follow to drive bogofilter, and CRM114 if you use it, for TOE training. The first, *unlearn_bogofilter.sh* shows how to apply TOE to bogofilter.

```
#!/bin/sh
#
#        Filter unlearning script.
#
#        Revision: $Revision: 1.24 $
#        Date:    $Date: 2011/08/25 15:12:18 $
#-------------------------------------------------
if test $# -eq 0
then
        echo "$0 [spam|nonspam] [email]"
        exit
fi

if test "$1" = "spam"
then
        echo "Retraining ham to spam"
        bogofilter -t -Ns -d ./.bogofilter < $2
else
        echo "Retraining spam to ham"
        bogofilter -t -Sn -d ./.bogofilter < $2
fi
```

This second script, *unlearn_crm114.sh* does the same thing with CRM114.

```
#!/bin/sh
#
#        Filter unlearning script.
```

```
#
#        Revision: $Revision: 1.24 $
#        Date:     $Date: 2011/08/25 15:12:18 $
#-----------------------------------------------------
if test $# -eq 0
then
        echo "$0 [spam|nonspam] [email]"
        exit
fi

if test "$1" = "spam"
then
        echo "Retraining ham to spam"
        ./mailfilter.crm --learnspam < $2
else
        echo "Retraining spam to ham"
        ./mailfilter.crm --learnnonspam < $2
fi
```

There is a script for training both bogofilter and CRM114 from a corpus given in full in the Appendix, p. 305 as it is a little long for the body of this book.

Spam Corpora

As a result of various initiatives, there are various spam corpora (i.e. spam collections) available on the web, which can be used for testing and training junk filtering techniques. These include

- TREC 2005, 2006, 2007[25]. Spam corpora collected as part of the TREC (Text REtrieval Conference) project. More details can be found here[26]. A later and related corpus is CEAS 2008[27].

- SpamAssassin spam corpora[28] A number of collections of spam and ham from between 2002 and 2005.

---

[25]http://plg.uwaterloo.ca/ gvcormac/treccorpus/about.html
[26]http://plg.uwaterloo.ca/ gvcormac/spam/
[27]http://plg.uwaterloo.ca/ gvcormac/ceascorpus/
[28]http://spamassassin.apache.org/publiccorpus/

- Webb spam corpus[29]. This is not specifically to do with e-mail but is worth mentioning anyway as it is a large collection of web pages which have been used to manipulate search engines and deceive Web users.

Whilst these are very important forensic sources, the nature of spam is that it is highly adaptive and also time and locale variant. The spam a particular receiving MTA receives over some given window of time may be somewhat different than another window of time and may be very different for another receiving MTA. In other words, junk filters trained on one spam corpus to perform well will not typically perform as well on another spam corpus without further (possibly significant) training.

It is important to appreciate however that individual junk filters trained on spam being delivered to many users in the same organisation using the same receiving MTAs still become very effective *for all those users* as amply demonstrated by [4].

There follow some personal quantitative experiences with testing locally trained filters on generic spam corpora.

Local v. generic training

After training the statistical filters used in the hybrid filtering system described on p. 232 for a population of around 500 spam messages and around 1,700 ham messages for the same domains over a period of some two months, they individually achieved around 99.3% efficiency. In comparison when they are used without further training on the first tranche of spam in the SpamAssassin spam corpus[30] which dates from 2002, the equivalent performance is little more than 90.0%.

Several points need making. First of all, the SpamAssassin corpus contains examples of spam which are rejected by other earlier tests in the hybrid filtering system described on p. 232 so the statistical filter components have no knowledge of them. Second, the nature of spam is changing on a time-scale of months so eight year-old spam may not be very representative of current trends unless cyclical. Third, as is described by numerous researchers, statistical filtering itself for a single filter tops out at about 99.95% more or less independently of whatever technique you use or how

---

[29]http://www.cc.gatech.edu/projects/doi/WebbSpamCorpus.html
[30]http://spamassassin.apache.org/publiccorpus/

you train it. Of course the essence of this book is that you can build a system from such components which is far more accurate and in the case of the one described later, this is currently operating at about 99.9995%. Finding this extra factor of hundred is also at the root of Yerazunis' perceptive ideas about inoculation discussed on p. 243.

6.7.3 Bayesian futures

The single great thing about Bayesian algorithms is that they adjust. As junk mailers change their attack vectors, continual training of Bayesian algorithms more than keeps pace.

There are theoretical ways in which they can be attacked however. For example, they could be poisoned by including lots of irrelevant words in and amongst the junk payload, a technique known as *Bayesian poisoning*[31]. In my experience, implementations like bogofilter seem relatively immune to this by focussing only on the 15 or so most significant words. Even more esoteric methods include using Bayesian methods to combat Bayesian methods[32]. For example, in papers presented at the MIT Spam conference in 2006, John Graham-Cumming and Stefano Brighenti demonstrated two forms of Bayesian poisoning - passive (no feedback available to the junk mailer about whether the message got delivered) and active (where the presence of a *web bug*, (c.f. p. 310), in the e-mail communicated back to the junk mailer that the message had been delivered).

Passive poisoning had almost no effect. Active poisoning however is more effective in that you can then train Bayesian junk mail generators to get past Bayesian filters, however, sensible MUAs today do not allow HTML to be displayed unless you trust it so that shuts off that particular vector. An even more exotic route is to intercept them, and then feed back a deliberately biased collection so their own anti-Bayesian filters train on deliberately biased parameters and are themselves poisoned. If you think too much about this however, you will need to have a lie down.

Further support is given for the effectiveness of Bayesian methods by Blosser and Josephsen [4] who describe the installation and tuning of a bogofilter-based system on a busy mail server of more than 2,000 accounts.

---

[31] http://en.wikipedia.org/wiki/Bayesian_poisoning, accessed 23-Aug-2010.

[32] Which presumably will lead to Bayesian methods to combat Bayesian methods to combat Bayesian methods ...

The overall mail load for this period back in 2004 is interesting. These 2,000 accounts led to a traffic of around 1.85 million e-mail messages on average per month of which around 70% were incoming and 30% outgoing. Based on filter logs and user feedback, the authors estimated that the incoming mail load comprised around 65-70% spam, which gives a total amount of junk of around 50% of all mail received or sent.

Let's just compare then the volumes on this busy hospital mail system in 2004 with my own primary mail server in 2010, (which handles around 20 accounts).

Item	Blosser and Josephsen	My server
Mail per month	1.85 million	1.2 million
Accounts	2,000	20
Incoming junk	65-70%	99.96%

This table makes the growth in junk through the first decade of the 21st century starkly obvious.

One of the challenges faced by Blosser and Josephsen is that as a hospital they receive genuine e-mails full of the kind of words which the rest of us (well, most of the rest of us) reject out of hand, such as Viagra, Cialis and all the other 'meds'. This places a particular challenge on statistical methods such as used by bogofilter and particularly on those which depend on word frequency rather than, for example, combinations and other word orderings.

In spite of this, bogofilter was a marked success story in this environment operating at around the 95% success rate with very, very few false positives. This is echoed by other sources anonymously referenced in their paper. We should recall that this is for a single serial filter operating a single vocabulary database for all it's users. Blosser and Josephsen also ask the question whether they themselves think that Bayesian filters are a permanent solution to all spam. They conclude no but the evidence of the last eight years of experience with this techique, including all my own experiments, suggest that it remains formidably effective even though we have to do a little more to match current junk mail levels and sophistication.

In summary, practical experience with them based on bogofilter implementations alongside the other methods described reveals them to be exceptionally powerful and difficult to defeat provided:-

- The population of spam and non-spam you use is sufficiently large, (in the order of thousands of messages although they are pretty effective when you start with hundreds).

- You train them on the messages which reach you rather than generic archives of junk.

- You retrain them on a regular basis.

- You do *not* respond to junk mailers. They must be deprived of any feedback at all or, as described above, carefully fed back biased data to poison their own efforts.

Where to use them ?

There is some disagreement here. Some argue that it is best if Bayesian methods occur very early in the filtering chain and therefore see everything. This way they rapidly build up their effectiveness on the initial deluge of junk mail. On the other hand, others argue that they should appear a little later in the chain as many junk mail messages are so easily rejected on the most trivial of criteria such as being unable even to say HELO properly.

I think this just depends on your interests as much as anything. If you are really interested in statistical filtering in general, then yes, it is beneficial to see just how well they can do. If, on the other hand, you are more interested in getting rid of junk by defence in depth, then you would likely place them later in the chain and train them on the sophisticated junk which got through your earlier defences.

Wherever you place them, the true bottom line for Bayesian and other statisical filtering techniques seems to be that they are effectively invincible. In preparing for this book, I read a lot of very good material on this subject, mostly written between 2002 and 2005, as referenced above by a number of pioneers, Graham, Robinson, Graham-Cumming and the rest. The works on Bayesian and statistical filtering, notably the papers by Blosser and Josephson [4] and the book by Zdziarski [56] basically concluded even then that sophisticated statistical filtering was capable of operating at sensitivity rates in excess of 99.9%[33]. All my experiments in the last 2-3 years conclude

---

[33]Zdziarski quotes an interview with Bill Yerazumis, the author of the well-known CRM114 that the techniques he used there were around 10 times better than a human, which is very impressive indeed. At first hearing, this sounds odd since a human generally *defines* what junk is. The statement should however be interpreted in the

that nothing has materially changed. They remain stunningly effective. With the resources the junk mail community has at it's disposal, if they were going to dent it significantly, it would have happened by now.

However, just in case they do (only fools dream of certainty), there are several other things which can be done as will be seen later including some really interesting stuff on semantic analysis.

6.7.4 Bayesian profiling and unscrupulous advertising

This might not be your cup of tea but it is really worth while knowing a little about just what you can do with these. Implementing so-called naive Bayesian filters is very simple, (about 100 lines of Perl will do it as eloquently exemplified by John Graham-Cumming[34]). This doesn't produce a very fast implementation but as we have seen there are much faster implementations freely available in C and C++ and they are astonishingly powerful.

This highlights a risk which an unscrupulous ISP could easily exploit[35]. Currently, just about every e-mail you send or receive is in plain text. As we have seen, your e-mail typically passes through four computers (and possibly more) - two MTAs and two MUAs, (Figure 2.1 on p. 19) on it's way from sender to receiver. If you are sending one, you compose in Outlook or whatever on your computer or increasingly often, using MUA software on your hand-held. You send it and your MUA transfers it (in plain text) to the sending MTA (usually your ISP). Their sending MTA sends it to it's destination handled by the receiving MTA. The recipient, sitting at their own computer or hand-held (MUA) then requests their mail from the receiving MTA and it is downloaded and they can then read it.

In reverse, your recipient responds and the response trails back through your ISP now acting as the receiving MTA and you pick up the response on your MUA. *Note that all mails, sent or received go through the MTAs of your ISP.* They read them. Not directly, but they analyse the text as part of any mail filtering services they are providing to you and also, it should not be forgotten, for governance purposes - they may have to check for any embedded illegal content such as pornography or worse in some legal frameworks.

---

same sense as adding 2+2 and getting 5 rather than failing to recognise the number 2.

[34] "Build your own Bayesian Spam Filter", 15 May, 2005, http://www.jgc.org/

[35] Note I am specifically not accusing anybody of doing this, I am just saying that they could.

Not to put too fine a point on it, your ISP is capable of knowing everything about you which you choose to reveal in your e-mail. Given that many people commit the most astonishing indiscretions in e-mail, this could be rather more than you would ever imagine.

Those multitude of you who have shopped with Amazon will know that Amazon use your browsing and purchase history to construct a profile of products you might be interested in. It can be astonishingly accurate. I do not mind this because they are as often as not, correct in their guesses about my shopping interests[36] and I have derived a lot of pleasure from stuff I have bought there. In short, there has never been evidence that they abuse this, so I don't mind. Should such evidence ever emerge in the future, I will re-assess.

Now imagine somebody having this kind of knowledge about your personal lives as revealed through your e-mail. That's the kind of profile an unscrupulous ISP could build up and it is very simple to do by adding a Bayesian categorising filter in a script such as allcontent.sh, (p. 153).

There are perhaps more legitimate reasons for such profiling, for example, if a company wishes to police the e-mails it's employees are sending and receiving in business hours. It is not after all unreasonable for an employer to expect the employee to be working on their behalf during such hours and it has to be said that some employees have not entirely grasped this concept.

6.8 e-mail trails: exploiting the Achille's heel

Bayesian classification methods can be used in many innovative ways including the seamier side of social engineering as we have just discussed. As we have also seen, they are extremely effective and can adapt. This raises the question of what other relevant junk aspects of e-mail could we train a Bayesian filter on? We must remember the maxim "data is king" and should never be wasted as has been noted in the context of junk mail by Paul Graham, [18].

The real Achille's heel of junk mail of course is that they have to get you to click on a link or visit a site, wittingly or unwittingly, either to hand over

---

[36]Although their guitar collection is rubbish. :-)

some money for something completely useless, or hand over some money because you are being scammed, or hand over your personal details for who knows what nefarious purposes. In other words, you have to respond in some way orchestrated by the junk mailer.

As a result of this, junk mail contains geographical information in the form of countries. This occurs either because they appear in the Received: header trail (although beware of spoofing of all but the most recent), in the From: header they want you to respond to, or contained within the body of the message itself, either as a link or as an e-mail address or both. However, using a simple IP database[37], we can look up which countries an e-mail directly or indirectly incorporates in it's payload. Furthermore, junk mail which employs mail addresses to respond to may be different from junk mail which contains links so we could further distinguish these by lower-casing the former and upper-casing the latter.

This turns out to be a productive thing to add to our armoury of junk mail detectors but first let's see an example. Figure 6.4 (p. 211) is a pretty obvious upfront fee scam. However, as interesting is the mixture of countries which appear in the From: and Received: header train and also the message itself. Extracting the IP addresses and looking them up in a IP to country database such as that described above reveals a country signature

`us/GBSG.SGNGUS`

In other words, it appears to start off in the USA (US), unreliably wanders off through Nigeria (NG), reliably travels through Singapore (SG) before finishing up with me, (remembering the final received link cannot be spoofed). On top of this it includes a contact e-mail address which is back in the USA. Even allowing for the potential unreliability of two of the links, it turns out that this pattern is sufficient to distinguish it when the Bayesian analyser is trained on a population of a few hundred scams, spams and hams. In this case, it outputs:-

`spam: globosity    1.58`

(I used globosity out of respectful admiration of the bogosity index of bogofilter.)

After training on the following population:-

---

[37]See for example http://software77.net/geo-ip/

```
     Date: 31/08/2009 13:38
[C]  From: POWERBALL LOTTERY Board <info@mail.com>
     To: undisclosed-recipients:;
[H]  Reply to: Powerballgames013@live.co.uk
[T]
[M]  POWERBALL LOTTERY
[L]  You have won
     £800,000,00 GBP

[M]  Lottery Officer
[e]  Mr John sherma
[s]  Email: Powerballgames013@live.co.uk
[s]  TELL: +447031964131
[a]
[g]  for claim with FULL NAMES/COMPLETE ADDRESS/AGE/SEX/OCCUPATION/TEL/COUNTRY
[e]  TICKET NUMBER:05-08-10-18-20-46-{43}.

     Regards
```

Figure 6.4: Although this classic upfront fee scam can be picked out using other techniques, analysis of the countries referenced in the From: and Received: header trails as well as embedded links reveals exploitable patterns.

Number of ham	Number of spam	Number of scam
1326	656	934

Table 6.8: Training population sizes for globosity measure.

The following results were achieved comparing scam against ham.

	True Scam	True Ham (i.e. non-scam)	
Pred. Scam	TP 40	FP 5	88.9% PPV
Pred. Ham	FN 3	TN 89	96.7% NPV
	sens. 93.0%	spec. 94.7%	

Table 6.8: Classification accuracy of scam globosity.

As can be seen, this table has been set out as a binary classification table, (see p. 82). A perfect discriminator has 100.0% for each of it's four measures, specificity and so on. The most dangerous one from the point of view of junk mail is considered to be FP (False Positive or Type I error), whereby a mail is identified as junk when it is not and therefore stands the risk of being thrown away unless quarantined, (and even then people do not look in their quarantine folders very often if at all). Although there are some FP measured here, the globosity measure is not a bad discriminator if used with other measures as it is measuring something which is not normally considered. Even after training on a relatively small population, this measure shows clear distinctions between ham and scams when it decides to choose, (which is about 64% of the time).

Interestingly, spam is much closer to ham in this measure and cannot be so discriminated as can be seen in the following table.

	True Spam	True Ham (i.e. non-spam)	
Pred. Spam	TP 13	FP 0	100.0% PPV
Pred. Ham	FN 18	TN 89	83.2% NPV
	sens. 41.9%	spec. 100.0%	

Table 6.8: Classification accuracy of spam globosity.

Although there are no false positives, giving perfect specificity, it's sensitivity is poor and most of the time (around 63%), it sits on the fence, so at this level of training, it is inadequate at distinguishing ham and spam although remains a very useful additional level of evidence when trying to identify scams since it operates with information which is not normally used.

6.9 Distributed initiatives

One of the most important emergent properties of the web is the sharing of resources which along with the open source movement has contributed a rich and rapidly evolving set of tools and resources. These have had a highly beneficial effect on our ability to defeat junk mail. The Perl and shell script fragments in this book were greatly influenced by other researchers and I freely pass my efforts on under the same conditions.

With regard to the sharing of resources, this benefits junk mail detection in several ways.

6.9.1 Software

Little need be said here. There is a vast amount of co-operating and freely available software of which we have seen only a tiny percentage here, (SpamAssassin, ClamAV, Postfix, Perl and so on). This situation will only get better and is a great source of comfort in battling junk mail.

6.9.2 Resources

Shared resources including farms of co-operating servers storing information about junk mail known as *signatures* are an important part of monitoring and protecting against it.

Junk signatures

It would clearly be an impossible task for co-operating servers to store junk mail in it's entirety. Instead different kinds of server store different kinds of information. On the one hand, RBLs store either IP addresses or domain names which might occur in junk mail headers and/or embedded within the content. On the other hand, some co-operating servers store compressed information about junk. This information usually takes the form of *hashed* information.

Hashed information is a short form of a particular piece of text which is designed to be as unique as possible so that if two hashes are the same, then the originating pieces of text were also the same. This ideal case is not generally realisable and there are so-called *collisions*. These occur when two different pieces of text produce the same hash.

A simple example of a hash is given by the *checksum*. A checksum can be computed in different ways. A very simple example would be to take the quotation "Now is the winter of our discontent" and add together the ASCII values of each letter, perhaps using modular arithmetic[38]. Using this, the word ROME produces the sum $82 + 79 + 77 + 69 = 307$. A common modular prime to use for hashing is 59 so $307 \bmod 59 = 12$ and 12 would be stored. Unfortunately, since MORE has the same letters but in a different order, it too would hash to 12. In other words ROME and MORE lead to a collision.

---

[38]Modular arithmetic is simply the remainder after dividing one number by another number, usually chosen to be a prime. For example $7 \bmod 5 = 2$ because 7/5 is 1 remainder 2 and we just keep the remainder.

This has led to much more sophisticated hashing algorithms such as MD5. MD5[39] was invented by Ron Rivest (the "R" in RSA public-key cryptography) in 1992. When fed any text, it generates a 128-bit number which is (almost)[40] collision resistant and is usually displayed as a 32-digit hexadecimal number. As an example, the following quotation from Henry V:-

> *And Crispin Crispian shall ne'er go by,*
> *From this day to the ending of the world,*
> *But we in it shall be remember'd;*
> *We few, we happy few, we band of brothers*

This generates the following MD5 hash

```
676666dbb8989f98af52c78ff2d54694
```

From a junk mail point of view, there is a problem however. MD5 hashes are exceptionally sensitive to small changes in the input. For example, if I change the word "brothers" to "sisters" in the above quotation, the resulting MD5 hash now becomes

```
53a597b464701ad411a05db3437656ce
```

which is completely different. This of course means that if a junk mailer makes slight changes to the body text of each mail they send (which doesn't cost very much), it effectively renders the signature useless as a means of identifying junk uniquely. Some hash-based databases recover from this somewhat by computing and storing separate MD5 hashes for the Subject:, Message-ID:, From: and other header lines as well as MD5 hashes for different parts of the body to de-sensitize the signatures.

Even with this de-sensitization however, they are markedly worse than any Bayesian approach.

There follow just a few examples of shared resources of various kinds.

---

[39] http://en.wikipedia.org/wiki/MD5

[40] It held out until 1996. By 2009, Tao Xie and Dengguo Feng demonstrated an attack which reduces the breakdown time of collision resistance to a few seconds on a PC, so for cryptographic use, it is considered broken. It is perfectly useable for junk mail signature generation though.

Co-operating Real Time Black Lists

I have discussed these elsewhere but most such lists are distributed around the net, hosted by willing volunteers and mostly free for non-commercial use. Of these I have found spamhaus.org, spamcop.net and surriel.com of particular use and extremely reliable with regard to FP (False Positive) problems, of which spamhaus.org is by far the most comprehensive, (c.f. p. 117).

Vipul's Razor

This is a distributed database[41] which contains signatures of spam e-mail against which you can compare any suspect messages you receive.

Although I have never used it, (only because I haven't needed to yet), it is quoted as being highly reliable and capable of recognising around 25% of all spam, [32].

Because only signatures are reported to the Razor servers, there is no loss of confidentiality but there are of course potential collisions. Providing that a signature is suitably comprehensive, the chance of this can be greatly reduced. A collision of course could lead to a FP (false positive) if a genuine message happened to lead to the same hash as a junk signature already in the database.

Second, there is a processing overhead so it is best not to overuse this. Although it has to be installed[42], it can be configured to run automatically from within SpamAssassin. Note however, that you might have to open port 2307 for TCP traffic in your firewall. Third, slight permutations change the checksum although considerable research has been expended to make them, at least to first order, insensitive to this.

Pyzor

This is similar to Vipul's Razor but is a single server and contains only signatures of bulk mail (UCE). Since it is written in Python, it's use also needs a working Python installation. It requires port 24441 to be opened for UDP traffic. I have not yet felt the need to use this.

---

[41]i.e. it is shared around many servers.
[42]http://www.iredmail.org/forum/topic481-install-pyzor-razor2-and-dcc-on-your-centosrhel-iredmail-server.html

DCC - Distributed Checksum Clearinghouse

This is similar to Pyzor in that it deals with all e-mails, junk or otherwise, but is distributed (hence the name). It is regarded as the most effective. It requires port 6227 to be opened for UDP traffic. Again I have not yet felt the need to use this.

6.10 Semantic analysis and blue sky stuff

Semantic analysis is a fascinating research area with a great deal of activity. Throughout the previous narrative, I have repeated the mantra that in sophisticated filtering, every single piece of information has to be used. In an e-mail, we have the envelope and we have the content. For the envelope, there are a number of sophisticated technologies for identifying the fingerprints of junk mailing; an incorrect spoof of an e-mail header or a blacklisted or proxied MTA somewhere in the mail transfer. For example, SpamAssassin is particularly good at identifying botched attempts to spoof headers. Unfortunately, as we have seen their success has driven junk criminals to attempt to sequester more and more zombies so that the envelope looks innocuous to a defensive filtering system. This means successful junk filtering requires that more and more dependence is placed on the analysis of the other part of an e-mail - the body.

I have alluded to simpler techniques in bygone days where filters might look for eponymous keywords such as "meds", "Viagra" or whatever. Junk mailers fairly quickly got round these and so adequate defence depends more and more on analysing the content of a junk mail as a whole. This is the domain of *semantic analysis*.

In it's simplest terms, we might just be interested in word counts. Indeed the earliest attempts to identify texts just used their distribution of vocabulary.

Then along came George Zipf, [57]. Zipf made the fascinating *observation* that if you measured the frequencies of words in texts and then arranged them in decreasing rank order of occurrence, that their frequencies obeyed a power-law in a surprisingly wide variety of circumstances. What does this mean ?

For reference, power-law behaviour can be represented in this case by the frequency n_r of the rth word appearing being given by a relationship like:-

$$n_r = \frac{k.n}{r} \qquad (6.10)$$

where k is a constant, n_r is the number of times the rth word occurs (i.e. word frequency), n is the total number of words and r is the rank order, (1 = most common, 2 = next most common and so on). On a log n_r - log r scale, this is a straight line with negative slope. Assuming that there are t distinct words, then we also have

$$n = \sum_{r=1}^{t} n_r \qquad (6.11)$$

We can derive an interesting relationship from this. Let us sum both sides of equation (6.10) from r = 1 to t. This leads us to

$$\sum_{r=1}^{t} n_r = k.n \sum_{r=1}^{t} \frac{1}{r} \qquad (6.12)$$

The right hand side of this is a well-known summation and evaluates to

$$k.n(\gamma + lnt + \frac{1}{2t} - \frac{1}{12t(t+1)}...) \qquad (6.13)$$

where $\gamma \approx 0.5772$ is Euler's constant. We will retain only the first two terms as t (the size of the vocabulary) is usually quite large in texts, (typically hundreds to thousands).

Now in most cases, the rarest type will only occur once so we can set $n_t = 1$ *in equation (6.10).* Then we get k = t/n and combining equations (6.11) and (6.13) leads us to

$$n = t(0.5772 + lnt) \qquad (6.14)$$

This is a very interesting result. It says that the total number of words in a text, n, is based on it's unique vocabulary of words, t. *In other words, from the unique words used, you can predict the approximate length of the text.*

If you do this for various texts, very interesting patterns emerge as can be seen by studying Figure 6.5 (p. 219). Here, adherence to equation (6.14) implies a value of around 1 on this figure (which plots n/t(0.5772 + ln t) for a number of texts taken from the splendid Project Gutenberg[43].

---

[43] http://www.gutenberg.org/

The most intriguing pattern about this figure is that certain kinds of text, (for example the works of Shakespeare) are very consistent with Zipf's work. Other kinds of text, such as religious works,(shown to the right of the figure) have very different behaviour.

What is happening here ? Perhaps the best interpretation is that Zipf's observations in some sense capture semantics, (they can be related to information theory, [8]). They must capture some essence because they can be used to classify at least some kinds of text very accurately. For example if a population of religious texts and the complete works of Shakespeare (and P.G. Wodehouse for that matter) are presented to a Zipfian classifier, it will very reliably distinguish between them. This should not really take us by surprise. Humans glancing through texts are pretty good at classifying them and we are certainly not counting the words.

It is obvious that power-law behaviour is at the heart of this mystery and as a result they have become very widely studied, see for example [46] (economic systems) and the excellent review by [36]. In software systems there has been significant activity, much of it recent, [9], [35], [34], [7], [16], [45], [2], [10] and myself in [23], all discuss power-law behaviour but in rather different contexts.

One of my own contributions is to prove that in constant size, constant information systems of any kind, however built, the probability of a component of t_i tokens in total appearing obeys a power-law in the unique set of tokens a_i used to construct it yielding

$$p_i \sim (a_i)^{-\beta} \tag{6.15}$$

A property seen in many software systems in various languages, (it also predicts another observed phenomenon, that defects in software systems are approximately distributed according to a power-law).

We have moved on considerably from Zipf's ground-breaking work. Classification of semantics can be done in a number of ways to take into account phrasing, ordering and semantic ties across entire texts.

6.10.1 Markovian processes

Markov processes sound very sophisticated but reflect fairly simple properties mathematically. In essence a Markov process, (named after the Russian

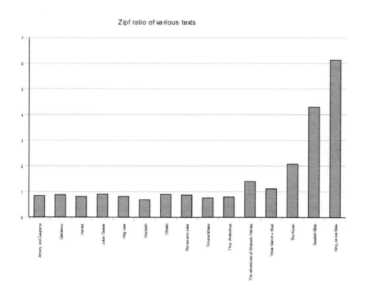

Figure 6.5: A variety of texts taken from Project Gutenberg and analysed for their adherence to Zipf's law.

mathematician Andrey Markov), is any kind of state system whose future state depends only on it's present state and not anything in it's past. In other words, it has no memory. As usual, Wikipedia is pretty good for this as can be seen with some of the simple examples at http://en.wikipedia.org/wiki/Examples_

These are implemented in CRM114 of which we have already heard, (along with a number of other techniques including, Bayesian Chain Rules, Orthogonal Sparse Bigrams, Winnow, Correlation, KNN/Hyperspace, Bit Entropy, CLUMP, SVM and Neural Networks).

To gain just a little insight into how these work, consider a very simple example. Supposing from a vast amount of messages we know are spam or ham, we calculate the probabilities of certain words occurring in the two forms of message.

Let P($word_i$,SC) be the probability of a word "$word_i$" occurring in a spam corpora and P($word_i$,HC) be the probability of the same word occurring in a ham corpora, (both calculated in the obvious way by dividing the number of times it occurs in all the relevant messages and dividing by the total number of words in those messages). Supposing we measure this for the M most popular words. To construct a Markov process from this, we simply have to build first what is called a transition matrix which is just the probabilities laid out as follows, noting that the sum of the probabilities in any row must be 1.0

$$\begin{bmatrix} P(word_1, SC) & ... & P(word_M, SC) \\ P(word_1, HC) & ... & P(word_M, HC) \end{bmatrix}$$

Suppose now that P($word_i$,M) is the probability of "word1" appearing in a newly arrived message, again calculated as it's frequency of occurrence in that message. Then from these and the transition matrix, we calculate the predicted state of the new message as the following matrix equation

$$\begin{bmatrix} P(S) \\ P(H) \end{bmatrix} = \begin{bmatrix} P(word_1, SC) & ... & P(word_M, SC) \\ P(word_1, HC) & ... & P(word_M, HC) \end{bmatrix} \begin{bmatrix} P(word_1, N) \\ \vdots \\ P(word_M, N) \end{bmatrix}$$

where P(S), P(H) are the probabilities of the new message being spam or ham respectively.

6.10.2 Latent Semantic Analysis (LSA)

Latent semantic analysis is a rapidly growing field. A detailed introduction can be found at [27] and a considerable number of other references, demonstrations and applications at http://lsa.colorado.edu/.

LSA takes word frequency analysis and adds sophisticated multi-dimensional statistical methods known as Singular Value Decomposition to look at a multi-dimensional dataset to determine it's characteristics[44].

Such methods can be criticised in that they do not take account of word order, an issue described in some detail by [28], however they conclude that the method still succeeds in capturing semantics in some sense even though word order is not a feature of the algorithm.

I have not found a need to use these algorithms yet, (at least not for this topic), so I will leave you to read more about it from the given references. Instead, I will address the issue of word ordering using an old familiar friend, the Nigerian 419 scam.

6.10.3 Word order and fast pattern recognition in C

For some kinds of filtering, the filters just have to be efficient. Perl is an estimable language for knocking up all kinds of things but for sheer execution speed, it's hard to beat writing it in C, the underlying language of Linux[45]. An excellent example of this is bogofilter itself. Bogofilter is really fast and an excellent example both of tight programming and the formidable power of modern processors when you make use of that power. It's also in my experience, one of the best statistical discriminators for junk mail.

So if you are not up to a bit of grinding in C, skip quickly to the next section (p. 229 if you're desperate to get away) before you are tempted to the dark side.

---

[44] You really don't need to know how to do this but it basically rotates an n-dimensional dataset until it looks at it's simplest. If you think about this too much you will have to have a lie down but mathematicians have always exploited coordinate transformations such as rotation to simplify problems. For example, would you rather think of a 3-dimensional sphere of radius a as $r = a$ (spherical coordinates) or $x^2 + y^2 + z^2 = a^2$ (rectangular or Cartesian coordinates).

[45] Please don't write to me if you are a devotee of C++, lisp, Etruscan or whatever. It's OK, you can get help. :-)

Although originally designed for writing compilers, there are two formidable free tools available on Linux to assist you in writing very fast pattern recognisers. They are called lex and yacc, [5]. They are enough to strike terror into any computer science student but for knocking up very fast pattern recognisers, they are hard to beat although debugging them sometimes leaves you with an overwhelming desire to bite the furniture.

Pattern recognition in compiler terms, (and this is the essence of compilers), is traditionally split up into two phases:-

- Lexical analysis. In this stage essential components of the patterns you are looking for are assembled from the raw characters. For example, if I was reading a book, I read the characters and assemble words. Words are tokens of the patterns I look for in a book. This process is unconscious to an adult but when a child is learning to read, they are naturally assimilating the appearance of characters by spelling letters out loud and hence, their contribution to words. The lexical analyser on Linux is called *lex*.

- Syntactic analysis. This stage describes the allowable ways in which tokens extracted from the lexical analysis stage may be combined. The syntactic analyser on Linux is called *yacc*.

For Windows users, all is not lost. Both lex and yacc have been ported to Windows machines in distributions like Cygwin[46] or DJGPP[47]. For the record, both are excellent, however if you can't be bothered, note that both lex and yacc generate C files as their *output*. This means you can simply take them over to a Windows environment and compile them as a command-line (Win32 console application) as easy as pie. Again I've had extensive experience of this[48], and it's no problem at all although you need to keep fairly close to the standard definition for C[49], although you would be mad to stray from it given the amount of money that portability saves you, but I digress.

Consider a very simple example. English sentence syntax in it's simplest form is *Subject Verb Object*, for example "Man likes dishwasher". In lexical analysis, the Subject token "Man" is assembled from the characters "M",

---

[46] http://www.cygwin.com/
[47] http://www.delorie.com/djgpp/
[48] http://www.saferc.com/
[49] ISO 9899:1990/9

"a" and "n" and so on. In syntactic analysis, the order of these tokens is checked against the grammar definition which in this case would be "Subject Verb Object" and if a match is found, the combination is passed as legal[50].

As a minor diversion, although exceedingly satisfactory for junk mail, syntactic analysis for natural (i.e. spoken languages) has proved a real challenge. In lex and yacc-able languages it's no problem by definition. In fact we generally try and design programming languages so that they are yacc-able to make it easier to write and maintain compilers. So languages like C are yacc-able. Sometimes we get a bit carried away with rampant feature-itis and the languages are not yacc-able and we have to use other syntactic analysis techniques such as recursive descent parsing as is the case with C++ and Fortran 77[51].

In yacc-able languages, there is a well-defined split between the lexical analysis stage and the syntactic analysis stage. In natural languages, this is simply not the case with analysis ebbing and flowing between the two stages until and if comprehension emerges. This is mostly unconscious in humans but consider for a moment the English phrase, "Fruit flies like a banana".

(Hello, are you still there ?)

This is parscable in at least three ways leading to three different semantic outcomes, (just pause in turn after the first, second and third words). Fortunately with junk mail we can define yacc-able patterns of great discriminating power which lead to parsers which do something a bit different than Bayesian analysers.

Switching back to the topic of junk mail and in particular 419s, it will immediately strike the reader studying examples like Figures 3.13 (p. 54) and 3.14 (p. 55), that they follow a traditional pattern which contains some or indeed all of the following themes:-

---

[50]I am deliberately glossing over another stage here, that of semantic analysis. A sentence which is lexically and syntactically correct may still be absurd semantically, for example, "Dishwasher bites man".

[51]I once wrote one for Fortran 77 called QA Fortran. It finished up containing over 100,000 lines of C. Life's too short to write one for C++, especially in it's latest 1300+ page standard incarnation. Yup, thats 1,3,0,0 - thirteen hundred, one thousand three hundred pages. This standard is the first in history which can measurably deflect light in it's gravitational field.

- DA_HELLO. Some form of greeting which other people never use.

- DA_INTRO. A feeble excuse for why they are contacting you.

- DA_GREATEST. A mixture of titles to impress you - the Reverend General Professor Chief Toejob or something.

- DA_SYMPATHY. Something to make you feel sorry for the halfwit sending this.

- DA_SOB_STORY. A tale of woe involving everybody in the family being killed by giant disgruntled lobsters or similar.

- DA_STING. The lure of riches untold.

- DA_PROMISE. Some kind of wish to do good with the untold riches.

- DA_BIG_SIGNOFF. End it with Best wishes unto God or other religious entity, which is a bit rich coming from a thief.

Other optional bits can appear like DA_HIDEY_HOLE (where they have secreted the riches). If we can find ways of characterising these and the order in which they appear then recognising 419s becomes trivial. It is of course perfectly possible to crank up a Bayesian filter to do this but generally these capture only the vocabulary and we are trying to find a quick way of identifying ordering as well since this too conveys important semantic information.

To write recognisers using lex and yacc, we need five components.

- A file describing how the tokens of the language are assembled from the letters. In this case, I will call it 419.l. This will be the input to lex.

- A file describing how the tokens themselves may be combined to form legal combinations which together capture the essence of a 419. In this case, I will call the file yacc419.y. This will be the input to yacc.

- A driver program to drive the generated lexical and syntactic analysers, main_419.c

- A recipe for building the executable file. I describe this using the VERY important *make* program of Linux.

- An input file or two to test it with.

We start with the 419.l file which follows. Note the regular expressions used to characterise the various concepts. In the case of DA_HELLO, I am using the simple appearance of the words "hello", "greeting" (optionally followed by an 's') or "compliments". It is important to note that these are not quite the same format as regular expressions in Perl[52]. However, they are extremely powerful going way beyond the very simple characterisation shown here as can be seen by consulting [5], for example.

```
#include <stdio.h>
#include "y.tab.h"
/*
 */
%}
num                [0-9]
%%
"hello"|"greeting"s?|"compliments"      {return(DA_HELLO);}
"i am"|"allow me to"|"introduce myself" {return(DA_INTRO);}
"rev"|"dr."|"chief"|"barrister"|"general" {return(DA_GREATEST);}
"widow"                                 {return(DA_SYMPATHY);}
"killed"|"crash"|"died"|"cancer"|"bitten off" {return(DA_SOB_STORY);}
"rebel"s?                               {return(DA_BADDIES);}
{num}+.*"million"                       {return(DA_STING);}
"bank".*"account"|"trouser leg"         {return(DA_HIDEYHOLE);}
"invest"                                {return(DA_PROMISE);}
"Christ"|"God"                          {return(DA_BIG_SIGNOFF);}


.                                       {;}
\n                                      {;}
%%
/******************************************************************/
/* A couple of utilities you need.                             */
int
yywrap( void )
{
     return    1;
}
/******************************************************************/
void
yyerror( char *s )
{
```

----
[52]One of the few things that irritates me in Linux.

```
/*
 * Do nothing.  Let it exit from the main() function if there is a
 * syntax error i.e. it is NOT a 419.
 */
}
/********************************************************************/
```

In the next file, yacc419.y, we define the grammar or the order in which the tokens can be combined in order to identify a 419 in the wild. This defines the names of the high-level tokens and then gives the order. For example a 419 starts with a hello of some kind, represented by the rule da_hello. This rule is defined as being either a DA_HELLO followed by a DA_INTRO or a DA_HELLO followed by a DA_INTRO followed by a DA_GREATEST. No other combination matches.

```
%token DA_BADDIES
%token DA_BIG_SIGNOFF
%token DA_INTRO
%token DA_GREATEST
%token DA_HELLO
%token DA_HIDEYHOLE
%token DA_PROMISE
%token DA_SOB_STORY
%token DA_SYMPATHY
%token DA_STING

%%

da_419   : da_hello da_windup da_tease da_end
     ;

da_hello  : DA_HELLO DA_INTRO
     | DA_HELLO DA_INTRO DA_GREATEST
     ;

da_windup : DA_SOB_STORY
     | DA_SYMPATHY DA_SOB_STORY
     | DA_SOB_STORY DA_BADDIES
     | DA_SYMPATHY DA_SOB_STORY DA_BADDIES
     ;
```

```
da_tease   : DA_STING
      | DA_STING DA_HIDEYHOLE
      ;

da_end     : DA_BIG_SIGNOFF
      | DA_PROMISE DA_BIG_SIGNOFF
      ;

%%
```

The driver, main_419.c follows. This just forms a harness for the lexical and syntactic analysis phases above. The variable lex_or_yacc allows me to do the lexical analysis phase alone or both by calling yyparse (which itself calls yylex internally).

```
#include <stdio.h>
#include <stdlib.h>

#include "y.tab.h"

extern    int       yylineno;
extern    char      yytext[];
extern    int       yydebug = 0;
extern    int       lex_or_yacc = 0;
static    int       token;
static    int       parse_result;

void output(char * msg) {printf("%s\n",msg);}

int
main(int  argc, char ** argv)
{
     if ( lex_or_yacc )
     {
          while(token = yylex())
               {printf("Token %d\n",token);}
     }
     else
     {
          if ((parse_result = yyparse()) == 0)
               {printf("419 !\n");}
```

```
        else {printf("Not a 419\n");}
    }

    exit(EXIT_SUCCESS);
}
```

In a Linux makefile[53], the meat of it might look like this. Typing *make* then makes the resulting executable main419.

```
main419: main419.o yacc419.o 419.o
        gcc -o main419 main419.o yacc419.o 419.o

419.o:    419.l
        lex -t 419.l > 419.c
        gcc -c 419.c

yacc419.o:    yacc419.y
        yacc -d yacc419.y
        yacc yacc419.y
        mv y.tab.c yacc419.c
        gcc -c yacc419.c
```

When we let it loose on a typical 419 this time from the good Reverend Toejob,

```
compliments of de day !:
i am rev toejob.  my left leg was bitten off by
a cheetah belonging to da rebels but i have
hid 10 million dollars in da empty trouser leg.
I wish to share it wid you.

Yours in Christ.
Milton Toejob.
```

we get

```
% main419 < msg1.txt
419 !
```

---

[53] John Graham-Cumming has written a good book on make available at http://www.lulu.com/product/paperback/gnu-make-unleashed/2937580.

This is a very simple example and could relatively easily be represented in a Perl analyser by using regular expressions, however eye-watering they may turn out to be. The point is however, that this technology is capable of producing far more sophisticated pattern recognisers and they run blisteringly fast. In content filtering, combining different views of the content and in particular the semantic connections as described here and next in Chance Discovery engines hold the key to reaching and exceeding Six Sigma as I will demonstrate later.

6.10.4 Chance Discovery and whispers

Chance Discovery is an exciting development in extracting semantic meaning from unstructured documents. So far we have seen the enormous impact of Bayesian filtering methods on reducing the spam problem. In their simplest terms, these are just vocabulary based. In other words from word frequencies in existing ham and spam, they use Bayes' theorem to predict whether a new message is ham or spam based on the comparative word frequencies.

However, word frequencies on their own give a pretty one-dimensional view of a document and only dimly hint at the semantics of that document. As more of a load is placed on the content of e-mails as a method of categorisation, so we need to explore richer semantic patterns. The well-known filter CRM114[54] provides facilities in this direction including Markovian models but here I will discuss Chance Discovery. I haven't (yet) found the need to use the power of Chance Discovery but it will give some insights into what we can yet exploit on the principle that it never does any harm to have extra techniques waiting in reserve.

The original work in Chance Discovery was carried out by [38], [37]. Note that in this sense, it is the discovery *of* chance not the discovery *by* chance which is the desired goal. In other words *chance* is used in the sense of an opportunity. However, the way it teases out phrases and in particular phrase correlations across sentences is particularly appealing when it comes to detecting junk. The algorithm works as follows.

Preparation

In order, the following semantic actions are performed.

---

[54]http://crm114.sourceforge.net/

Word selection and stemming It is first of all assumed that a document is comprised of N sentences, $s_0, s_1, ..., s_{N-1}$. Each sentence consists of a number of words, terminated in some way, such as full stop ".". Prior to any processing, a list of non-significant words of little meaning (the *stopword* list) is prepared in the manner described by [38] and might include words such as "and" or "the". In conventional Chance Discovery, words are also optionally pre-processed with a stemming function M(). A stemming function simply reduces related words, for example *run, running* and *runs*, to a common stem in the manner described by [44]. I wrote a fast version of one of these for English in C which is freely downloadable[55]. For junk mail identification however, *it is best if they are not stemmed.*

Phrase selection *Phrases* are defined to be sequences of words separated by *stopwords*. Finally, if a phrase consists of several words, each combination of words which is a true subset of the original phrase is optionally included as a phrase candidate. So if a phrase contains the words (abc), then *generated phrases* (ab) and (bc) could also be added.

Significant term extraction The document is then analysed and a list of words and phrases in decreasing order of occurrence is produced. There are a number of ways in which such ordering can be carried out.

- Generated phrases in the document are culled in favour of the phrase they are generated from if they occur at the same frequency again in the manner described in [38]
- The phrases could be sorted strictly inversely to the number of words they contain
- Some combination of phrase frequency and their length can be used

The net result of this is that the M most frequently occurring words or phrases are retained by whatever measure is used. These are known as *terms*, $t_0, t_1, ..., t_{M-1}$. All other terms are discarded.

The original work of [38] then extracted concepts it defined as *foundations, columns* and *roofs* (keyword extractions) from a document and graphs these based essentially on co-occurrence, i.e. when terms occur together in different locations in the document and how they are linked together. For computational efficiency and to give fuzzy phrase recognition, I

---

[55] http://www.leshatton.org/wordstem_2006.html

modified this approach in [21] to treat it in a rather different way with co-occurrence being generalised to co-proximity and then treated formally as cross-correlation. Co-proximity is defined as belonging to the same sentence or a nearby sentence.

Application

As an example, consider the following text extracted (after parsing out various creative HTML tags) from an obfuscated spam. In this case, an online casino offer has been tastefully decorated by extracts from "Sense and sensibility" by Jane Austen, a use for which the original author would probably not have foreseen.

```
CAS1NO ONL1NE 1000. EURO start bonus, over 250 games,
start winning now. Get your EURO start bonus now.
Visit us at http://dwarfurl.com/b2d88f.
Download the free playing software Register as guest
or player and get your 1000 EURO start bonus right now.
Three  thousand  pounds!  he  could  spare  so
considerable  a  sum  with little of her intention to
her mother-in-law, arrived with her  child and their
attendants. No one could dispute her right to come;
the house was her husbands from the moment of his fathers
decease;  but invited and received into his house the
family of his nephew Mr. Henry Dashwood, the legal
inheritor daughters. The son, a  steady respectable young
man,  was amply provided for  by the fortune of  his
succession to the Norland estate was not so  really
important as to his sisters; for their  fortune,
independent of what might arise to them  from
their fathers inheriting that property, could  be but
small. Their mother had nothing,  and their father only
seven  thousand pounds in his own disposal; The family
of Dashwood had long been settled in Sussex. Their
...
```

If you pass this into the algorithm described above and display the links graphically using the excellent graphviz[56], the diagram shown in Figure 6.6 (p. 232) results. Junk mailers pack e-mails with this kind of unrelated content to attempt to de-rail Bayesian statistical analysis. In fact it has the

---

[56]http://www.graphviz.org/

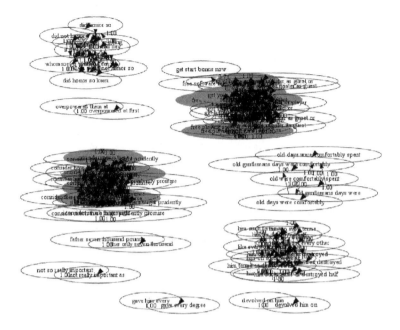

Figure 6.6: A spam message hidden in obfuscated text when fed to a chance discovery algorithm can automatically be split into semantically related clusters. The Casino semantics is the cluster in the top right. (My apologies for the congestion, I haven't yet figured out how to make graphviz de-congest itself, if indeed this is possible.)

opposite effect and it also helps other kinds of semantic separation filtering as we have seen here.

Now we have discussed a number of ways of looking at an e-mail, I will introduce an important concept from engineering.

6.11 Six sigma filtering

Six sigma is a manufacturing concept. In this context, sigma means standard deviation and the notion of six sigma is derived from the normal distribution curve of classical statistics[57]. A Motorola trademark, it was

---

[57]http://en.wikipedia.org/wiki/Six_Sigma

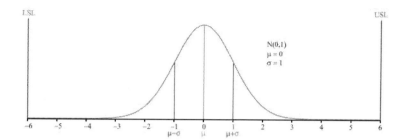

Figure 6.7: A normal distribution curve annotated with integral multiples of the standard deviation which appears in http://en.wikipedia.org/wiki/Six_Sigma. LSL and USL are the lower and upper specification limits and correspond to -/+ six sigma.

originally developed by them in the early 1980s to describe the number of faults in a manufacturing process and is based on the pioneering 1931 work [50] of the father of modern statistical process control, Walter A. Shewhart. Six sigma refers to the area under a normal distribution curve which is more than six standard deviations away from the mean, Figure 6.7 on p. 233.

As you can see, this area is very, very small. In fact it contributes only 0.0000002% of the whole area). In parts per million, this corresponds to .002 per million. If this was applied to manufacturinig, it would describe a process which produces no more than .002 failures per million items manufactured. However six sigma manufacturing quality is always quoted as 3.4 failures per million, (0.00034%). The reason for this discrepancy is that it is observed that processes which meet six sigma in the short term, drift as time passes by about one and half sigma, reducing the distance to the specification limits to four and half sigma. So in manufacturing, six sigma is really taken as four and a half sigma, which is where the 3.4 failures per million comes from. If we build memory chips to a "six sigma standard", then at most 3.4 will fail in a million on average. It is considered the state of the art in manufacturing[58].

---

[58]If you consider this a bit of a distortion of statistical language, I completely agree with you. Six sigma is six sigma is six sigma. Not four and a half. It is a mathematical measurement. If it was four and a half sigma, then in mathematics, this means four and half sigma, not six. Consider it a symptom of 21st century arithmetic as reinvented by accountants and bankers - Bistromath as the late, great Douglas Adams used to call it.

The concept passes over easily to a junk mail filtering process where it can simply be taken to mean no more than 3.4 mistakes (FP + FN) per million messages. This is entirely appropriate for a junk mail filtering process because they of course drift due to the ever-changing nature of junk mail. On my own mail server at average volumes over the year, this would correspond to no more than 3 per week. This seems a reasonable level at which to aim. We would not like to see more than this really as each such message carries with it a risk of financial loss, system hi-jacking or theft of personal details. Ideally we would like to see less[59] but, as we will now see, it turns out that a single filtering system is not enough to achieve this, by about a factor of 300.

In other words, *we need at least six sigma levels of filtering accuracy at current junk mail volumes*[60]. How are we to achieve this ?

Figure 6.8 (p. 235) shows a typical multi-layered filtering system comprising both serial filters (back to back) and filters acting in parallel. There is a limit to the quality of a single filter in junk mail content filtering and for the best Bayesian methods, (see p. (195)), this appears to be around the human level of accuracy, 99.9%, [18], [4].

Whilst this is exceptionally good, it is under threat by the sheer volume of junk. On my mail server, 99.9% accuracy (a failure probability of 0.001) means 1,000 false positives and negatives a week, shared amongst perhaps 20 e-mail addresses, (although much of the abuse is aimed at my e-mail address[61]). Since false positives (labelling something genuine as junk with the attendant possibility of losing it) are anathema in mail filtering, this means that filtering bias should be arranged so that these are all false negatives (not labelling something as junk when it is junk), each e-mail address on my server will receive around 7 junk mails a day which is close to what I receive on my university system.

---

[59] Actually six and a half sigma would be nice because including the drift, that gives a target of around 0.4 per million.

[60] Well I do. To see what you need to achieve, just set what you would think would be a reasonable level - say 5 per week and then divide by the total volume of mail aimed at you during the week. If this is only 1,000, then you only need around four sigma (or two and half sigma including the drift) and a single Bayesian filter can give you this. If you get 10,000, you need another sigma or so and a single Bayesian filter can't give you this.

[61] I'm not bitter.

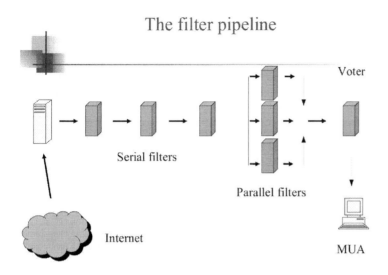

Figure 6.8: Illustrating how filters can be glued together in a receiving MTA to filter junk mail. Both serial and parallel combinations are possible and indeed necessary as we will see.

This perhaps should not exercise us particularly but perhaps half of these will be scams and people might get fooled accordingly so it is still too much and we can do much better as we will now see by applying a little filter theory.

To achieve higher levels of detection, we have to combine filters in interesting ways as shown in Figure 6.8 (p. 235). These ideas come essentially from redundant designs common in safety-critical systems, [20].

First, to make things simple, I will assume that every filter is independent and has the same probabilities of failure p_{FP} and p_{FN} for false positive and false negative respectively. The argument can easily be generalised to other probabilities and loss of independence, but it proves interesting to consider FP and FN separately. What we are trying to do of course is to reduce (FP+FN) to negligible levels.

6.11.1 Filters in series

If I combine q such filters in series as in the first part of Figure 6.8 (p. 235), the probability of any FN passing through unscathed is given by considering that the message must travel all the way through without triggering a detection. The probability that the chain fails to detect this is therefore

$$F_{FN}^{series} = p_{FN}^q \tag{6.16}$$

However, if this is a FP failure, then we are looking at the probability that the message is junked incorrectly. It therefore must not survive the chain. This it does by failing at the first or the second and all way up to the qth filter. The probability of this happening is therefore 1 - the probability of it surviving the whole chain which is

$$F_{FP}^{series} = 1 - (1 - p_{FP})^q \tag{6.17}$$

To simplify things a bit, let's assume our filters are pretty good in which case $p_{FP}, p_{FN} \ll 1$. In this case, the probability that the system will fail (FP or FN) is

$$F^{series} \equiv F_{FN}^{series} + F_{FP}^{series} = p_{FN}^q + 1 - (1 - p_{FP})^q \simeq p_{FN}^q + q p_{FP} \tag{6.18}$$

This is an interesting result. If $p_{FP} \sim p_{FN}$, then for q = 1, i.e a single filter, false positives and false negatives are treated symmetrically. However as q increases under the same conditions, we are led to

$$p_{FN}^q + q p_{FP} \simeq q p_{FP} \tag{6.19}$$

In other words the failure of a set of filters in series *is dominated by FP failures*. This embodies the problem for serial filters. As q increases for fixed p_{FP}, F^{series} increases, so the chance of false positive failures when glueing together filters in series just gets higher as the number of filters increases. In contrast the contribution of false negative failure *decreases* as the number of filters increases.

The *only* case for which this is not true is when $p_{FP}, p_{FN} = 0$, in other words the filter is perfect in how it treats FP and FN. Then the system as a whole is perfect whatever the value of q.

The implication is that if you wish to avoid any false positives, the only filters which you can string together in series are the perfect ones. Furthermore, a serial system is much more sensitive to false positive failure than to false negative failure.

Two practical classes of "perfect" filter arise.

- Filters which give a warning to the sending MTA in the event of rejection. An example of this is a filter which checks RBL (Real-time Black Lists). It is exceedingly rare on my server for a legitimate sending MTA to get onto a RBL[62]. However, if they have a temporary relapse, a responsible receiving MTA will issue a warning that they are listed with a web-site address giving details of how to de-list. Although the filter is possibly failing a genuine e-mail however remote the possibility, to all intents and purposes we can consider this perfection because a genuine sender is being given the chance of re-sending and they are not left in the dark. Since the sender's address has not been spoofed by definition, the feedback reaches the intended original sender.

- Filters for patterns which are 100% guarantees of spam. There are a number of examples of these. A perfect example is those ridiculous dictionary attacks with exotic users like FruitFliesLikeBananaCrumble@oakcomp.co.uk. My server gets tens of thousands of these a day. They can be silently discarded as they couldn't possibly be the business address of a genuine user[63]. They are specifically designed to exploit mail servers which by default accept all messages to a domain name. The fact that they still occur in such quantities is mute testament to how many servers must still be so configured.

This has the implication that we do have to allow for a small amount of finger trouble with e-mail addresses, (see also the discussion on p. 96).

For both of these categories, we make the implicit assumption that $p_{FP} = p_{FN} = 0$. In the former because the administrator of the sending MTA has the opportunity to correct it and try again and in the latter, it forms part of the standard policy either to feed back nothing to a junk mailer or false information to screw up their own Bayesian systems.

Now we come to the majority of filtering methods. These are enormously effective but evade perfection by various degrees. This is not a limiting factor fortunately as there is a very considerable literature in computing

---

[62]One of the RBLs I trust that is.
[63]Or if they are, they are asking for their e-mail to be lost.

science, notably in the area of safety-critical systems design, where somewhat less than perfect sub-systems can be combined together in interesting ways to form systems which are much more reliable as we will hear more of shortly. The technique is called parallelism.

6.11.2 Filters in parallel

When filters operate in parallel as in the right hand part of Figure 6.8 (p. 235), we get very different behaviour to serially combined filters. In this case, we can use a voting system as indicated. *Every* filter configured in parallel gets a go at the incoming message and we go with whatever that majority decision might be. For an obvious junk message, they will very likely all agree. For less obvious ones, some may disagree or not be sure. The probability that the system fails is then given by all the ways that the majority might get it wrong. Let us simplify this by computing for odd values of q, so that there must be a majority[64].

Once again assuming separate probabilities for FP and FN and *assuming that individual filters fail independently*, we note immediately that unlike the serial deployment case, *the parallel system treats FP and FN failures the same way*. The system probability that a majority vote of q filters in parallel gets it wrong and fails is therefore

$$F_{FP}^{parallel} = \sum_{q/2+1}^{q} C_r^q p_{FP}^r (1 - p_{FP})^{q-r} \qquad (6.20)$$

and

$$F_{FN}^{parallel} = \sum_{q/2+1}^{q} C_r^q p_{FN}^r (1 - p_{FN})^{q-r} \qquad (6.21)$$

where C_r^q is the group combinatorial operator for choosing groups of r objects from a total of q.

---

[64] It is slightly more complicated than this as most Bayesian filters for example are not two-valued as in Yes or No. They are three-valued as in Yes, Unsure or No. This is not of itself harder to deal with, you just need a policy for deciding how Unsure should be counted. One way of doing this is to assign numerical values of 1, 0.5 and 0 to Yes, Unsure and No respectively and add up the filter results and decide to pass if it is more than a certain number. Another way is to treat Unsure as being in favour of acceptance not rejection to err on the side of caution.

The combined failure probability is therefore

$$F^{parallel} = F^{parallel}_{FN} + F^{parallel}_{FP} \tag{6.22}$$

giving

$$F^{parallel} = \sum_{q/2+1}^{q} C_r^q \{(p^r_{FN}(1 - p_{FN})^{q-r}) + (p^r_{FP}(1 - p_{FP})^{q-r})\} \tag{6.23}$$

Now we are in entirely different territory. Consider a simple example with $p_{FP} = p_{FN} = p$. For imperfect filters $p > 0$. However for fixed p as q, the number of filters employed in parallel increases, $F^{parallel}$ now *decreases*. For q = 3 the system will fail if any two channels fail or all three channels fail. There are three ways that two channels of three can fail (1,2), (1,3) or (2,3) so the probability of failure is therefore

$$F^{parallel} = 2(3(1 - p)p^2 + p^3) \tag{6.24}$$

However the failure probability of a single channel is 2p for symmetric FP/FN failures so using equation (6.24) we can construct the following table

Probability	1 ch. failure	3-way ch. failure
0.01	0.02	0.0006
0.001	0.002	0.000006
0.0001	0.0002	0.00000006

Assuming independence, our six sigma target (0.0000034) is therefore almost achieved by having a 3-way parallel system operating at 99.9% single channel accuracy which as we have seen can be achieved by Bayesian filters. As we will see, this is *very* close to the actual achieved performance as described on p. 253 over a several month period, strongly supporting the above analysis.

Returning briefly to the argument that Bayesian filters should appear earlier in the chain to see most spam, this is the reason why you shouldn't do this. If you want to hit six sigma, (and you have to given the current and expected volume of junk), then you would have to put a 3-way Bayesian filter in the path of the whole tidal wave. That might challenge even today's servers somewhat.

You don't need to. The point is that Bayesian filters appear to asymptote to around 99.9% whatever diet they are fed on, so if you want to achieve a six sigma system, this diet has to be pre-filtered by single-channel filters which are perfect in the sense described in the previous section before being directed into a parallel filtering system.

However, we are not quite finished. One of the assumptions made in getting to the result of equation (6.21) is that channels fail *independently*. Sadly they don't always. For example, unless we can differentiate the diet fed to our proposed individual filters, it is perfectly possible that they will fail on the same inputs, indeed you would expect it even if their internal mechanisms are slightly different. It turns out that we can indeed differentiate the diet fed to each and even allowing for some dependent failure between channels, it is still possible to get very significant improvements in parallel filtering. All we need to do is to combine filters which take rather different looks at each e-mail.

An example of a similar environment is that of dependent failure in computer programs written by different people to the same specification. This is not the place to raise this subject but have a look at the following references to get a feel for the expected degradation, [26], [20], [52], [53]. It's perhaps a factor of 10. In the junk mail filtering implementation described here, the degradation appears to be less, implying there is enough independence in what each cooperating filter takes from it's common junk mail diet that the six sigma target was still met, as will be seen later (with a little help from the voter). Note that supporting evidence for significant statistical difference between filters fed the same diet is also given by [11].

The voter

Referring back to Figure 6.8 (p. 235), the parallel filters do nothing other than annotate the mail and pass it on to the voter. Normally the voter in a parallel system does that and nothing else; it just votes and goes with the majority. In my implementation, the voter does some significant heavy lifting. The essential reason for this is that there are often additional clues which do not form part of the information registered by any of the parallel filters, (at present). As a result, my current voter runs to some 3,300 lines of Perl and is still actively growing as new lines of defence become available. It is based on the full MIME parsing Perl program shown in Appendix .1 on page p. 285.

This additional information proves to be important because on it's own the 3-way parallel system can't quite reach six sigma. The voter tips the balance by using this extra information. The voter therefore contains intelligence about the following:-

- Private IP blacklists. These are the tens of thousands of IP addresses which have attacked the mail server in the last three years. This is not enough to reject the mail in the sense of RBLs[65] but it is sufficient evidence to me that their administration is less than perfect even if they are legitimate. As a result, this contributes to tipping the scales when the parallel system fails to achieve a majority verdict.

- An extensive vocabulary of words to help it discriminate between spam and scams on the grounds that a spam is simply annoying and a scam is positively dangerous. The user can therefore do with a little extra help if it can be made available reliably. The 3-way parallel filter is very good at identifying junk. The voter simply decides on the basis of this what kind of junk it is.

- Geographic IP databases. A full IP to country map is included internally for the reasons described earlier. Country information adds real discriminating power and is used for both embedded link analysis as well as country paths.

- Attachment parsing. Common attachments are parsed and their vocabulary placed into the internal discriminator.

- Link visiting with both shallow and deep parsing. This is described on page 194.

Capture-recapture

I mention this in passing but when you have parallel systems testing the same input stream, you can use something known as capture-recapture to predict the total number of junk mails and therefore estimate what you might have miscategorised without even looking.

The concept of capture-recapture originated amongst marine biologists trying to count the number of fish in a lake[66]. In essence it works like this.

---

[65] Recall that if these are trusted they are assumed to be perfect and therefore appear as serial filters earlier on.

[66] http://en.wikipedia.org/wiki/Mark_and_recapture

You visit a lake and you capture a certain number of fish and tag them and put them back. On a second visit, you capture some more fish and *you measure how many are tagged*. An estimate of the total number of fish in the lake can then be obtained using the Lincoln-Petersen method and is given by

$$N_{estimated} = \frac{C_1 C_2}{T} \tag{6.25}$$

where

- $N_{estimated}$ is the estimate of the total number of fish.

- C_1 and C_2 are the total numbers of fish caught on the first and second visit respectively.

- T is the total number of tagged fish, i.e. those caught on both visits.

It's remarkably good. I have used it to estimate the total number of defects undiscovered during parallel code inspections, [22]. A variant of this method was used to predict the total number of tanks produced in World War II from the serial numbers of captured tanks[67]. These estimates turned out to be very much better than those made from intelligence reports[68] as can be seen from the following table:-

Month	Statistical estimate	Intelligence estimate	German records
June 1940	169	1000	122
June 1941	244	1550	271
August 1942	327	1550	342

This now of course gives you an important handle on how to predict the total number of junk messages without having to check all the ones that were missed. It proceeds as follows.

Let

- f_1 and f_2 be the number of junk messages identified by parallel filters 1 and 2 respectively.

- T be the total number of messages identified as junk by both.

---

[67] http://en.wikipedia.org/wiki/German_tank_problem

[68] A problem not unknown today. The military use of the word intelligence appears to be somewhat different to the conventional use.

Then the total number of junk messages is estimated by:-

$$J_{estimated} = \frac{f_1 f_2}{T} \tag{6.26}$$

Let's make a few observations before we stick some numbers in. If both filters are perfect and there are a total of J junk messages, then $f_1 = f_2 = J$, and $J_{estimated} = J'$ as we would hope.

For a slightly more realistic scenario, supposing that $f_1 = 9997$, $f_2 = 9990$ and T $= 9984$, then $J_{estimated} = 10,003$. In practice, it is relatively simple to keep track of the individual and combined scores of the filters and for numbers around 99.9%, it is remarkably accurate.

Inoculation

This idea is due to Bill Yerazunis, the author of the eponymous CRM114 filter, (and a lot of other interesting stuff[69]). It is very similar to parallel filtering but it works like this. Since junk comes out in waves, then if the first to receive it trains on it and then immediately passes on the training data to others *before it reaches them,* then if one early warning person achieves this for 100 others and this person changes randomly as various junk waves flow over us, then the overall effect is that on average, one person sees 100 times less junk.

Very briefly it works like this.

- User A receives a mis-filtered spam

- User A labels the spam and forwards it to B

- User B's mail agent verifies A as privileged and is therefore sending it spam for good reasons.

- User B's mail filter then learns the particulars of this new spam

- User B's filter is now inoculated against this spam before it received it from a non-privileged mail agent, (i.e. as conventional spam).

---

[69]http://www.merl.com/people/yerazunis/

Trials of this by Yerazunis demonstrated promising results[70]. It includes subtleties like spam minefields where lots of honeypots anticipate the wave of spam to give time for the inoculation to take effect. *However, even without honeypots, there is a very obvious way of slowing down the spam wave and that is if everybody uses greylisting as described on p. 139. Greylisting will typically add several minutes and often rather longer before an e-mail is redelivered and accepted. On it's own, it is a very good spam filter so that only pretty sophisticated ones using botnets might get through. Since grey-list retries will be fairly randomly distributed in time, this will also slow down the wave for long enough for the first recipient to analyse it, tag it and distribute it's characteristics to allow others to be protected.*

6.11.3 Throttling spammers - FFB

Whatever your personal feelings about junk mail, this title doesn't mean quite what you expect, so if you feel a little disappointed, just move on to the next chapter.

Throughout this book, I have counselled against providing junk mailers with any feedback at all unless you can be sophisticated enough to send them false information. There are a couple of potentially interesting exceptions to this, one of which Paul Graham calls FFB[71]. FFB is an acronym for *Filters Fight Back*. The idea is very simple. Many junk mails try to get you to click on an embedded link. However junk mailers expect very few people actually to do this out of the millions of junk mails they send and those they expect to fleece in some way. It is perfectly feasible to parse out these embedded links, have a digital sniff at them for toxicity, and if they emit the sour reek of junk, wander off to their web-site to fetch the contents and then bin them[72].

In other words all you are doing is what the junk mailer wants but in a quantity they are simply not prepared for. Furthermore, the content of their junk has no effect because your automatic retrieval does nothing with it. However, and this is what I mean by throttling, if the junk mailer sends out lots of e-mails to FFBs, the end result is that their customer's web-site is brought to it's knees; the biter bit.

---

[70] http://www.merl.com/papers/docs/TR2004-091.pdf
[71] http://www.paulgraham.com/ffb.html, http://www.paulgraham.com/ffbfaq.html
[72] Paul Graham even talks of having a robot visit all the pages.

As Paul Graham describes, this could impact the economics of junk mailing so disastrously for the junk mailer that it would put them out of business. Naturally, a little forensic care and attention would be necessary to masquerade your fetch so that it does not look like a robot but the idea of self-limiting the junk volume like this has a number of attractions although care would be taken to handle re-directs and to make sure you didn't hit a legitimate planted link instead, although in my experience, it is pretty obvious what the dirty links are.

It's very easy to do within a Perl program. Here is a fragment linkvisit.pl, which can quite easily be glued into the Perl harness in the Appendix.

```perl
#
#  You might have to get this with cpan -i LWP::UserAgent
#
use LWP::UserAgent;

my $ua = new LWP::UserAgent;
#
#  Give up after 120 seconds.
#
$ua->timeout(120);
#
#  This toxic link is mentioned in the next chapter.
#  Feel free to contact them.  I'm sure they are
#  desperate to hear from you.
#
my $url='http://www.skype-upgrade.com/';

my $request  = new HTTP::Request('GET', $url);
my $response = $ua->request($request);
my $content  = $response->content();
#
#  Here we print it but we could do anything with it
#  including just bin it, or if iturns out to be a
#  refresh, parsing it and accessing that and so on.
#
print $content;
```

7 The bottom line - how well can we do ?

This chapter first of all brings together the above discussions and presents them alongside data collected from my main mail server over the last few months using the mail architecture shown in Figure 6.8 (p. 235) and described above. For most of this time, a three-way parallel filter was used with an intelligent majority voter. The three-way parallel filter consists of

- SpamAssassin *not* using Bayesian filtering but with a very rich set of rules.

- Bayesian filtering based on single word content using bogofilter (p. 150).

- Various kinds of statistical filtering provided by CRM114, as described on p. 218 leading to a cumulative index.

Bogofilter and CRM114 are both trained using TOE (Train On Error) and training is still done on a weekly basis as the junk mail threat gradually evolves. Training is very simple using the scripts described in the appendix on p. 305 and takes little time.

This three-way system is fed into a voting engine which itself has considerable intelligence as described on p. 240. In particular, shallow and deep embedded link parsing to mine extra vocabulary from a suspect mail stops single embedded link spam from making any headway at all, whether it tries to do clever referrals or not.

This architecture is easily extensible to other filtering possibilities and a Chance Discovery engine as described on p. 229 is being trained in parallel[1]. In addition, an implementation of SpamProbe as described on p. 200 is

---

[1]This appears to provide a different view of e-mails to that provided by single word Bayesian engines or Markovian systems like CRM114 because it looks at phrase correlations across sentences in order to extract phrases of significant semantic content.

being trained on a differentiated set of spam. Both of these are showing early promise at being able to take the overall engine to maybe six and half sigma (including the drift, around 0.4 per million as described earlier), but it's early days and it takes a long time to build up statistical evidence of such an ambitious target. All that can be said so far is that it is beginning to look feasible.

7.1 A preliminary note on scoring

Historical data are not much use unless you know how they are arrived at, so here are a few notes on how the various categories of TN, TP, FN and FP were marked with reference to the annotations added to incoming e-mail as described on p. 89. Since serial filters as shown in Figure 6.8 (p. 235) are defined to be perfect, the process is as follows.

1. All dictionary attacks (idiotic addresses) are *defined* to be TP and are discarded rather than rejected to starve the perpetrators of feedback. Their content is never inspected. This gets rid of around half of the total mail volume.

   All servers masquerading as my server are *defined* to be TP. Their content is never inspected. This is now a significant amount of the total with considerable recent growth, (something like 2,000 a day at the time of writing).

   All incorrect HELO transactions are rejected with an instructive message rather than discarded to give innocent parties a chance to respond. They are *defined* to be TP but their content is randomly inspected although I have never thus far detected an FP here.

   Anything flagged by the RBL checks is rejected with a warning[2]. Their content is still randomly sampled on a weekly basis but I have detected no FPs here with this setup in the last year, (although the RBLs don't stop as much as they used to). Should FPs ever occur at levels which prejudice the six sigma target of the entire system, these can always be backed off to accept with warning rather than reject with warning. Reject with warning in a sense is not a FP unless the server is incorrectly listed as it gives the sender a detailed message as to what is wrong and how to respond.

---

[2]I have experimented with many in the last three years to check their FP rates but only use Spamhaus currently in this role. Other RBLs are not so reliable and are accepted for further processing.

After these, mails drop into the parallel voting system and their subject lines annotated according to their content as described on p. 89.

2. Based on these annotations and their junk categorisation of Table 4.2.3, p. 91, I use the MUAs customisable rules (in my case kmail) to split incoming mail into nominal TN (not junk) and TP (junk) folders which I will call TN' and TP' respectively.

3. Every day, the contents of TN' and TP' are dual inspected and errors recorded; participating individual filters in parallel retrained on Unsure and Error; and then FN and FP are incrementally populated from any errors in TN' and TP'. Everything remaining has been correctly classified by definition and TN' and TP' become TN and TP respectively.

4. Finally once a week, the Postfix mail server logs and the grey-listing logs are inspected for FPs before the complete binary classification table is computed from the processed data before display as shown in the next section.

To complete the picture, regular impact analysis (turning rules on and off in test streams as described on p. 259) is applied to see how the filter chains re-balance and how sensitive FP/FN detection is.

In the early days, this scoring system was very time consuming but as the filtering performance has crept up, it is now far less than the time I used to spend trying to find valid e-mails in and amongst the junk.

7.2 Historical performance examples

Now the scoring system is clear, there follow examples from various periods in 2010 up to just before this book went to press.

The full data for a typical week (22-28 Aug 2010) taken directly from the log follow.

	Junk mail	Good mail	
Flagged as junk	560,410	0	PPV 100.0%
Flagged as good	1	910	NPV 99.89%
	Sens. 99.9998%	Spec. 100.00%	

The corresponding (Spam-Hit, Ham-Strike) doublet of p. 85 is:-

Spam-Hit	Ham-Strike
0.999998	0.000000

Note that the figure of 560,410 includes all the low-grade spam immediately rejected or discarded as junk by my MTA because it is a crude dictionary attack or can't do the SMTP transaction properly, (the vast majority of it).

To give a temporal viewpoint, here is the equivalent data for 2 months later this time taken for the whole month from mid-October 2010.

	Junk mail	Good mail	
Flagged as junk	1236440	0	PPV 100.00%
Flagged as good	6	488	NPV 98.79%
	Sens. 99.9995%	Spec. 100.00%	

The corresponding (Spam-Hit, Ham-Strike) doublet of p. 85 is

Spam-Hit	Ham-Strike
0.999995	0.000000

Note that here, the weekly volume is running at around 54% of it's volume in August and around 35% of it's volume around May, so it's obvious that some big spammers have been taken offline or have been taking an extended leave[3].

7.3 The current situation

First of all, raw data for recent months are shown in the following table.

---

[3] Although you still get big spikes. The day before this section was completed, (Sunday 7th November 2010, an extraordinary 105,000 messages were received (and rejected) in a 7 hour period.

End Week	TP serial	TP parallel	TN	FP	FN
20101016	355773	77	111	0	3
20101023	313977	71	130	0	1
20101030	307270	77	128	0	1
20101106	259129	66	119	0	1
20101113	401784	72	119	0	2
20101120	219352	83	97	0	0
20101127	242911	82	129	0	0
20101204	332742	71	145	0	1
20101211	354248	87	102	0	7
20101218	207869	93	114	0	1
20101225	223511	63	88	0	0
20110101	93568	32	79	0	0
20110108	78126	69	78	0	2
20110115	160691	86	86	0	1
20110122	206719	72	116	0	0
20110129	228449	94	79	0	0
20110205	212631	81	82	0	1
20110212	175183	72	103	0	1
20110219	167022	67	111	0	1
20110226	185205	77	64	0	1
20110305	178142	83	97	0	1
20110312	166506	81	106	0	1
20110319	119902	98	85	0	0
20110326	93498	115	141	0	0

Table 7.3: Raw mail server data for the most recent period before completion of this book.

Here, the category *TP serial* is those messages which were automatically rejected or discarded by the MTA on the basis that they are *defined* to be TP using the principles defined in the previous section. The remaining categories were all identified by the parallel annotating system and populated using the principles defined earlier.

From these data, the standard binary classification data can then be calculated and these are shown in the following table as sensitivity, specificity, positive predictive value (PPV), negative predictive value (NPV) and the Spam-Hit (SH) and Ham-Strike (HS) parameters.

Total	Sens.	Spec.	PPV	NPV	SH	HS
355964	0.999992	1.000000	1.000000	0.973684	0.999992	0.000000
314179	0.999997	1.000000	1.000000	0.992366	0.999997	0.000000
307476	0.999997	1.000000	1.000000	0.992248	0.999997	0.000000
259315	0.999996	1.000000	1.000000	0.991667	0.999996	0.000000
401977	0.999995	1.000000	1.000000	0.983471	0.999995	0.000000
219532	1.000000	1.000000	1.000000	1.000000	1.000000	0.000000
243122	1.000000	1.000000	1.000000	1.000000	1.000000	0.000000
332959	0.999997	1.000000	1.000000	0.993151	0.999997	0.000000
354444	0.999980	1.000000	1.000000	0.935780	0.999980	0.000000
208077	0.999995	1.000000	1.000000	0.991304	0.999995	0.000000
223662	1.000000	1.000000	1.000000	1.000000	1.000000	0.000000
93679	1.000000	1.000000	1.000000	1.000000	1.000000	0.000000
78275	0.999974	1.000000	1.000000	0.975000	0.999974	0.000000
160864	0.999994	1.000000	1.000000	0.988506	0.999994	0.000000
206907	1.000000	1.000000	1.000000	1.000000	1.000000	0.000000
228622	1.000000	1.000000	1.000000	1.000000	1.000000	0.000000
212795	0.999995	1.000000	1.000000	0.987952	0.999995	0.000000
175359	0.999994	1.000000	1.000000	0.990385	0.999994	0.000000
167201	0.999994	1.000000	1.000000	0.991071	0.999994	0.000000
185347	0.999995	1.000000	1.000000	0.984615	0.999995	0.000000
178323	0.999994	1.000000	1.000000	0.989796	0.999994	0.000000
166694	0.999994	1.000000	1.000000	0.990654	0.999994	0.000000
120085	1.000000	1.000000	1.000000	1.000000	1.000000	0.000000
93754	1.000000	1.000000	1.000000	1.000000	1.000000	0.000000

Table 7.3: The matching processed binary classification mail server data for the most recent period before completion of this book.

The aggregate performance as a binary classification table over this entire period is shown next.

	Junk mail	Good mail	
Flagged as junk	5286077	0	PPV 100.00%
Flagged as good	26	2509	NPV 98.97%
	Sens. 99.999508%	Spec. 100.000000%	

The Spam-Hit and Ham-Strike ratios follow.

Spam-Hit	Ham-Strike
0.999995	0.000000

This aggregate period over several months is very close to six sigma performance with zero false positives, the original stated goal[4].

To make this a little more digestible, Figure 7.1 on p. 254 shows the total mail volume plotted against the FP+FN score, per week, for the most recent few weeks.

Finally, before leaving this section, the data for the last month (Feb-Mar 2011) before completing this section is shown below. Again, this is very close to six sigma performance and almost exactly that predicted by the analysis of parallel filtering systems described on p. 238.

It remains to be seen how the threats will develop in 2011 and whether the asymptotic performance can be improved a little more.

	Junk mail	Good mail	
Flagged as junk	743707	0	PPV 100.00%
Flagged as good	3	493	NPV 99.40%
	Sens. 99.999597%	Spec. 100.000000%	

Spam Hit	Ham Strike	
0.999996	0.000000	

---

[4]It is interesting to reflect on the power of standardisation here. The main reason for the shortfall from six sigma in the past few months is a single burst of 7 bounced messages in the week ending the 11th December 2010 in a format different from previously bounced messages. This inflates the false negative (FN) score just beyond six sigma, (the six sigma Spam-Hit rate corresponds to 0.9999966). If there was a standard for this, it would not have been breached. A private cryptographically signed volatile header was added in January 2011 to all outgoing e-mail. Provided bounced messages include headers, there will be no more occurrences of this as it can not be copied by junk mailers. If bouncing mailers do not include sufficient information, it may take a little more time and experience to assimilate the different ways mail servers present this information.

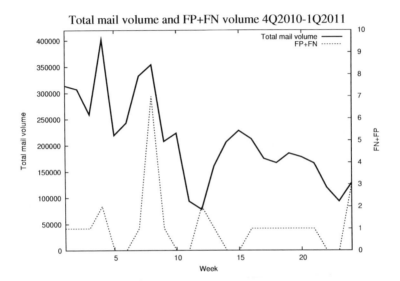

Figure 7.1: A graphical summary of the total mail volume per week experienced in the most recent few weeks prior to this book being published. The FP+FN score is also shown. The spike due to the burst of bounced messages described in the text can clearly be seen in the FP+FN graph as can the significant reduction in mail volume.

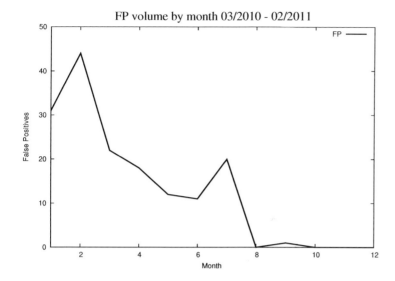

Figure 7.2: A graphical summary of the FP rate for each of the last 12 months until Feb 2011. The parallel architecture was initially implemented in month 8 of this picture and further refined in the last 3 months although this refinement represents discriminating power still held in reserve.

By the way, if you are a little wary about the absence of false positives in the above, the last one recorded was on 5th October 2010. Prior to that they were at around the level of 10-20 a month until August 2010. In mid-August 2010 I implemented the first two parallel channels and in September I added a third and the parallel architecture really began to bite rapidly, approaching the theoretical performance derived on p. 238. The 5th October 2010 false positive was caused by an error in the voter and since then, touch wood, nothing[5]. In the meantime, I have two other parallel channels trained up and hungry for spam as described in the previous chapter. In the four months since the last false positive, the voter has grown from 1318 lines of Perl to 3736 lines so there is hopefully plenty of intelligence in reserve.

The impact of parallel architectures on the FP rate is dramatic to say the least as can be seen by looking at Figure 7.2 on p. 255.

---

[5]Over the same period, note that the total spam volumes declined and then rose a little but this does not correlate with the disappearance of false positives.

7.3.1 Some general observations Mar 2010 - Feb 2011

It has been stated throughout this book that the threat landscape changes
with time. In this one year period, there is a very noticeable drop in total
quantity and a change in the nature of junk. By November 2010, junk levels
were at about 25% of their equivalents in March 2010 - a 75% drop in eight
months.

By the end of 2010, the situation changed yet again as several of the big
botnets appeared to be resting with a drop to the lowest levels I have seen
in three years. This lull lasted just two weeks and activity picked up again
with a blizzard of low-quality[6] phishing e-mails as can be seen below, (all
to my own e-mail address).

```
r Jan 9 04:30:18 -- security@paypal-security.org.uk
r Jan 9 04:32:49 -- billing@ronnebeck.com
r Jan 9 04:32:49 -- claude.sampol@sofresid.com
r Jan 9 04:34:55 -- security@paypal-security.org.uk
r Jan 9 04:35:39 -- security@paypal-security.org.uk
r Jan 9 04:44:49 -- security@paypal-security.org.uk
r Jan 9 05:24:24 -- security@paypal-security.org.uk
r Jan 9 05:40:19 -- security@paypal-security.org.uk
r Jan 9 05:56:02 -- security@paypal-security.org.uk
r Jan 9 05:59:27 -- security@paypal-security.org.uk
r Jan 9 06:20:49 -- security@paypal-security.org.uk
r Jan 9 06:46:13 -- security@paypal-security.org.uk
r Jan 9 06:50:21 -- security@paypal-security.org.uk
r Jan 9 07:05:51 -- security@paypal-security.org.uk

...

r Jan 9 10:58:04 -- security@paypal-security.org.uk
r Jan 9 11:30:21 -- security@paypal-security.org.uk
r Jan 9 11:32:12 -- security@paypal-security.org.uk
r Jan 9 11:43:55 -- security@paypal-security.org.uk
r Jan 9 11:44:51.-- security@paypal-security.org.uk
r Jan 9 12:19:17 -- security@paypal-security.org.uk
r Jan 9 12:40:19 -- security@paypal-security.org.uk
r Jan 9 12:54:50 -- security@paypal-security.org.uk
r Jan 9 12:55:26 -- security@paypal-security.org.uk
```

---

[6]In the sense that they were rejected in the serial filter stage of the pipeline of Figure
6.8 on p. 235 for general SMTP incompetence before they even got to the parallel
system.

```
r  Jan 9 13:02:55 -- gbvwyk@yahoo.com
r  Jan 9 13:32:24 -- security@paypal-security.org.uk
r  Jan 9 13:44:10 -- security@paypal-security.org.uk
r  Jan 9 13:50:20 -- security@paypal-security.org.uk
r  Jan 9 14:04:50 -- security@paypal-security.org.uk
r  Jan 9 14:19:43 -- security@paypal-security.org.uk
r  Jan 9 15:00:19 -- security@paypal-security.org.uk
r  Jan 9 15:06:17 -- security@paypal-security.org.uk
r  Jan 9 15:14:54 -- security@paypal-security.org.uk
r  Jan 9 15:19:32 -- security@paypal-security.org.uk
r  Jan 9 15:43:17 -- notify@hsbcbanking.co.uk
r  Jan 9 15:44:09 -- security@paypal-security.org.uk
r  Jan 9 15:53:19 -- notify@hsbcbanking.co.uk
r  Jan 9 16:05:22 -- noreplyaca@fibertel.com.ar
r  Jan 9 16:10:19 -- security@paypal-security.org.uk
r  Jan 9 16:15:31 -- notify@hsbcbanking.co.uk
r  Jan 9 16:24:57 -- security@paypal-security.org.uk
...
```

Notice all the paypal-security.org.uk rubbish. In the week, there were many hundreds of these, (basically every 5 minutes for most of the week). In one sense, it is pleasing to note these because they show that the perpetrator is highly inefficient by continually trying to deliver the same junk to the same address. In another sense, it is dismaying to realise that it is our bandwidth that they are wasting. Ultimately of course, it may turn out that the cost to the infrastructure of bandwidth wastage is far higher than the amount lost due to successful scamming attacks.

On Jan 10, a phishing attack purporting to come from @hsbcbanking.co.uk started (you can see the beginnings above) and over the week, about half of all the series filter rejected junk was scamming attacks. In comparison, just to show how diverse incoming junk can be even on the same mail server, here is a sample of series filter rejections (i.e. the same point in the filtering flow) from a different user on the same server in the same period. In this case, there are no phishing attacks and it was predominantly unwanted pharmaceutical products, a very different junk mail profile.

```
r  Jan 9 11:02:57 -- korucit@modus-center.com
r  Jan 9 11:03:36 -- gl_ljeffers@seovec.org
r  Jan 9 15:50:12 -- lyde@lmcmc.com
r  Jan 9 15:50:12 -- surgeon@oxford.net
```

```
r Jan 10 05:48:37 -- phungnatalyass@elad.co.il
r Jan 10 23:58:10 -- ably33@three.com.au
r Jan 10 23:58:30 -- bilrice@pacbel.net
r Jan 11 21:54:35 -- cixevyj@antal.org
r Jan 12 02:28:50 -- sophistcl4@kronoplus.com
r Jan 12 02:33:03 -- elliptictdh@kroeg.com
r Jan 12 03:20:56 -- disquietwg056@kronbergwall.com
r Jan 12 03:21:51 -- baydn9@kropas.com
r Jan 12 03:30:11 -- ganglyko5@kropacmedia.com
r Jan 12 03:30:41 -- winterierbt@kroon-bier.com
r Jan 12 03:54:11 -- deflectorh@krmcn.com
r Jan 12 03:55:01 -- hobblemr1@krogenyachts.com
r Jan 12 10:35:05 -- fontenot@kevlau.com
r Jan 12 16:22:45 -- picecus@chori.dol.ru
r Jan 13 02:32:40 -- sylovon@orion.extech.msk.su
r Jan 13 02:35:40 -- stepaniecolettabs@mygothicblog.com
r Jan 13 02:36:27 -- katherinamistieiz@homesweb.com
r Jan 13 02:36:36 -- bglindams@starnursery.com
r Jan 13 06:20:15 -- catafalques@kron.net
r Jan 13 06:21:10 -- exterminated6402@kromeplanet.com
r Jan 13 06:38:28 -- unsteadyml5@krothco.com
r Jan 13 06:39:26 -- healthye0@kroeck.com
r Jan 13 19:40:39 -- cinunyt@decta.ru
r Jan 13 23:17:18 -- ulide@aatc.org
...
```

To summarise then, the most recent period is characterised by considerably lower volumes of mail. It is also characterised by increased scamming, mostly of purported bank communications, attempts at self-HELO and also hacking attempts on the server itself. Moreover, there has been a significant increase in the percentage of junk emanating from botnets with little or no blacklisting and generally marking very low in SpamAssassin (in the range -1.0 to +1.0 with a comprehensive ruleset) indicating heavy use of SpamAssassin by these perpetrators.

Whilst this has partially neutralised SpamAssassin, and also sender verification techniques such as SPF and Domain Keys, the adaptive properties of the Bayesian components and the intelligence and deep parsing in the voter as well as the fundamental robustness of parallelism have self-adjusted and ensure that the system is still operating at or very close to the six sigma mark even through this significant shift in junk content and volume.

This essentially reflects the findings of Blosser and Josephsen, [4] in that the overall filtering system worked equally well for all users against the backdrop of a temporally changing junk landscape without specifically catering for different types of junk mail to each. This is very reassuring and continues to confirm the original insights of Paul Graham and others that adaptive techniques represent a formidable barrier to a junk mailer.

This success of course is absolutely predicated on revealing either no information or only misleading information to the junk mailer who attacks your system.

7.4 Impact testing: turning rules on and off

Impact testing is a standard engineering technique for complex systems. It is very simple and I wish programmers would do it more often in the systems they deliver to the public[7]. In essence, you pick a rule, turn it off and see what happens.

What this teaches you is how sensitive your system is. Complex systems such as that necessary for mail filtering are full of surprises. Turning off some rules can have little or no effect in that the multi-layered defence in depth behaviour of junk mail filtering simply means that an offending mail is picked up by a different rule somewhere else. This may be more expensive or cheaper, (as I found to my cost with my first experiences with RBL checking - see p. 117). The only way to find out reliably is to try it and see - not once but on a regular basis as the threat environment changes very quickly. The warn_if_reject feature of Postfix is very useful here. Using it places a warning in your log but allows the message through, (unless it gets blocked by another rule).

The whole point of this exercise is to discover how your system might respond to an ever-changing threat environment *before* genuine mail recipients are compromised.

7.4.1 Turning off self HELO

A good example of impact analysis can be seen here where the self HELO check has been turned off in Postfix. As you may recall, the self HELO

---

[7]http://www.leshatton.org/ for extensive ramblings on this subject.

check is present to reject those sending MTAs which try to pass themselves off as the receiving MTA. This is a guaranteed 100% test in that anybody doing this is bound to be doing it for nefarious purposes. It should therefore be a standard serial "perfect" filter in the sense defined as shown in Figure 6.8 (p. 235). Surprisingly, too many receiving MTAs do not implement it for some reason.

It is significant as can be seen from the table on p. 131. In the data there it was close to 1% (a big number when you receive a million a week). In last week's logs for comparison (two months later), it was 3%. Since the junk mail world is a highly adaptive system, this confirms that too many receiving MTAs are not implementing this check because it is obviously proving successful and the junk mailers are exploiting it more.

The listing below shows what happens in the logs when I turned the self HELO check off.

```
Sep 15 11:52:09 localhost postfix/smtpd[21034]:
 NOQUEUE: reject:
 RCPT from unknown[116.73.102.57]:
 554 5.7.1 <oakcomp.co.uk>:
 Helo command rejected: You cannot be SERIOUS.;
 from=<claraholder06@warpdriveonline.com>
 to=<brobtpa@oakcomp.co.uk>
 proto=SMTP helo=<oakcomp.co.uk>
Sep 15 11:54:02 localhost postfix/smtpd[21028]:
 NOQUEUE: reject:
 RCPT from unknown[117.197.164.227]:
 554 5.7.1 <oakcomp.co.uk>:
 Helo command rejected: You cannot be SERIOUS.;
 from=<idawhitlock37@ispnetinc.net>
 to=<bwo@oakcomp.co.uk>
 proto=SMTP helo=<oakcomp.co.uk>
Sep 15 11:55:30 localhost postfix/smtpd[21028]:
 NOQUEUE: reject:
 RCPT from unknown[144.122.163.102]:
 554 5.7.1 <oakcomp.co.uk>:
 Helo command rejected: You cannot be SERIOUS.;
 from=<lorettaspain15@myacc.net>
 to=<bttzp@oakcomp.co.uk>
 proto=SMTP helo=<oakcomp.co.uk>
```

```
+++++++ Self HELO check turned off at 11:56:00 +++++++

Sep 15 11:56:12 localhost postfix/smtpd[22475]:
NOQUEUE: discard:
RCPT from unknown[95.58.118.188]: <canier@oakcomp.co.uk>:
Recipient address CATCH-ALL DISCARD;
from=<estherthompson49@storm.ca>
to=<canier@oakcomp.co.uk> proto=SMTP helo=<oakcomp.co.uk>
Sep 15 11:57:07 localhost postfix/smtpd[22478]:
NOQUEUE: discard: RCPT from unknown[117.242.206.54]:
<carolinesotoobscene@oakcomp.co.uk>:
Recipient address CATCH-ALL DISCARD;
from=<deannapurcell98@hotmail.co.uk>
to=<carolinesotoobscene@oakcomp.co.uk> proto=SMTP
helo=<oakcomp.co.uk>
Sep 15 11:59:10 localhost postfix/smtpd[22474]:
NOQUEUE: discard: RCPT from unknown[194.186.222.242]:
<c233dc57@oakcomp.co.uk>: Recipient address CATCH-ALL DISCARD;
from=<ashleylackey45@verizon.net>
to=<c233dc57@oakcomp.co.uk> proto=SMTP helo=<oakcomp.co.uk>
```

As can be seen, another check (in this case a separate check which discards dictionary attacks on the domain oakcomp.co.uk) takes over the load. Even after several hours, nothing additional got through. This is simply because the self HELO junk mailers in this case are tending to do dictionary attacks. If a self HELO junk mailer attacked a defined address such as lesh@oakcomp.co.uk, then another part of the system would take over. However, this might be a more expensive check to apply, (for example content filtering, the last line of defence), so it is better to reinstate this as it is a guaranteed winner.

As a short postscript to this section, as of the time of writing, (February 2011), self HELO is becoming a major junk vector with around 10% of all junk trying to masquerade as a local user in the initial SMTP conversation. Here is an example taken from the mail logs on 8th February 2011 by mid morning when 935 out of a total of 10,000 have appeared already. These are always delivered in bursts of at most 20 presumably to get round outgoing restrictions applied by many ISPs.

```
Helo command rejected: Self-HELO (total: 935)
```

```
20    61.94.155.175
20    178.44.130.112
20    58.145.51.132
20    95.57.15.252
20    95.69.175.63
20    59.103.222.46
20    183.105.92.18
20    123.236.238.188
20    123.238.84.3
20    188.18.223.110
20    112.197.240.141
20    113.20.16.225
20    113.78.80.205
20    82.151.102.37
20    115.96.103.97
20    115.242.223.252
20    115.249.84.50
20    83.139.39.87
20    117.192.38.161
20    117.195.15.177
20    117.197.67.47
20    85.122.70.70
. . .
```

7.4.2 Switching self HELO from reject to discard

The rapidly growing rise in early 2011 of the self-helo masquerade[8] (up again to 20% just before publication of this book) prompted an impact test of switching the status of the response to such masquerades from reject to discard. As will be recalled from the discussion on p. 96, a discard spoofs the sender into believing the mail has been delivered. This has a significant effect on the mail load.

When you reject a message using my original response

```
88.208.247.158  REJECT  You cannot be SERIOUS (coki)
```

, you are of course informing the sending MTA that you are rejecting the message. The response of a spamming MTA is a blizzard of further attempts in the fond hope that one will get past your defences as follows.

---

[8]See p. 131

```
May 14 15:51:30 localhost postfix/smtpd[18149]: NOQUEUE: reject:
 RCPT from unknown[95.189.50.61]: 554 5.7.1 <88.208.247.158>:
 Helo command rejected: You cannot be SERIOUS (coki);
 from=<Avila@ictcsc.net> to=<ashfouad@oakcomp.co.uk>
 proto=SMTP helo=<88.208.247.158>
May 14 15:51:30 localhost postfix/smtpd[18149]: NOQUEUE: reject:
 RCPT from unknown[95.189.50.61]: 554 5.7.1 <88.208.247.158>:
 Helo command rejected: You cannot be SERIOUS (coki);
 from=<Avila@ictcsc.net> to=<ashidah@oakcomp.co.uk>
 proto=SMTP helo=<88.208.247.158>
May 14 15:51:30 localhost postfix/smtpd[18149]: NOQUEUE: reject:
 RCPT from unknown[95.189.50.61]: 554 5.7.1 <88.208.247.158>:
 Helo command rejected: You cannot be SERIOUS (coki);
 from=<Avila@ictcsc.net> to=<ateglia@oakcomp.co.uk>
 proto=SMTP helo=<88.208.247.158>
May 14 15:51:33 localhost postfix/smtpd[18149]: NOQUEUE: reject:
 RCPT from unknown[95.189.50.61]: 554 5.7.1 <88.208.247.158>:
 Helo command rejected: You cannot be SERIOUS (coki);
 from=<Avila@ictcsc.net> to=<attern@oakcomp.co.uk>
 proto=SMTPhelo=<88.208.247.158>
May 14 15:51:34 localhost postfix/smtpd[18149]: NOQUEUE: reject:
 RCPT from unknown[95.189.50.61]: 554 5.7.1 <88.208.247.158>:
 Helo command rejected: You cannot be SERIOUS (coki);
 from=<Avila@ictcsc.net> to=<asuzieq@oakcomp.co.uk>
 proto=SMTP helo=<88.208.247.158>

... almost ad infinitum.
```

Switching the appropriate response in Postfix (p. 131) from REJECT to DISCARD as in

```
88.208.247.158  DISCARD  Self-helo attempt on 88.208.247.158
```

Only the first response is sent as the sending MTA believes it has been delivered. At self-helo masquerade levels of 20%, this is well worth it and the result is a significant reduction in the junk load on the server. The simple discard draws the teeth of the junk mailer without giving them any worthwhile feedback. It is also very satisfying to know that you are spoofing a spoofer.

7.4.3 Reflections on viruses

It has been stated elsewhere that one of the important effects of six sigma levels of junk mail filtering is that viruses just about disappear, (none have made it to an end user in the last two years). It was clear quite early on that this would be the case. This was revealed by an impact experiment in September 2008 where the serial filters (see Figure 6.8 on p. 235) for automatic discard for stupid addresses, RBL checking AND greylisting were all turned off to see how the back end parallel content filter would cope, (note that the back end content filter at the time contained the principle virus checking via ClamAV but only a rather primitive 2-channel parallel filter).

The results are dramatic indeed. The table below shows the average monthly rate at which viruses reached the virus checking stage.

Discard, RBL check and greylist OFF	Discard, RBL check and greylist ON
299 per month	0.5 per month

Table 7.4.3: The dramatic effect on monthly virus rates reaching the parallel content filter when the serial filters for auto-discard of stupid addresses, RBL checking and greylisting are switched off compared with the same filters switched back on.

At the rate of 299 per month, the content filters at the time did not keep up and some reached end-user mailboxes. The rate of 0.5 per month after September 2008 has declined slowly since down to around 0.3, and none have reached an end user as the parallel content filter has adapted. To all intents and purposes, viruses have effectively disappeared, certainly for the moment.

7.4.4 Turning off HSBC string rejection

We saw earlier, (p. 143), that it is very unlikely for responsible banks to e-mail you and if they do, it will be from specific addresses. Junk mailers however know that many people don't know this and continue to spoof almost any plausible-looking "From:" address with examples such as accounts@hsbc-onlin-co.uk, account@barclays-marine.co.uk and for all I know, accounts@jolly-plausible-lloyds.co.uk and accounts@not-at-all-spoofed-halifax.co.uk. You can see some of the variations the junk mailers use in the log extract shortly.

You have several choices for treating such addresses. You can

- Pick them up globally using rules in the receiving MTA (Postfix in my case) as mentioned on p. 143 and reject them sending a message back so that if your bank really has been daft enough to e-mail you, they will realise and write to you instead[9]. You could argue I suppose that this is not a FP (false positive) but that might be stretching it a bit far.

- Allow them all and hope to pick them up later in your filter chain. Although this will not induce FPs, it might well induce FNs allowing through a particularly nasty form of scamming. This is actually a counter-example to the accepted wisdom that it is better to have a FN than a FP. In this case, it is reasonable to argue that allowing a FP and forcing a legitimate bank to contact you in more secure ways, is safer than allowing a potentially dangerous FN scamming attack. To repeat my caveat above, this assumes that the rejection is passed through correctly to the original sender of course using language which allows them to see what is the problem and actually do something about it.

- Allow the addresses which might be legitimately used and reject or even discard the rest. This is probably the best compromise but we need to know the implied load of allowing some through on the rest of the filter chain. We need to know that if we allow any baddies through, they will still get caught somewhere.

To measure the impact of allowing selective ones through, I switched off the global rejection of hsbc as shown in the data extracted from the receiving MTAs logs. (Note that this cannot lead to FPs on my system because the user I selected was myself and I don't bank with HSBC in the UK at the moment.) This data is that part of the mail flow which actually reached the content filtering. I have indicated my mail address lesh@oakcomp.co.uk as $< LH >$ to fit.

---

[9]I am making some fairly ambitious assumptions about the general competence of banks here. I have yet to receive a response from any bank when I have on occasions tried to do this.

******* Some hsbc blocked at this stage. *********

2010-05-20 19:32:08+01:00,<LH>,spam,notice@hsbccreditcard.com
2010-06-01 23:43:30+01:00,<LH>,spam,notice@hsbccreditcard.com
2010-06-04 16:35:17+01:00,<LH>,spam,notice@hsbccreditcard.com
2010-06-06 23:09:11+01:00,<LH>,spam,alert@hsbcmortgageservices.com
2010-07-07 12:01:34+01:00,<LH>,spam,notice@hsbcnet.com
2010-07-08 02:02:38+01:00,<LH>,spam,notice@hsbcnet.com
2010-07-16 12:13:52+01:00,<LH>,spam,notice@hsbcplc.co.uk
2010-07-16 12:59:29+01:00,<LH>,spam,notice@hsbcplc.co.uk
2010-07-16 18:36:56+01:00,<LH>,spam,hsbc@online.co.uk
2010-08-14 11:13:37+01:00,<LH>,spam,hsbc@ibanking.co.uk
2010-08-16 12:50:05+01:00,<LH>,spam,hsbc@onlinesecure.com
2010-08-30 10:28:45+01:00,<LH>,spam,Security@hsbc.co.uk
2010-08-31 12:03:34+01:00,<LH>,spam,customers@hsbc.co.uk
2010-08-31 15:47:57+01:00,<LH>,spam,customers@hsbc.co.uk
2010-09-01 12:15:57+01:00,<LH>,spam,security@hsbc.co.uk

******* All hsbc allowed through from now. *********

2010-09-03 13:29:10+01:00,<LH>,spam,onlinemail@hsbcbanking.co.uk
2010-09-06 20:40:47+01:00,<LH>,spam,alert@hsbc-online.co.uk
2010-09-09 04:50:31+01:00,<LH>,spam,alert@hsbc-online.co.uk
2010-09-10 08:21:17+01:00,<LH>,spam,hmail@hsbconlinebanking.co.uk
2010-09-11 23:19:11+01:00,<LH>,spam,hmail@hsbconlinebanking.co.uk
2010-09-12 03:46:12+01:00,<LH>,spam,hmail@hsbconlinebanking.co.uk
2010-09-14 09:14:36+01:00,<LH>,spam,security@hsbc.co.uk
2010-09-15 10:33:17+01:00,<LH>,spam,survey@hsbc.co.uk
2010-09-15 14:08:36+01:00,<LH>,spam,alert@hsbc-online.co.uk
2010-09-16 04:30:23+01:00,<LH>,spam,notify@hsbcbanking.co.uk

As can be seen, using the rules of p. 143, some hsbc spoofs always got into
the content filtering before meeting their doom because the imagination of
junk mailers knows no bounds. When I let any pattern with "hsbc" in it
through after 2010-09-03, the load on the content filtering increased slightly,
(from around 1-2 per week up to around 5 per week). This is scarcely going
to trouble the server and the result of this impact analysis is that rejecting
in the receiving MTA rather than later in the content filtering makes hardly
any difference, (in either case, none ever reached their intended victims).

Impact analysis is a vital part of any engineering process however you have to be careful not to disrupt or expose any normal users to these experiments. This is another example of the value of honeypots. With a good selection of mature honeypots, (i.e. attracting lots of junk), switching rules on and off *only* for honeypots allows you to gauge the ongoing effectiveness of your filter chain without affecting normal users.

Most if not all rules are switchable like this. For example, if you wanted to test the efficacy of RBL checking, this is a little more difficult to set up because it is usually based on IP address. However you could switch it to warn_if_reject in Postfix (p. 138), and pick up these warnings in the Postfix log and allow through only the honeypot ones. Provided your honeypots attract enough junk, this will reflect the mainstream flow of mail sufficiently well that your impact experiments are statistically valid.

If you are a really big ISP and concerned that however much care you take you could put a few normal users' noses out of joint with your experiments, then you should set up a separate mail server running the same filtering chain as your production servers to which you divert your honeypot traffic. You can then experiment away to your heart's content without disrupting anybody[10]. Furthermore any changes resulting from these experiments can be propagated into the production servers when they are settled down nicely.

As one final note, keep examples of the logs (or their processed forms) before and after the impact for future reference. Don't ever make assumptions about things - measurement is a wonderful thing.

---

[10]Be careful however about feeding back anything useful or even anything at all to a junk mailer. Receiving no feedback is a junk mailer's worst nightmare.

7 The bottom line - how well can we do ?

8 Where is this all going ?

Perhaps the most obvious statement I can make is that some junk mailers will get better. There's lots of evidence of this but fortunately not all of them will. The usual idiotic 419s and so on will continue whilst there continue to be people daft enough to fall for them but from a filtering point of view, they are trivial to deal with as we have seen as their payload is so obvious even if delivered from compromised legitimate machines on botnets. The real threat comes from the smaller number of smart junk mailers who are technically at least as proficient as the defenders. This has always been the real threat and it will remain so. It is why it is appropriate to consider junk mail as an arms race. It is an arms race between the most technically proficient on either side of the fence.

The junk mailers, however ingenious, will always have their Achilles heel, which is that they have to get you to do something you would not normally do - giving away personal details, money, being a party to a shady deal, taking up the offer of illusory work, buying products you don't need, laundering or whatever. This is their sting.

Unfortunately, the defenders also have an Achilles heel and that is the continual absorption of IP addresses which are otherwise clean into botnets. This undermines initiatives such as better verification of envelope details (SPF etc.) for the sending MTA and takes away one of the more important productive approaches that defensive measures can exploit. It seems to me from the degree of growth in botnets and the persistent attempts to close vulnerabilities whilst opening up others, that we have lost this battle. Windows has always been the most attacked and indeed attackable but the ingenuity of botmasters keeps pace with whatever technical blocks are introduced. It is probably fair to say that this particular battle is unwinnable for the goodies because if you really try to clamp down the hatches on any machine, (and you can make Windows as secure as any other[1]), then you also shut out genuine but more technically naive users.

---

[1] I am not a fan of Windows but it would be unfair to paint it as insecure. That is far too trivial. Microsoft needs to spread access to as many users as possible for their business model. When they are forced into over-reacting (as they

It is exactly the same as the FP (throw away good ones) v. FN (keep bad ones) battle of junk mail. You *have* to let through a few FNs to make sure you don't have any FPs, (not many but it's not zero)[2]. Similarly with machine security, you *have* to favour access for the naive user over keeping all hackers out. Ergo, you have botnets. You will *always* have botnets so you must learn to live with them. *This will inevitably result in placing a much greater load on the receiving MTAs for advanced content filtering.* The good news is that there is a lot of CPU power going spare in a modern mail server allowing some very heavy duty content filtering without troubling the mail handling load too much. Time will tell but *all engineering processes require feedback to exact improvement,* [42], [41] and [43]. Exactly the same is true for dark-side engineering processes, so it will always remain important to deprive the junk mailer of any useful feedback or, if you are sophisticated enough, to feed them false information, which is far more satisfying.

As an example of the need for vigilance, here is an example of a very recent attack which wriggled through almost all of my defences. These are the ones you learn from.

8.1 Case study of a sophisticated junk mail campaign

The first time this particular attack appeared, it almost reached the last line of my defences and was triggered only by a back-end voting system I use which amongst other things, uses a Bayesian filtering system based on e-mail country trails described earlier as well as some dubious properties of it's embedded link. Part of the e-mail is shown in Figure 8.1 (p. 275). The English is good and the embedded link is believable. Let's study this in a little more detail and it will allow me to introduce some tools for flushing out the details you need.

---

were with Vista which makes it very difficult for genuine users as well), they stray too far in the wrong direction. I do however despair at their seemingly never-ending and ultimately unsuccessful attempts to make Internet Explorer safe, http://www.scmagazineuk.com/microsoft-will-patch-critical-flaws-in-internet-explorer-and-windows-next-week/article/195682/?DCMP=EMC-SCUK_Newswire. The best advice seems to be, simply don't use it.

[2]Recall that this asymmetry is a direct result of equation (6.19) p. 236

8.1.1 Useful forensic tools

Largely as a result of the unsung heroes of the open source movement, there are a number of simple command-line tools available which can tease out all kinds of useful information about domains which allows us to categorise potential toxicity. Probably the most useful (at least, I use them all the time) are as follows:-

nslookup IP-address/domain-name This tool searches the DNS system to map between the IP address and the domain-name, depending on which one you enter. A simple example of it's use looks like:-

```
% nslookup pdf-adobe-upgrade.com     (which returns ...)
...
Non-authoritative answer:
Name:   pdf-adobe-upgrade.com
Address: 194.85.61.54
```

or

```
% nslookup 194.85.61.54              (which returns ...)
...
Non-authoritative answer:
54.61.85.194.in-addr.arpa     name = wf1.nic.ru.
```

The *non-authoritative* bit means that the information has been returned by a name server (actually a local one of mine), which has cached the request[3] but is very likely correct. You need to a do a little more digging to get the authoritative answers. Which brings me to the next tool.

dig IP-address type An all-purpose way of digging out all the different kinds of record associated with the Domain Name System, A records (the principle ones), NS records (Name server), MX records (Mail exchange), PTR (reverse names) and so on. If you want to do much of this, you will need to get into the DNS system rather more than I have space to do here. I can recommend Liu and Albitz [30].

---

[3]Caching is a standard technique in the DNS system and just means answers are stored locally for a little while to reduce the hit on the authoritative servers.

An example of a dig use for name servers is:-

```
% dig wf1.nic.ru NS    (which returns ...)
...
;; QUESTION SECTION:
;wf1.nic.ru.                            IN      NS

;; AUTHORITY SECTION:
nic.ru.                   10800   IN      SOA     \
ns.RIPN.net. noc-dns.nic.ru. \
            650128220 14400 3600 2592000 86400
...
```

It's not uncommon when looking at spamming machines to find name servers scattered all over the planet.

host IP-address/domain-name A nice quick way of looking at the DNS records.

```
% host pdf-adobe-upgrade.com    (which returns ...)

pdf-adobe-upgrade.com has address 194.85.61.54
```

or

```
% host 194.85.61.54   (which gives the following)

54.61.85.194.in-addr.arpa domain name pointer wf1.nic.ru.
```

Note that a correctly set up domain name with reverse DNS just goes round in a circle so that host(host(domain_name)) = domain_name.

whois IP-address/domain-name This is where it goes downhill a little. The whois system tells you all you need to know about the registration of a domain name and also where it's IP address lives. The problem is that the output is free-form and is quite difficult to parse as different parts of the whois system respond in different ways.

A whois query on the IP-address reveals where the IP-address lives. A whois query on the domain-name tells you who the domain is registered to, (in both cases, amongst a lot of other information such as who to report abuse to). I won't give any examples of this as you can easily do it yourself on either Windows (in a command line shell with the Run command) or Linux systems (any terminal window).

Each of these tools produces useful output but some of it is voluminous and a little hard to understand. To make things somewhat easier, the Perl script *domain_forensics.pl* of the Appendix (p. 303) extracts the information we need very quickly.

8.1.2 The attacks

Chronologically, the attacks appear as:-

13-Sep-2010

The e-mail, part of which is shown in Figure 8.1 on p. 275, appeared for the first time. For forensic completeness, let's have a closer look at the e-mail headers of the first appearance.

> **First note that although SpamAssassin picks up the nasty embedded link as a brand new one, (URIBL_RHS_DOB), the SPF passes from the sending server (74.63.47.117) allay it's fears. It also greylists correctly.**
>
> Return-Path: <bounce-2340694-457178-xxx=juniperhillblues.co.uk@mcsv114.net>
> X-Spam-Checker-Version: SpamAssassin 3.3.1 (2010-03-16) on localhost.oakcomp.com
> X-Spam-Level:
> X-Spam-Status: No, score=0.3 required=5.0
> tests=HTML_MESSAGE,MIME_QP_LONG_LINE,
> SPF_HELO_PASS,SPF_PASS,T_RP_MATCHES_RCVD,
> URIBL_RHS_DOB autolearn=disabled
> version=3.3.1
> X-Greylist: delayed 1804 seconds by postgrey-1.33 at localhost.oakcomp.com;
> Mon, 13 Sep 2010 04:59:32 BST
> Received: from mcsv114.net (mcsv114.net [74.63.47.117])
> by localhost.oakcomp.com (Postfix) with ESMTP id 24FE865965
> for <xxx@juniperhillblues.co.uk>; Mon, 13 Sep 2010 04:59:29
> +0100 (BST)
>
> **The remaining headers are plausible but toxic.**
>
> Received: by mcsv114.net (PowerMTA(TM) v3.5r15) id
> hhmgq80ik18r for
> <xxx@juniperhillblues.co.uk>; Sun, 12 Sep 2010 23:29:23 -0400
> (envelope-from
> <bounce-2340694-457178-
> xxx=juniperhillblues.co.uk@mcsv114.net>)
> Subject: Download VOIP Addons for Skype Free Talks
> From: "Skype Support" <service@skype-upgrade.com>
> Reply-To: "Skype Support" <service@skype-upgrade.com>
> To: <xxx@juniperhillblues.co.uk>
> Date: Sun, 12 Sep 2010 23:29:23 -0400

It is worth adding a small note on the generation of the URIBL_RHS_DOB message by SpamAssassin here. In essence this states that SpamAssassin analysed the www.skype-upgrade.com link and looked up the corresponding

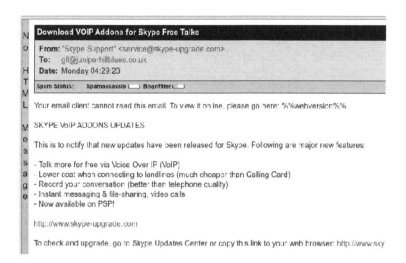

Figure 8.1: A sophisticated attack claiming to allow me to update my Skype details. It comes from a server in Russia hosting a number of equally dubious domains.

IP address. This is listed in the DOB (Day Old Bread) list maintained by www.support-intelligence.com. In English, this means that it has been registered in the last few days, a common technique used by the junk mailers shortly before a junk run. Of course you can tune SpamAssassin to elevate the importance of this message but as noted on the web site, this list is in beta and may induce FPs (false positives). In essence, as intended by the junk mailer, Spamassassin in it's non-Bayesian mode is rendered impotent by this attack.

In addition, the vocabulary led to an inconclusive test in the Bayesian filter channels so the IP country database tie-breaker built into the voting system of Figure 6.8 on p. 235 proved instrumental in identifying this particular threat, (as it happened, a false embedded postal address is given to enhance credibility and can therefore be parsed. This gave an inconsistency about where the site actually lives).

Let's check it out with the domain_forensics.pl script of p. 303. This gives an output of

```
% domain_forensics.pl -d skype-upgrade.com   (which returns ...)
```

```
Domain     :     skype-upgrade.com
IP         :     194.85.61.54
PTR        :     wf1.nic.ru.
Creation   :     11-sep-2010
Creation   :     2010.09.12
Country R  :     US
Country R  :     US
Country I  :     RU
```

You can see two things immediately. It's a brand new registration and the registrant claims to be in the US but the site is in Russia as can also be seen by the reverse DNS record, PTR. (The two creation dates which appear are because of the way they are displayed by the underlying whois used by the domain_forensics.pl script.

8.1.3 13-Sep-2010, a few hours later

A very similar message appears but this time offering an Adobe upgrade and with an embedded link www.pdf-adobe-upgrade.com. This time it sets off the newly-trained statistical filters and is tagged as junk before reaching the geographic IP address analysis, demonstrating why adaptive systems are so important.

```
Domain     :     pdf-adobe-upgrade.com
IP         :     194.85.61.54
PTR        :     wf1.nic.ru.
Creation   :     12-sep-2010
Creation   :     2010.09.13
Country R  :     US
Country R  :     US
Country I  :     RU
```

It's exactly the same as before and on the same IP address. In fact, a bit of *IP rummaging*[4] reveals that this IP address hosts around 1,000 domain names, some of them with very dubious names.

---

[4]http://www.robtex.com/ip is really excellent.

8.1.4 30-Sep-2010

A very similar message appears again offering an Adobe upgrade and with an embedded link www.adobe–upgrade.com. Again it sets off the statistical filters and is tagged as junk.

```
Domain     :    adobe--upgrade.com
IP         :    194.85.61.54
PTR        :    wf1.nic.ru.
Creation   :    29-sep-2010
Creation   :    2010.09.30
Country R  :    GB
Country R  :    GB
Country I  :    RU
```

Same IP address and brand new again but this time they claim to be in the UK. I live in the UK so let's have a look at the address.

```
Registrant ID:           ZA5XXWT-RU
Registrant Name:         John Terry
Registrant Organization: John Terry
Registrant Street1:      1729 Park Way
Registrant City:         London
Registrant Postal Code:  H38LA92
Registrant Country:      GB
Contact Phone:           +1 800 3892039
```

It's a bogus address - the postcode is illegal, the address does not exist and the contact phone number is an 800 number in the US. John Terry is (or was - I don't really care for football) the England football captain so at least they read the papers. In short, this wouldn't fool a child if you dig into it a little.

Spurred on by this, it turns out that not surprisingly, the quoted Registrant addresses for the previous effort in the USA are also bogus.

8.1.5 28-Oct-2010, and also a few hours later

Rolling on the clock a few weeks, a very similar message appears once again offering an Adobe upgrade and with an embedded link www.official-adobe-software.com.

Figure 8.2: A nasty little e-mail from the plundered yahoo.co.uk account of a friend. I have sanitised this to remove the e-mail list which the perpetrators also stole.

```
Domain    :      official-adobe-software.com
IP        :      109.70.27.4
PTR       :      uf1.nic.ru.
Creation  :      27-oct-2010
Creation  :      2010.10.28
Country R :      US
Country R :      US
```

Here we go again. Brand new and this time a different IP address. It's easy to see that in the next few hours there will be more of this nonsense from 109.70.27.4[5]. The adaptive Bayesian filters recognised it immediately.

So, nice try but no cigar. If the junk mailer fails at the first hurdle, he or she should not get a second chance as the power of parallel Bayesian filters steps in and learns much quicker than the junk mailer can adapt. By giving them as little feedback as possible, (the above doesn't tell the perpetrator any more than he or she already knows but it helps potential victims to identify this sort of sewage more easily), they cannot easily respond.

8.2 Sometimes it just isn't worth complaining

For a number of weeks now, I have been receiving e-mails from the plundered e-mail account of a friend and I am on a mailing list of about 20 people who also receive this. A little of the header and the body is shown as Figure 8.2 (p. 278).

In order to throw deeper analysis off, the link is just a HTML refresh which itself points to a new site, http://bedtime-heroes.com/. No prizes for what this lot are selling. The spammer has gone to considerable trouble

---

[5]IP rummaging reveals that this IP address is a particularly erudite one hosting a number of scams to come - adobe-acrobat-new-download.com as well as enduring classics such as blackonasianporn.com.

to hack this account and the prize is that the e-mail is coming from a trusted source as can be seen by inspecting the Spamassassin header line below.

```
X-Spam-Status: No, score=0.7 required=5.0
    tests=DKIM_SIGNED,DKIM_VALID,
 DKIM_VALID_AU,FREEMAIL_FROM,LOCAL_MSG_HAS_CC,
    MISSING_SUBJECT,RCVD_IN_DNSWL_NONE,
    T_TO_NO_BRKTS_FREEMAIL autolearn=disabled version=3.3.1
```

Fortunately, as this hero has been at it for several weeks, the statistical filters have been trained on it and this along with other analysis tools including plundering the actual content of the site, have no trouble identifying it as junk.

I have been receiving it for several weeks and have learned as much as I need. Unfortunately, the others on the mailing list remain vulnerable so at this point, I decided to involve Yahoo to ask them to close the account, (my friend has ceased to use it because of all this). After complaining to their Yahoo! help site, explaining the circumstances, giving them a complete example with all headers and basically telling them what to do, I received this response.

```
Hello Les,

Thank you for writing to Yahoo! Mail.

It appears as though you have received one or more
emails containing a  "worm" virus. These types of
viruses spread themselves by mass sending
an email with an infected attachment to addresses
found in an infected  computer's address book, local
files, etc. The virus hopes the infected emails reach
unsuspecting recipients and entice them to open the
attachment thus infecting the recipient's computer.

If you feel that your account has been compromised,
we encourage you to update your password and any
other information on your Yahoo! account.
For useful information and resources regarding
```

online security, please visit the Yahoo! Security
Center at the following location:

...

(Much more of this irrelevant nonsense follows
making it perfectly clear that they hadn't read any
of my original e-mail. I love the Hello Les bit.)

No there was no "worm" virus and yes there are times when I feel that
the English I speak and write has long since disappeared. They might as
well have responded by:-

Hello Les,

Thank you for writing to Yahoo! Mail. We didn't
read a word you said but felt you would feel much
better if we responded quickly with a completely
irrelevant statement which nevertheless might prove
valuable one day if you take part in those oddly
British eccentricities like pub quizzes, so here goes.

Did you know that the Capital of Burkina Faso is
Ouagadougou ? Awesome.

Have a nice day pondering why on earth we bother
responding at all.

Peace and Love.

Yahoo! customer irritation center.

I responded pointing out that their mail was completely useless and my
problem was nothing to do with a worm, (I will spare you the tiresome
details) and a couple of days later they responded again with instructions on
how to tell them all about it, (I had already). Sadly, these were impossible
to carry out as I pointed out below.

Hello again Yahoo:

Thank you for your response. Unfortunately we are
not doing too well here.

```
Your first response went on about a non-existent worm.

This second response is asking me to send details of
the offending e-mail (which I actually included in the
original mail) to the following link:-

http://help.yahoo.com/l/uk/yahoo/mail/classic/spam.htm

This however requires me to be a Yahoo user. I'm not.


Are you telling me that there is no way that a non Yahoo
user being spammed by a compromised Yahoo account can
submit an offending e-mail ? Seems a bit of an oversight.

Thank you in advance,
Les Hatton.
```

Here it has all sadly ground to a halt.

Certainly in the West, (I don't know what it's like elsewhere), customer support in the 21st century has basically evolved into the rapid response of completely useless and irrelevant information, call-centres in cheap parts of the world or the mind-mangling telephone menu systems which leave you losing the will to live. These will no doubt allow the respective managing directors and CEOs to tick the box marked "customer response" with their pretty coloured pencils. This might sound a little brutal but you can't find out about how good your customer service is without pretending to be a customer. If you are a CEO, try it and prepare yourself for the shocking decline in technical staff capable of answering questions without passing it off to another customer service executive[6].

8.3 The shape of things to come

So are we winning ? If we are, will we carry on winning ? Let me emphasise a few points.

---

[6]You might also have a look at http://www.leshatton.org/ for lots of examples of trying to check-in at airports, complain to telecommunications and utility companies and teasing social services out of their bureaucratic nest.

8.3.1 Conventional junk

> In a highly-adaptive environment, the threat landscape mirrors
> the weaknesses which it finds. If 419s are still being sent, some-
> body is being careless enough to respond to them and MTAs are
> still not adequately protecting against them. The fact that Spa-
> mAssassin is gradually becoming less effective, (as it has on my
> junk corpus accumulated over the last 3 years) mirrors the fact
> that everybody is using it, including the junk mailers. It still has
> very considerable value but on it's own, it is not as effective as it
> was say 5 years ago. On the other side of the coin, the fact that
> botnet junk is on the increase mirrors the success of blacklists and
> greylisting.

So botnet acquisition will continue as a major growth industry. Of course
the major threat vector to achieve this is e-mail so I expect sophisticated
attacks to increase rapidly to maintain access to the large population of
potential victims junk mailers need. This means more zombie machines.

Apart from blacklists and greylisting, other drivers for this include SPF
(Sender Policy Framework) which forces junk mailers to look for machines
which, by communicating through a trusted MTA with SPF, appear to be
innocent.

In other words, the defence methods we have developed now determine
the nature of the junk we receive[7]. This has been a relatively slowly moving
process. Sending junk is gradually becoming more expensive. By throttling
junk using various methods such as greylisting, rapidly reacting RBLs and
so on, this forces the junk mailer to expend more energy per junk mail
sent, so the total volume drops. This is very obvious on my server where
the current junk level is only about 25% of it's levels a year ago. There is
no reason to suppose they are avoiding me so the level must be dropping
everywhere.

Perhaps this is the end of the first phase of junk where the great volumes
of unsophisticated junk will gradually give way to lower volumes of more
sophisticated fare.

---

[7] For an original science fiction adaptation of this theme, try the excellent "Deathworld"
by Harry Harrison, http://en.wikipedia.org/wiki/Deathworld

Perhaps the best news is that over the almost 10 year period since they first appeared, adaptive Bayesian filters appear undiminished in their power although a single filter seems to top out at around 99.9% efficiency independently of what we do or how we train them. This is impressive to say the least but given the volumes, this isn't good enough. However, as this book shows, there are ways of combining them or networking them as in Bill Yarazounis's inoculation schemes, which can take you up into six sigma performance which is where we need to be for junk to be a very occasional and non-threatening distraction. We should not forget however that

> The success of adaptive Bayesian filters depends on *not giving any feedback at all*, (or only misleading feedback if you can), to the junk mailers. That way they CANNOT improve systematically - we have the theory of statistical process control to thank for that.

One other important thing I should say relates to email-born toxic payloads such as viruses, trojans and all the other stuff which a resourceful criminal community can think up.

> If e-mail is filtered properly at the six sigma level as described here, viruses become a thing of the past even if they are passed on by a friend, i.e. *friendly fire*. In the system described here, nothing has reached the virus checking stage for many months in spite of continual virus waves from the various botnets.

8.3.2 New junk vectors

So where is the growth area for junk mailers ? I won't say much about this but I get a bit gloomy about Facebook, Twitter and the seeming death-wish of an entire generation to reveal it's innermost secrets to anybody who wants to know them.

It's not just in social networking where you find a dismal approach to security. It seems that marketing organisations (even big ones) in their desperate efforts to sell you anything also throw any caution to the winds. The following is an excerpt from a marketing mail sent to me immediately before Xmas 2010 by O2, a *very* big telecommunications supplier in the UK. I wondered at first why it had been flagged as suspicious. When I checked the logs of the mail filtering system I discovered the following embedded snippet.

> ...
>
> To clearly communicate all important details, O2 have created a
> <a   href="http://service.o2.co.uk/IQ/SRVS/CGI-
> BIN/*WEBCGI.EXE*?New,
>
> ...
>
> </a>highlighting the impact by product. ...

Notice that they have included an embedded link to an executable file !
This of course sets the alarm-bells in SpamAssassin off as well as several
other filters. Will they ever learn ?

8.3.3 Caveat Emptor

At the end of the day, and as always in security related issues, the limit is
set by human gullibility and naivety. There isn't much you can do about
that other than make sure the exposure is minimal. A continuing theme in
this book is that if junk gets through, particularly scams, somebody will
fall for it. This is why 99.9% success is simply not good enough. A perfect
example of this appeared just before this book went to press[8]. Dozens
of undergraduates at Sheffield-Hallam university were robbed of tens of
thousands of pounds by an e-mail scam on the student loan scheme. In
essence, it was a simple scamming mail requesting identification codes and
national insurance numbers, timed to coincide with the payment of student
loans for the summer term. Unfortunately, it got through.

The good news is that on balance, we are capable of winning with judi-
cious use of technology, as I hope I have demonstrated in this book. However, there is no end to conflict in an adaptive environment, so unfortunately
we can't, and will probably never be able, to relax.

---

[8]*Daily Telegraph*, 04-Apr-2011.

Appendices

.1 Skeleton Perl content filter

This Perl program[9] performs full MIME parsing of an e-mail revealing all the necessary locations where forensic rules can be applied. Just read the embedded comments.

```
#!/usr/bin/Perl
#
#     Prototype full MIME handler for e-mail parsing.
#
#     This is based on ideas from many sources on the web.
#     The code can be used under the same terms as Perl
#     itself.
#     It comes with absolutely NO WARRANTY and you use at
#     your own risk.
#
#     Copyright 2010, Les Hatton.
#
#     Revision: $Revision: 1.24 $
#     Date:     $Date: 2011/08/25 15:12:18 $
#--------------------------------------------------------
use strict;
use warnings;
#
#     Pull in Perl packages.  If these are not installed
#     you will have to install them yourself for example
#     by:-
#
#     # cpan -i Unicode::Map8
#     # cpan -i HTML::Strip
#     # cpan -i CAM::PDF
#     # cpan -i String::Random
```

---

[9]Available at http://www.leshatton.org/emailforensics.html

```
#
use Getopt::Std;
use Socket;
use MIME::Parser;
use MIME::Base64;
use MIME::WordDecoder;
use Unicode::Map8;
use HTML::Strip;
use IO::File;
use String::Random;
use CAM::PDF;

my    ($wd, $message, $unimap, $msg);
my    (%opt);
my    (@all_received);
my    ($tempdir);
my    ($h_image, $sender);

$tempdir       = "/var/book/TEMP/";
$h_image       = 0;
$sender        = "lesh\@oakcomp.co.uk";

#-----------------------------------------------------
getopts('bhm:t:s:z', \%opt);

sub usage_die
{
    my $msg = <<EOF;
Usage: mimetotext.pl [-hp] -m email -t tempdir -s sender
-b print mail body
-h print basic headers
-m file containing email
-s sender (passed by MTA usually)
-t Specify temporary directory
-z Output synopses of pdf and word files.
EOF
    ;
    $msg .= shift;
    die $msg, "\n";
}
#-----------------------------------------------------
```

```
usage_die("-m email is a required option\n")
     unless $opt{m};

my   $fname    = $opt{m};

if ( defined $opt{t} )   {$tempdir    = $opt{t};}
if ( defined $opt{s} )   {$sender     = $opt{s};}
#========================================================
#--  Instantiate the various parsers.
#
#--  Set up the Unicode character map to 8-bit.
#
$unimap = Unicode::Map8->new('ASCII')
     or die "Cannot create character map\n";
#
#--  We now set up a MIME parser to extract each of the
#     parts.
#
my $mimeparser = new MIME::Parser;
$mimeparser->ignore_errors(1);
$mimeparser->extract_uuencode(1);
#========================================================
#     Start class HTMLStrip and base it HTML::Parser.
#     This brings in the new constructor from there whilst
#     we override the start, end comment and text methods.
#
package   HTMLStrip;
use   base "HTML::Parser";
#
#--  Set up the HTML stripper.
#
#     Process <tag ...
#
sub   start
{
     my ($self, $tag, $attr, $attrseq, $origtext) = @_;

     unless ($tag =~ /^a$/)          {return;}

     if (defined $attr->{'href'})
     {
```

```
            my    $uri = $attr->{'href'};
            print $uri if $opt{b};
        }
}
#------------------------------------------------------------
#
#     Process between tags.
#
sub   text
{
      my ($self, $text) = @_;

      $text      =~ s/ //g;

      print $text if $opt{b};
}
#------------------------------------------------------------
#
#     Process </tag>.
#
sub   end
{
      my ($self, $tag, $origtext) = @_;
}
#------------------------------------------------------------
#
#     Process <!- .. ->.
#
sub   comment
{
      my ($self, $comment) = @_;
}
#------------------------------------------------------------
my    $htmlparser    = new HTMLStrip;
#
#     End of class, return to main namespace.
#
package    main;
#============================================================
#     Output text
#
```

```perl
sub   output_text
{
    my ($text) = @_;

    print $text if $opt{b};
}
#-------------------------------------------------------
#    Setup the character decoder.
#
sub setup_decoder
{
#
#    Unless one is specified on the Content-type header,
#    default to Western European.
#
    my $head = shift;
    if ( defined $head->get('Content-Type')
        and $head->get('Content-Type') =~
        m|charset="([^\"]+)"|)
    {
        $wd = supported MIME::WordDecoder uc $1;
    }
#
#    This might not be supported so just default to Western
#    European.
#
    if ( ! defined $wd )
    {
        $wd = supported MIME::WordDecoder "ISO-8859-1";
    }
}
#-------------------------------------------------------
#
#    Map to 8-bit.
#
sub unicode8
{
    if ( defined $wd )
    {
        $unimap->to8($unimap->to16($wd->decode(shift||'')));
    }
```

```
}
#-----------------------------------------------------------
#
#     Process the entities in each part.
#
sub process_entities
{
    my $entity = shift;

    if (my @parts = $entity->parts)
    {
        &process_entities($_) for @parts;
    }
    elsif (my $body = $entity->bodyhandle)
    {
        my $type = $entity->head->mime_type;
#
#        It's the MIME preamble, set the decoder for
#        this bit.
#
        &setup_decoder($entity->head);

        if ( $type eq 'text/plain' )
        {
#
#            Extract the words.
#
            my $bodystring =
                unicode8($body->as_string);

            &main::output_text($bodystring);
        }
        elsif ($type eq 'text/html')
        {
            my $bodystring =
                unicode8($body->as_string);

            my $clean_text =
                $htmlparser->parse($bodystring);
            $htmlparser->eof;
```

```
#              &main::output_text($clean_text);
          }
          elsif ($type eq 'application/zip'   ||
                 $type eq 'application/pdf'   ||
                 $type eq 'application/msword'    )
          {
#
#             Extract an allowed attachment.
#
              if ( $opt{z} )
              {
#
#                 ***** You may wish to analyse this for viral
#                 ***** content.
#
                  if ($type eq 'application/pdf')
                  {
#
#                     Create a temporary file in tempdir
#                     and load the string into it.

                      my   $fname     = new String::Random;

                      my   $tempfname = $tempdir .
                           $fname->randregex(
                           '[A-Z]{4}[a-z]{4}[0-9]{4}\d'
                           ) . ".pdf";

                      my   $fh =
                           IO::File->new($tempfname, "w");

                      if (defined $fh)
                      {
                          print $fh $body->as_string;

                          $fh->close;
#
#                         We now process some of the text
#                         of this .pdf file.  Just use
#                         first two pages.
#
```

```
                my    $doc = CAM::PDF->new($tempfname);
                my    $pdftext  = "";
                if ( defined $doc )
                {
                    foreach my $p
                       ((1 .. $doc->numPages()))
                       {
                           my $str =
                             $doc->getPageText($p);

                           $pdftext   .= $str;

                           last if ($p == 2);
                       }

                       &main::output_text($pdftext);
                }
                else
                {
#
#                          If we can't read it, just
#                          silently give up for now.
#
                    }
#
#                      Remove the temporary file.
#
                    unlink $tempfname;
                }
                else
                {
                    die "\nExiting .. Can't open
                       temporary file $tempfname\n";
                }
        }
        elsif ($type eq 'application/msword')
        {
                my    $bodystring    = $body->as_string;
#
#                  Render it into (mostly) ASCII.
#                  Limit to first 3K characters.
```

```
#
                        $bodystring   =~ tr/\x80-\xFF//d;
                        $bodystring   =~ tr/\x00-\x1F//d;
                        $bodystring   =
                            substr($bodystring, 0, 3000);
                        $bodystring   .= "\n";
#
#                       Pick out words.
#
                        my  $wordstring   = "";
                        while( $bodystring =~
                                /([a-z0-9]{1,20})/ig )
                        {
                              $wordstring   .= $1 . " ";
                        }

                        &main::output_text($wordstring);
                    }
                }
            }
            elsif ($type =~ /image\//i )
            {
                $h_image  = 1;
            }
            else
            {
#
#               Handle any other attachments as required.
#
#               &main::output_text(
                    "Attachments of type $type NOT yet handled.");
            }
        }
    }
}
#=============================================================
#-- ACTION.
#-- Open the supplied email message.
#
open(FL, $fname)      || die("Could not open input email");

local    $/;        # Absorb whole file mode.
```

```perl
$msg       = <FL>;   # Gobble, gobble.
close($fname);
#
#--  Parse the MIME structure catching any parsing errors.
#
eval { $message = $mimeparser->parse_data($msg); };
my $error = ($@ || $mimeparser->last_error);

if ($error)
{
    printf "PARSING ERROR: $error\n" if $opt{b};

    exit(1);
}
#
#--  Initialise the decoder.
#
&setup_decoder($message->head);
#
#--  Process the headers.
#
if ( $opt{h} &&
   defined $message->head->get('from') )
{
    print "From: " . $message->head->get('from');
}
if ( $opt{h} &&
   defined $message->head->get('return-path') )
{
    print "Return-path: " .
        $message->head->get('return-path');
}
if ( $opt{h} &&
   defined $message->head->get('to') )
{
    print "To: " . $message->head->get('to');
}
if ( $opt{h} &&
   defined $message->head->get('subject') )
{
    print "Subject: " . $message->head->get('subject');
```

```perl
}
if ( $opt{h} &&
   defined $message->head->get('x-spam-status') )
{
     print "X-Spam-Status: " .
        $message->head->get('x-spam-status');
}
if ( $opt{h} &&
   defined $message->head->get('x-bogosity') )
{
     print "X-Bogosity: " .
        $message->head->get('x-bogosity');
}
if ( $opt{h} &&
   defined $message->head->get('received')      )
{
     @all_received = $message->head->get('received');
     foreach   my $elem  (@all_received)
     {
         print "Received: " . $elem;
     }
}
if ( $opt{h} )
{
     printf "Envelope-From: %s\n\n", $sender;
}
#
#--   Traverse the rest of the MIME structure, parsing
#     the entities.
#
&process_entities($message);
#========================================================
#
#     Clean up the temporary MIME files msg-*.
#
$mimeparser->filer->purge;

exit(0);
#-------------------------------------------------------
```

.2 C string closeness comparator

This C program[10] will compare two strings for closeness. It's pretty fast so it can be used on a big mail server to decide how close a misspelt name must be to a genuine name to be accepted. Of course, the spammers will just read this and the good ones will adjust their names accordingly in which case just discard everything which does not match genuine names. The lazy ones won't bother so it will help to reduce the chance of genuine finger-trouble being rejected whilst being *much* better than leaving the default open as still seems common.

Just read the embedded comments for instructions for use. You might decide that anything returning 2 or less is close enough.

```
/*
 *    String closeness.
 */
#define   EQ(s,t)                      (strcmp(s,t) == 0)

#define   STRINGS_SAME                 0
#define   STRINGS_HAVE_TRANSPOSE       1
#define   STRINGS_HAVE_ONE_DIFF        2
#define   STRINGS_HAVE_MULT_DIFF       3
#define   STRINGS_HAVE_OZERO_DIFF      4
#define   STRINGS_HAVE_LONE_DIFF       5
#define   STRINGS_HAVE_2ZED_DIFF       6
#define   STRINGS_HAVE_5ESS_DIFF       7
#define   STRINGS_HAVE_SNSH_DIFF       8



/*
 *    Compute the "distance" between two names using the
 *    following metric:
 *
 *         Copyright Les Hatton 2010-.  Released under
 *         the GNU Public Licence.
 *
 *         Return STRINGS_SAME if the strings are
```

---

[10]Available at http://www.leshatton.org/emailforensics.html

```
*          identical.
*          Return STRINGS_HAVE_TRANSPOSE if the strings
*              differ by one character transposed.
*          Return STRINGS_HAVE_ONE_DIFF if the strings
*              differ by one character, wrong, added or
*              deleted.
*          Return STRINGS_HAVE_OZERO_DIFF if the strings
*              differ by an O - zero replacement.
*          Return STRINGS_HAVE_LONE_DIFF if the strings
*              differ by an l - one replacement.
*          Return STRINGS_HAVE_MULT_DIFF if the strings
*              differ by some other amount.
*/
int
myc_spell_dist(
    char *    s,            /* String one    */
    char *    t             /* String two    */
)
{
    while (*s++ == *t )
    {
        if ( *t++ == '\0' )
            /*    identical      */
            return (STRINGS_SAME);
    }
/*
*    Here if not identical.
*/
    if ( *--s )
    {
        if ( *t )
        {
            if ( s[1] && t[1] &&
                *s == t[1] && *t == s[1] &&
                EQ(s+2,t+2) )
            {
                /*    transposition      */
                return(STRINGS_HAVE_TRANSPOSE);
            }
            if ( EQ(s+1,t+1) )
            {
```

```
                        /*    1 character mismatch*/
                        if ( (*s == '0' && *t == 'O') ||
                             (*s == 'O' && *t == '0')   )
                        {
/*
 *                          0 - zero difference.
 */
                            return(STRINGS_HAVE_OZERO_DIFF);
                        }
                        else if ( (*s == '1' && *t == 'l') ||
                                  (*s == 'l' && *t == '1') )
                        {
/*
 *                          ell - 1 difference.
 */
                            return(STRINGS_HAVE_LONE_DIFF);
                        }
                        else if ( (*s == '2' && *t == 'Z') ||
                                  (*s == 'Z' && *t == '2') )
                        {
/*
 *                          2 - Z difference.
 */
                            return(STRINGS_HAVE_2ZED_DIFF);
                        }
                        else if ( (*s == '5' && *t == 'S') ||
                                  (*s == 'S' && *t == '5') )
                        {
/*
 *                          5 - S difference.
 */
                            return(STRINGS_HAVE_5ESS_DIFF);
                        }
                        else if ( (*s == 'n' && *t == 'h') ||
                                  (*s == 'h' && *t == 'n') )
                        {
/*
 *                          n - h difference.
 */
                            return(STRINGS_HAVE_SNSH_DIFF);
                        }
```

```
                else
                {
                        return(STRINGS_HAVE_ONE_DIFF);
                }
            }
        }
        if ( EQ(s+1,t) )
        {
            /*   extra character    */
            return(STRINGS_HAVE_ONE_DIFF);
        }
    }
    if ( *t && EQ(s,t+1) )
    {
        /*   missing character   */
        return(STRINGS_HAVE_ONE_DIFF);
    }
    else
    {
        /*   other differences   */
        return(STRINGS_HAVE_MULT_DIFF);
    }
}
```

.3 Example of mail relaying

A mail relay is when the sender tries to use your server to deliver an e-mail to another server which has nothing to do with you, i.e from Bad-die → Mug → Victim, where you are the unlucky Mug in the middle. Unless you set up Postfix to reject relays by correct positioning of the reject_unauth_destination parameter, (it is the default), sooner or later, somebody will do this, tainting your own server.

You can test your own server with a transaction like the one shown in Figure .3 (p. 300). You should get the "Relay access denied" for any receiving domains which are not handled directly by the receiving MTA.

Layered protection and postfix
- essentials

- **Reject as early as possible in the transaction**
- **No open relays**

> **Connect** mail.receive.com (an MTA responds)
>
> HELO mail.send.com
>
> (an MTA responds ...)
>
> MAIL FROM: alice@totallybogus.com
>
> 250 Ok
>
> RCPT TO: bob@notonyourserver.com
>
> 554 bob@notonyourserver.com Recipient address
> rejected: Relay access denied

Figure .3: An example of a telnet dialog with a receiving MTA which correctly rejects my attempt to relay mail through it from send.com to receive.com, neither of which is handled by this MTA.

.4 Installing postgrey on a Centos 5.X server

The following is how I installed postgrey and integrated it with Postfix. I started off with a

```
# yum install postgrey
```

(# is the root prompt on the server). If this doesn't work, check here[11] for advice on how to do this. When you get it installed, (yum is generally a painless way of updating software on Centos systems), do the following

Add following line to smtp_recipient_restrictions= in the Postfix file main.cf, (p. 134).

```
check_policy_service unix:postgrey/socket,
```

Now create /etc/sysconfig/postgrey and add

```
OPTIONS="--unix=/var/spool/postfix/postgrey/socket
   --delay=300"
```

The 300 is the delay in seconds from the first attempt before which postgrey will not allow a retry. Finally, crank it all up by

```
# /sbin/service postgrey start
# /sbin/service postfix
# /sbin/chkconfig --levels 345 postgrey on (for reboot)
# /sbin/service postgrey start
```

Some other useful snippets follow.

List current contents of fly-paper Issue the command

```
# cat /var/log/maillog | postgreyreport \
| awk '{print $1}' | sort | uniq -c \
      | sort -nr | head -n20
```

List everything fatally greylisted Issue the command

```
# cat /var/log/maillog
         | /usr/sbin/postgreyreport delay=300
```

---

[11]http://wiki.centos.org/HowTos/postgrey

Extending time before retry accepted Edit /etc/sysconfig/postgrey and change
delay on line

```
OPTIONS="--unix=/var/spool/postfix/postgrey/socket
  --delay=180"
```

then

```
# /sbin/service postgrey start
```

If messages from big ISPs get stuck Most of the big ISPs load balance
(i.e. swap services between servers according to current loads). It is
perfectly possible that a retry of a grey-listed message will be sent
from a different IP address than the first attempt. If this is the case,
postgrey currently treats this as another first attempt and a valid
message never gets free of the fly-paper. Losing valid messages is the
ultimate sin in e-mail filtering so this needs to be handled properly.
Postgrey ameliorates this by only using the top three numbers of the
IP address (the A, B and C classes) allowing retries from the 255 IP
addresses which have this in common. If this isn't enough, you can
white-list IP address ranges. I have only ever had to do this once with
virgin.net. You just add this as an entry to

```
/etc/postfix/postgrey_whitelist_clients.local
```

Not forgetting to remake the access lists (using postmap) and reload-
ing postfix with

```
# postfix reload
```

.5 Some interesting SMTP status codes

Actually I use the word "interesting" somewhat advisedly. You can find
them on the web in about 1000 different places[12] but it won't do any harm
to quote some of them again which you might like to know about.

---

[12]See for example, http://www.greenend.org.uk/rjk/2000/05/21/smtp-replies.html, accessed 29-Aug-2010, which has them nicely grouped numerically, via command and
so on.

Code	Meaning
200	(nonstandard success response, see rfc876)
220	*domain* Service ready
250	Requested mail action okay, completed
251	User not local; will forward to *forward-path*
354	Start mail input; end with CRLF.CRLF
421	*domain* Service not available, closing transmission channel
450	Requested mail action not taken: mailbox unavailable
451	Requested action aborted: local error in processing
452	Requested action not taken: insufficient system storage
500	Syntax error, command unrecognised
501	Syntax error in parameters or arguments
502	Command not implemented
503	Bad sequence of commands
504	Command parameter not implemented
521	*domain* does not accept mail (see rfc1846)
550	Requested action not taken: mailbox unavailable
551	User not local; please try *forward-path*
552	Requested mail action aborted: exceeded storage allocation
553	Requested action not taken: mailbox name not allowed
554	Transaction failed

.6 A forensic Perl program to investigate domain names

This is a very simple Perl program, (as an exercise to the reader, you can make it a little more sophisticated). However, it reveals important forensic details about domain names very simply and efficiently. The embedded whois calls in the middle, (see the open DATA lines), query the whois system and attempt to parse out the bits you need. *This output varies depending on who is servicing the whois response so you might have to fiddle with the pattern matching.*

```
#!/usr/bin/Perl
#
#    Extract information about a domain name in a
#    forensically useful manner.
#
#    Revision: $Revision: 1.24 $
#    Date:     $Date: 2011/08/25 15:12:18 $
```

```perl
#----------------------------------------------------------
use strict;
use Socket;
use Net::DNS;
use Getopt::Std;

my   (%opt);

getopts('d:', \%opt);
die("-d [domain-name] is a required option\n")
    unless $opt{d};
my   $dom = $opt{d};

my   $lup = gethostbyname($dom);
if ( defined $lup )
{
    my   $ip_address = inet_ntoa( $lup );
    my   $res = Net::DNS::Resolver->new;
#
#   Create the reverse lookup DNS name.
#
    my   $target_IP = join('.',
                   reverse split(/\./, $ip_address))
                 . ".in-addr.arpa";

    my   $query = $res->query("$target_IP", "PTR");

    if ( $query )
    {
        printf "Domain    :      %.40s\n", $dom;
        printf "IP        :      %s\n", $ip_address;

        foreach my $rr ($query->answer)
        {
            next unless $rr->type eq "PTR";
            printf "PTR       :      %.40s\n",
                $rr->rdatastr;
        }

        open DATA, "whois $dom |"   or
            die "Couldn't execute program: $!";
```

```perl
while ( defined( my $line = <DATA> )  )
{
      chomp($line);

      if ( $line =~ /Creation Date:\s+(\S+)/i )
      {
            printf "Creation  :       %.40s\n", $1;
      }

      if ( $line =~ /Country:\s+(\S+)/i )
      {
            printf "Country R :       %.40s\n", $1;
      }
}
close DATA;

open DATA, "whois $ip_address |"
      or die "Couldn't execute program: $!";
while ( defined( my $line = <DATA> )  )
{
      chomp($line);

      if ( $line =~ /country:\s+(\S+)/i )
      {
            printf "Country I :       %.40s\n", $1;
      }
}
close DATA;
}
else
{
      warn "query failed: ", $res->errorstring, "\n";
}
}
```

.7 A simple shell script to train unsure filters

When you are training statistical filters, you need a simple interactive script
to teach them when they are unsure. Here is such a script which can be
used to train both bogofilter and CRM114 when they are unsure.

```sh
#!/bin/sh
#
#     Filter training script.
#
#     Revision: $Revision: 1.24 $
#     Date:     $Date: 2011/08/25 15:12:18 $
#-------------------------------------------------

echo "Training Bogofilter ..."
read reply

if [ "$(ls -A UNSURE/BOGO)" ]
then
     for file in UNSURE/BOGO/*.flt
     do
          vi   $file
          echo "Is this spam (y or n ?)"
          read reply
          if test "$reply" = "y"
          then
               bogofilter -t -s -d ./.bogofilter < $file
               mv $file SPAM
          else
               bogofilter -t -n -d ./.bogofilter < $file
               mv $file HAM
          fi
     done
else
     echo "... No files to test"
     echo
fi

echo "Training CRM114 ..."
read reply

if [ "$(ls -A UNSURE/CRM114)" ]
then
     for file in UNSURE/CRM114/*.flt
     do
          vi   $file
          echo "Is this spam (y or n ?)"
```

```
            read reply
            if test "$reply" = "y"
            then
                    ./mailfilter.crm --learnspam < $file
                    mv $file SPAM
            else
                    ./mailfilter.crm --learnnonspam < $file
                    mv $file HAM
            fi
        done
else
        echo "... No files to test"
        echo
fi

echo "Now testing BOGOFILTER"

if [ "$(ls -A SPAM)" ]
then
        for file in SPAM/*.flt
        do
                echo "Spam file .. $file"
                bogofilter -p -d ./.bogofilter < $file \
                    | egrep X-Bogosity
        done
fi

echo

if [ "$(ls -A HAM)" ]
then
        for file in HAM/*.flt
        do
                echo "Ham file .. $file"
                bogofilter -p -d ./.bogofilter < $file \
                    | egrep X-Bogosity
        done
fi

echo "------------------"
echo "Now testing CRM114"
```

```
if [ "$(ls -A SPAM)" ]
then
     for file in SPAM/*.flt
     do
          echo "Spam file .. $file"
          crm ./mailfilter.crm --fileprefix=./ < $file \
               | egrep X-CRM114-Status
     done
fi

echo

if [ "$(ls -A HAM)" ]
then
     for file in HAM/*.flt
     do
          echo "Spam file .. $file"
          crm ./mailfilter.crm --fileprefix=./ < $file \
               | egrep X-CRM114-Status
     done
fi
```

.8 Web bugs

Web bugs take several forms but are usually 1x1 pixel size images so you can't see them. These are fetched from a different server than the rest of your message. When you allow an HTML format e-mail message, you are allowing your MUA to process the message like a browser and in so doing, fetching this effectively hidden image from where it lurks. The server it lurks on then records the fact that you have read the message in it's own logs where it can be analysed by the junk mailer. Here is an example as it would appear embedded in your e-mail message somewhere.

```
<img width='1' height='1'
src="http://www.nasty.place/spying.asp?
catid=20100823215913\&email=lesh@oakcomp.co.uk" alt=" ">
```

If you tell your MUA (Outlook or whatever) to render HTML mails to produce pretty e-mails, this image will be fetched and the server at nasty.place will record this fact in it's own access logs as in for example:-

```
aaa.bbb.ccc.ddd - - [30/Dec/2009:04:15:17 +0000]
    "GET /hiddenimage.jpg HTTP/1.1" 200 18914
```

showing that an IP address aaa.bbb.ccc.ddd accessed the image hidden-image.jpg on the 30th December 2009. It is pretty easy to scour the logs automatically looking for which IP addresses have accessed a particular image.

Sadly, this is becoming a trend with otherwise legitimate bulk mailers doing it as well, in their increasingly sophisticated attempts to map out your spending habits to hoover more money out of you.

A screenshot taken from my annotated message folder for a few days in December 2010 is shown as Figure .4 (p. 310). This includes both junk and non junk messages but as you can see, the majority are trying to store information about my reaction to these e-mails without telling me. This I am sure will only get worse unless some kind of legislation is passed preventing marketing companies from doing this or at least forcing them to tell people what they are doing.

It may also of course be self-limiting as most MUAs now allow images to be left on the server without being fetched at all, ruining it's value as a metric for open rates.

.9 Regular expressions

These are described in countless places with tutorials far better than I should be trying to achieve in a book so I will do no more than list some really good sources. There have been different implementations over the years and one of the few areas of Linux which used to really irritate me was the profileration of such implementations in grep, lex, Perl and so on. There has been some convergence in recent times however to the Perl model so that is the one I will deal with here.

[WARN: contains hidden image] Governme...	SC Magazine	Friday 12:08:18
[DANGER: Spyware content] Email-exclusi...	Healthspan	Friday 12:35:57
[WARN: contains hidden image] Millions of ...	Google AdSense	Friday 13:40:51
[INFO: Likely bulk mail] Front Row - Londo...	London 2012 ...	Friday 13:51:40
[INFO: Likely bulk mail] Leslie, Avoid the C...	Gear4music.com	Friday 14:36:58
[WARN: contains hidden image] runbritain	UK Athletics	Friday 17:17:09
[DANGER: Spyware content] The UK's low...	Anna James ...	Friday 17:24:22
[WARN: contains hidden image] EE Times ...	EE Times	Friday 19:57:57
[WARN: contains hidden image] Includes: ...	IT Security Bull...	Yesterday 09:48:24
[WARN: contains hidden image] Still delive...	Andertons Music	Yesterday 10:19:40
[WARN: contains hidden image] Win a Pan...	IT Storage Bull...	Yesterday 10:49:05
[WARN: contains hidden image] Les Hatto...	Amazon.com	Yesterday 11:58:48
[WARN: contains hidden image] Amazon.c...	Amazon.co.uk	Yesterday 12:32:28
[INFO: Likely bulk mail] HAMSTERS CANC...	Feenstra Maili...	Yesterday 12:42:14
[WARN: Likely spam] Buy U.G.G Boots Onl...	desgroseilliers1	Yesterday 18:01:41
[WARN: contains hidden image] Amazon.c...	Amazon.co.uk	Today 09:50:34

Figure .4: A screenshot of my annotated message folder for a few days in December 2010. Note that it is now the norm for companies, even responsible ones to glean as much information out of you as possible without telling you they are doing it. This seems offensive to me.

The definitive reference is Wall and Schwartz [54]. There are also some excellent tutorials on the Web[13][14][15] and about a zillion others. Be prepared to be patient. There are Perl regular expressions which can turn your brain inside out, but persevere, content in the knowledge that:

Good digital forensic investigators have to be comfortable with regular expressions as it is often the first thing you might use.

.10 Forensic investigation of release of e-mail addresses under FOIA 2000

.10.1 Glossary

The following abbreviations are used:-

- DPA, (Data Protection Act, 1998)

---

[13]http://www.troubleshooters.com/codecorn/littPerl/Perlreg.html, accessed 11-Jan-2011.
[14]http://Perldoc.Perl.org/Perlre.html.
[15]http://www.cs.tut.fi/~jkorpela/Perl/regexp.html

- ICO, (Information Commissioner's Office of England and Wales)

- FOIA (Freedom of Information Act, 2000)

- PECR (Privacy and Electronic Communications EC Directive 2003)

- RBL (Real-time BlackList. One of a significant number of lists maintained on the Internet to record spamming IP addresses and domain names)

- HEI (Higher Education Institute)

.10.2 Background

In the period March-April 2010, requests were apparently issued to every HEI in the UK stating the following[16]:-

> "FOI Request Staff E-mail Addresses I would like to request the following information under the provisions of the Freedom of Information Act. I would ask you to send your response by e-mail. A list of the workplace e-mail addresses for all staff. By workplace I am referring to corporate e-mail addresses ending in .ac.uk. By staff I am referring to all individuals employed by your institution. Please note that I do not require any segmentation of the list or any associated details."

The request emanated from the beneficial owner of the website academic-foi.com, a site presenting itself as "Investigating UK Universities through Freedom of Information", and therefore fulfilling an apparent public service. Indeed the request makes it clear that the resulting acquired email lists would be used for occasional bulk-mailing purposes and on being queried by the ICO, the applicant later stated

> "I requested the list of staff e-mail addresses in order to inform staff about my website AcademicFOI.Com. This site investigates higher education matters through FOI requests and publishes the results. University staff are invited to suggest in confidence topics worthy of investigation. I attach an outline of the wider aims of the project."

---

[16] For full details, try http://www.ico.gov.uk/ /media/documents/decisionnotices/2011/fs_50344341.ashx and http://www.ico.gov.uk/ /media/documents/decisionnotices/2011/fs_50315973.ashx.

So far all apparently laudable, but unfortunately, there are some more worrying features. A simple investigation for a few minutes on the 16th March 2011 carried out by myself using tools described elsewhere in this Appendix revealed the following:-

- The corresponding IP address 213.165.84.172 appeared on at least one RBL, spamcannibal.org, (although this is not widely used)[17].

- Reverse DNS and whois enquiries reveals that the beneficial owner of academicfoi.com also owns at least the following domain names, *also resident on the same server.*
  - mediasalesbulletin.com
  - whatemployersreallywant.com
  - zerobudgetmedia.com

- The requester states "I have no intention of selling, passing on or publishing any lists of university staff e-mail addresses." Note that he does not say that he will not do this under any circumstances, he just says he has no intention. With respect that is no guarantee. Even if the requester stated that *he would not in any circumstances release such information,* his systems could still be penetrated unknowingly.

- In the Sheffield-Hallam ruling of the 14 February, 2011, the ICO quotes that the requester knew that there were 226,000 e-mail addresses on the 148 HEI sites in the UK. In other words he has already deployed scraping software[18]. This is confirmed by the successful University of Glasgow rebuttal where the Scottish Commissioner "did not require the university to provide the information requested because Mr .... now has a software programme capable of producing a list of the email addresses making them reasonably obtainable". It has to be said that the possession and use of scraping software is itself somewhat questionable.

It must be stressed that there is nothing currently illegal in the UK about these activities providing certain procedures are followed. The requester even states that he will follow these procedures but the larger worry stems from the fact that *successful FOIA requests are considered to place the corresponding information with the **public at large**,* in which wider context

---

[17] At the time of writing on 11th July 2011, it is not so listed.

[18] A simple web robot which visits pages and looks for patterns which match e-mail addresses. Obfuscation of e-mail address such as writing lesh@oakcomp.co.uk as lesh (at) oakcomp (dot) co (dot) uk slows the process of diffusion down but does not stop it.

they are often deployed for illegal purposes. There is nothing to stop later and perhaps less well-intentioned requests from other parties from garnering the same information and selling it on.

It should further be noted that a successful request amongst all HEIs would yield probably close to 1,000,000 validated (i.e. genuine) e-mail addresses, a very valuable asset in the murky world of junk mail where addresses are sold on at a current rate of perhaps 50 pounds sterling per thousand validated e-mails.

.10.3 Current status of this request

To my knowledge, at the time of writing, (11 July 2011), only Sheffield-Hallam and my own institution, Kingston University have managed to block the request. In both cases, this was based on legitimate concerns about the impact on the ability to perform their public duties of an inevitable increase in successful scamming attacks as such information percolated in the public domain.

It should be noted that the Scottish Commissioner has already upheld the objections of Edinburgh, Glasgow and the University of West Scotland against releasing this information.

Rather worryingly, the ICO stated in their analysis of Sheffield-Hallam

"While it must be noted that the application of an exemption is discretionary, the Commissioner must consider whether the prejudice has been overstated by this public authority given the alternative approach by the others."

and

"The motivations of the complainant are therefore irrelevant."

In other words, there is evidence that precedent may be a significant issue **and** nobody cares what happens to the information when released.

This feels most uncomfortable given the level of current threats as described elsewhere in this book.

For example, in the case of universities, assuming roughly the same relative levels, publishing the actual validated addresses would lead to them inevitably getting into the hands of the junk mailers either through leakage or later vexatious request, and the total number of junk mails getting through the primary line of defence would more than double. Much of this would be directed to people who did not previously appear on university web-sites (only around 25% of all e-mail addresses appear to be revealed on such sites). This class of user must be considered more vulnerable to sophisticated phishing attacks for the following reasons:-

- They will normally not receive much external mail except from people to whom they have given their address.

- It is quite likely that they will not be accustomed to receiving spam, scams and phishing e-mails. It can be argued that they will be used to this with their home addresses but many people use Google mail which although not perfect, is particularly well protected.

- By having their names released this way, *almost all* of the resulting new mail they will receive will be junk. Furthermore that junk may contain phishing payloads which the university's protection systems may not detect. The ICO accepts that such systems are not perfect.

.10.4 Personal data and DPA 1998

The problems with the DPA start here. The Act states (I have left a subclause out):-

> "personal data" means data which relate to a living individual who can be identified amongst other things:-
>
> - from those data, AND (my caps)
>
> - includes any expression of opinion about the individual ...

On the face of it then e-mail addresses are not personal data. However postal addresses *are* considered personal data, so the role "opinion" plays here is murky to say the least. It seems entirely reasonable to accord the same status to e-mail addresses as to personal addresses *given that acts of criminal behaviour can and are directed at both.*

.10.5 Personal data and FOIA 2000

Part 1, section 2, subsection (3) of the FOIA specifically states that a number of provisions are to be regarded as providing absolute exemption from the need to disclose information by a public authority following a request under the FOIA. One of these is section (f) which covers personal information under the conditions of section 40 of the FOIA.

Section 40 refers to personal information as specifically covered by the provisions of the DPA. Section 40 of FOIA then goes on to state under provisions 2(a)(b) and 3(a)(i)+(ii), that data which contravenes any of the data protection principles or any data whose release is likely to cause damage or distress to the data subject under section 10 of the DPA is absolutely exempt.

Going on, section 10 of the DPA states that data subjects can specifically require the data controller, (which is the public organisation), not to begin processing of personal data, (in this case it's e-mail addresses) for a specified purpose or in a specified manner for the following specified reasons:-

- section 10 1(a), covers data "likely to cause substantial damage or distress to him or another".

- section 10 1(b), that "damage or distress is or would be unwarranted".

Furthermore section 10 of the DPA references section 11 of the DPA and paragraph 1 of that states:-

> "An individual is entitled at any time by notice in writing to a data controller to require the data controller at the end of such period as is reasonable in the circumstances to cease, or not to begin, processing for the purposes of direct marketing personal data in respect of which he is the data subject".

It seems therefore that any individual in a public organisation could instruct their data controller not to release their e-mail address and the data controller must comply with the following legislative trail:-

FOIA 1/2/3f → FOIA 40 2(a)(b)/3(a)(i)+(ii) → DPA section 10 → DPA section 11/1.

In general however, the rulings by the ICO seem to imply that 40(2) is not to be relied on as a reason for withholding an e-mail address although it is hard to see how the above would not apply if each data subject responded in this way.

FOIA section 36

The only successful all-encompassing arguments raised so far in England and Wales appear to be those employed by Sheffield-Hallam and Kingston Universities using arguments from the earlier EA/2006/0027[19]ruling. This makes use of section 36 of the FOIA which deals with "Prejudice to effective conduct of public affairs.".

Such a defence is built on the impact of spam, scam and phishing attacks on the individual. It makes sense and it is helped if there is quantitative evidence from the organisation on

- Potential increase in such activity

- Costs of dealing with such activity

- Evidence of previous occurrences causing personal loss or distress or reducing the ability of a public organisation to use it's e-mail systems, on which it depends for satisfactory conduct of it's duties.

In the case of Sheffield-Hallam and Kingston, the ICO decided that on balance it was not in the public interest to release any e-mail addresses because of this and did not consider any other avenues. In other words, it was sufficient. Further arguments based on sections 31(1)(a) (Law enforcement) or 40(2) (Personal data) were not needed.

To conclude, releasing e-mails indiscrimately to FOIA requests, vexatious or otherwise, is a very poor idea. It should be reconsidered such that either there is a standard response or the law should recognise that the vast majority of e-mail passing across the internet is either unwanted or positively dangerous in that it seeks to trick recipients into giving away money and/or personal details.

---

[19]http://www.informationtribunal.gov.uk/DBFiles/Decision/i101/MoD.pdf

Any increase in scamming and phishing attacks, particularly the large increase threatened here will claim more victims and reduce their confidence in the value of e-mail in doing their job. Given that most organisations completely depend on e-mail, the section 36 FOIA defence isn't just a convenient way of blocking information, it is an essential part of the public benefit equation.

.11 SpamAssassin Clown of the Year

It has to be said that some of the more challenged spammers haven't quite got the hang of SpamAssassin. Note this fine performance:

```
X-Spam-Report:
* 2.1 DNS_FROM_RFC_BOGUSMX RBL: Envelope sender in
*    bogusmx.rfc-ignorant.org
* 2.1 URIBL_WS_SURBL Contains an URL listed in the WS SURBL blocklist
*    [URIs: areice.com]
* 2.9 URIBL_JP_SURBL Contains an URL listed in the JP SURBL blocklist
*    [URIs: areice.com]
* 2.1 URIBL_OB_SURBL Contains an URL listed in the OB SURBL blocklist
*    [URIs: areice.com]
* 2.5 URIBL_SC_SURBL Contains an URL listed in the SC SURBL blocklist
*    [URIs: areice.com]
* 1.0 EXTRA_MPART_TYPE Header has extraneous Content-type:...type= entry
* 4.4 HELO_DYNAMIC_IPADDR2 Relay HELO'd using suspicious hostname (IP addr
*    2)
* 0.5 FH_HELO_EQ_D_D_D_D Helo is d-d-d-d
* 1.7 INVALID_DATE Invalid Date: header (not RFC 2822)
* 1.6 TVD_RCVD_IP TVD_RCVD_IP
* 0.0 SUBJECT_DRUG_GAP_C Subject contains a gappy version of 'cialis'
* 3.9 DATE_IN_FUTURE_96_XX Date: is 96 hours or more after Received: date
* 2.9 MSGID_OUTLOOK_INVALID Message-Id is fake (in Outlook Express format)
* 4.3 FB_SOFTTABS BODY: Phrase: Softabs
* 0.0 FB_GVR BODY: Looks like generic viagra
* 2.8 FB_CIALIS_LEO3 BODY: Uses a mis-spelled version of cialis.
* 1.3 HTML_IMAGE_ONLY_32 BODY: HTML: images with 2800-3200 bytes of words
* 1.2 TVD_FW_GRAPHIC_NAME_MID BODY: TVD_FW_GRAPHIC_NAME_MID
* 0.0 HTML_MESSAGE BODY: HTML included in message
* 2.2 RCVD_IN_BL_SPAMCOP_NET RBL: Received via a relay in bl.spamcop.net
*    [Blocked - see <http://www.spamcop.net/bl.shtml?92.113.159.62>]
```

```
* 2.5 URIBL_SBL Contains an URL listed in the SBL blocklist
*    [URIs: areice.com]
* 0.5 RCVD_IN_PBL RBL: Received via a relay in Spamhaus PBL
*    [URIs: areice.com]
        [92.113.159.62 listed in zen.spamhaus.org]
* 2.9 RCVD_IN_XBL RBL: Received via a relay in Spamhaus XBL
* 0.9 URIBL_RHS_DOB Contains an URI of a new domain (Day Old Bread)
*    [URIs: areice.com]
* 0.6 DRUGS_ERECTILE Refers to an erectile drug
* 0.0 DRUGS_DIET Refers to a diet drug
* 2.0 FROM_EXCESS_BASE64 From: base64 encoded unnecessarily
* 0.1 RDNS_NONE Delivered to trusted network by a host with no rDNS

Total 49.0
```

Better luck next time.

Bibliography

[1] Ross J. Anderson. *Security Engineering: A Guide to Building Dependable Distributed Systems.* Wiley, 2008.

[2] G. Baxter, M. Frean, J. Noble, M. Rickerby, H. Smith, M. Visser, H. Melton, and E. Tempero. Understanding the shape of java software. *OOPSLA '06*, 2006. http://doi.acm.org/10.1145/1167473.1167507.

[3] R. Beverly and K. Sollins. Exploiting transport-level characteristics of spam, Feb 2008. MIT report MIT-CSAIL-TR-2008-008.

[4] J. Blosser and D. Josephsen. Scalable Centralized Bayesian Spam Mitigation with Bogofilter. In *LISA XVIII*, November 2004.

[5] D. Brown, J. Levine, and T. Mason. *lex and yacc, Second Edition.* O'Reilly, 1992.

[6] Sean M. Burke. *LWP and Perl.* O'Reilly, 2002.

[7] D. Challet and A. Lombardoni. Bug propagation and debugging in asymmetric software structures. *Physical Review E*, 70(046109), 2004.

[8] Colin Cherry. *On Human Communication.* John Wiley Science Editions, 1963. Library of Congress 56-9820.

[9] D. Clark and C. Green. An empirical study of list structures in lisp. *Communications of the ACM*, 20(2):78–87, 1977.

[10] G. Concas, M. Marchesi, S. Pinna, and N.Serra. Power-laws in a large object-oriented software system. *IEEE Trans. Software Eng.*, 33(10):687–708, 2007.

[11] G. Cormack and T. Lynam. On-line Supervised Spam Filter Evaluation. *ACM Transactions on Information Systems*, 25(3), 2007.

[12] Kyle D. Dent. *Postfix: the definitive guide.* O'Reilly, 2004.

[13] C. Dwork and M. Naor. Pricing via Processing or Combatting Junk Mail. In *Advances in Cryptology*, pages 139–147. Springer-Verlag, 1992.

[14] R.P. Feynman. *Quantum Electrodynamics.* Perseus, 1998.

[15] Julian Field. *Mailscanner: A user guide and training manual.* www.lulu.com, 2007.

[16] A.A. Gorshenev and Yu. M. Pis'mak. Punctuated equilibrium in software evolution. *Physical Review E*, 70:067103–1,4, 2004.

[17] Paul Graham. A plan for spam, 2002. http://www.paulgraham.com/spam.html.

[18] Paul Graham. Better bayesian filtering, 2003. http://www.paulgraham.com/better.html.

[19] J. Graham-Cumming. Build your own Bayesian spam filter. *Web*, 2005. http://www.jgc.org/writing.html.

[20] L. Hatton. Are n versions better than one good version ? *IEEE Software*, 14(6):71–76, 1997.

[21] L. Hatton. An implementation of a chance discovery algorithm using cross-correlation and varimax weighting, 2006. http://www.leshatton.org/.

[22] L. Hatton. Testing the value of checklists in code inspections. *IEEE Software*, 25(4):82–88, 2008.

[23] L. Hatton. Power-law distributions of component sizes in general software systems. *IEEE Transactions on Software Engineering*, July/August 2009.

[24] Craig Hunt. *TCP/IP Network Administration.* O'Reilly, 2002.

[25] R.V. Jones. *Most Secret War.* Penguin, 2009. ISBN 9780141042824.

[26] J.C. Knight and N.G. Leveson. An experimental evaluation of the assumption of independence in multi-version programming. *IEEE Transactions on Software Engineering*, 12(1):96–109, 1986.

[27] T.K. Landauer, P. Foltz, and D. Laham. Introduction to latent semantic analysis. *Discourse Processes*, 25:p.259–284, 1998.

[28] T.K. Landauer, D. Laham, B. Rehder, and M.E. Schreiner. How well can passage meaning be derived without using word order ? In M.G. Shafto and P. Langley, editors, *Proceedings of the 19th annual meeting of the Cognitive Science Society*, pages p.412–417, New York, NY, USA, 1997. Erlbaum.

[29] B. Laurie and R. Clayton. "proof-of-work" proves not to work. *In WEIS 04*, 2004.

[30] C. Liu and P. Albitz. *DNS and BIND*. O'Reilly, 5th edition, 2006. ISBN 0-596-10057-4.

[31] Andrew Kachites McCallum. Bow: A toolkit for statistical language modeling, text retrieval, classification and clustering. http://www.cs.cmu.edu/ mccallum/bow, 1996.

[32] Alistair McDonald. *SpamAssassin: a practical guide to configuration, customization and integration*. PACKT publishing, 2004. ISBN 1-904811-12-4.

[33] R.B. Mellor. Receiving spam depends on the occurrence of the e-mail address in hyper text and on the nature of the link to the file containing the e-mail address., 2005. Kingston University Research reports, KURIR-2005-4: Pages 31 - 39.

[34] Michael Mitzenmacher. A brief history of generative models for power-law and lognormal distributions. *Internet Mathematics*, 1(2):226–251, 2003.

[35] Christopher R. Myers. Software systems as complex networks: Structure, function and evolvability of software collaboration graphs. *Physical Review E*, 68(046116), 2003.

[36] M. E. J. Newman. Power laws, pareto distributions and zipf's law. *Contemporary Physics*, 46:323–351, 2006.

[37] Y. Ohsawa. Chance discoveries for making decisions in complex real world. *New Generation Computing*, 20:143–163, 2002.

[38] Y. Ohsawa, N.E. Benson, and M. Yachida. Keygraph: Automatic indexing by co-occurrence graph based on building construction metaphor. *Proc. of advanced digital library conference*, pages 12–18, 1998.

[39] P. Pantel and D. Lin. SpamCop– a Spam Classification and Organization Program. In *Proceedings of AAAI-98 Workshop on Learning for Text Categorization*, 1998.

[40] John Allen Paulos. *Innumeracy: Mathematical Illiteracy and Its Consequences*. Hill and Wang, 2001. ISBN 0809058405.

[41] Charles Perrow. *Normal Accidents: living with high risk technologies.* Princeton University Press, 1999.

[42] Henry Petroski. *To Engineer is Human: the role of failure in successful design.* Vintage, 1992.

[43] Henry Petroski. *Success through Failure: the paradox of design.* Princeton University Press, 2008.

[44] M.F. Porter. An algorithm for suffix stripping. *Automated Library and Information Systems*, 14(3):130–137, 1980.

[45] A. Potanin, J. Noble, M. Frean, and R. Biddle. Scale-free geometry in OO programs. *Comm. ACM.*, 48(5):99–103, May 2005.

[46] P.K. Rawlings, D. Reguera, and H. Reiss. Entropic basis of the pareto law. *Physica A*, 343:643–652, July 2004.

[47] A-F Rutkowski and C.S. Saunders. Growing pains with information overload. *IEEE Computer*, 43(6):95–96, June 2010.

[48] A-F Rutkowski and M. van Genuchten. No more reply-to-all. *IEEE Computer*, 41(7):94–96, July 2008.

[49] M. Sahami, S. Dumais, D. Heckerman, and E. Horvitz. A bayesian approach to filtering junk e-mail. In *Proceedings of AAAI-98 Workshop on Learning for Text Categorization*, 1998.

[50] W.A. Shewhart. *Economic Control of Quality of Manufactured Product.* ASQC, 1980.

[51] Simon Singh. *The code book.* Fourth Estate, 2000.

[52] Meine van der Meulen and Miguel A. Revilla. The effectiveness of software diversity in a large population of programs. *IEEE Trans. Software Eng.*, 34(6):753–764, 2008.

[53] Meine J.P. van der Meulen. The effectiveness of software diversity. Ph.D. Thesis, City University, London, 2008.

[54] L. Wall and R.L. Schwartz. *Programming Perl.* O'Reilly, 1990.

[55] D. Wessels. *Squid: The definitive guide.* O'Reilly, 2004.

[56] Jonathan A. Zdziarski. *Ending Spam.* No Starch Press, 2005. ISBN 1-59327-052-6.

[57] G.K. Zipf. *Psycho-Biology of Languages.* Houghton-Miflin, 1935.

Index

Made in the USA
Charleston, SC
29 September 2011